Lecture Notes in Computer Science　13124

More information about this subseries at https://link.springer.com/bookseries/7408

Roderick Bloem · Rayna Dimitrova ·
Chuchu Fan · Natasha Sharygina (Eds.)

Software Verification

13th International Conference, VSTTE 2021
New Haven, CT, USA, October 18–19, 2021
and 14th International Workshop, NSV 2021
Los Angeles, CA, USA, July 18–19, 2021
Revised Selected Papers

Springer

Editors
Roderick Bloem
Graz University of Technology
Graz, Austria

Chuchu Fan (iD)
Massachusetts Institute of Technology
Cambridge, MA, USA

Rayna Dimitrova
CISPA
Helmholtz Center for Information Security
Saarbrücken, Germany

Natasha Sharygina
Faculty of Informatics
Università della Svizzera italiana
Lugano, Switzerland

ISSN 0302-9743   ISSN 1611-3349   (electronic)
Lecture Notes in Computer Science
ISBN 978-3-030-95560-1   ISBN 978-3-030-95561-8   (eBook)
https://doi.org/10.1007/978-3-030-95561-8

LNCS Sublibrary: SL2 – Programming and Software Engineering

This Springer imprint is published by the registered company Springer Nature Switzerland AG
The registered company address is: Gewerbestrasse 11, 6330 Cham, Switzerland

VSTTE 2021 Preface

This volume contains the papers presented at the 13th Working Conference on Verified Software: Theories, Tools, and Experiments (VSTTE 2021), held virtually during October 18–19, 2021. The conference was co-located with the 21st Conference on Formal Methods in Computer-Aided Design (FMCAD 2021).

The Verified Software Initiative (VSI), spearheaded by Tony Hoare and Jayadev Misra, is an ambitious research program for making large-scale verified software a practical reality. VSTTE is the main forum for advancing the initiative. VSTTE brings together experts spanning the spectrum of software verification in order to foster international collaboration on the critical research challenges.

There were 17 submissions to VSTTE 2021, with authors from 11 countries. The Program Committee consisted of 23 distinguished computer scientists from all over the world. Each submission was reviewed by three Program Committee members in single-blind mode. In order to obtain domain-specific expertise, we also involved seven external reviewers: Robby Findler, Antti Hyvärinen, Makai Mann, Andres Noetzli, Rodrigo Otoni, Alex Ozdemir, and Daniel Riley. After a comprehensive discussion on the strengths and weaknesses of papers, the committee decided to accept seven papers. The technical program also included two invited talks by Tom Henzinger (IST Austria) and Michael Whalen (Amazon Web Services and University of Minnesota, USA), as well as two invited tutorials (joint with FMCAD) by Matteo Maffei (TU Wien, Austria) and Frits Vaandrager (Institute for Computing and Information Sciences, Radboud University Nijmegen, The Netherlands). We greatly appreciate the help we got from the members of the Formal Verification Lab of the University of Lugano, Switzerland, and in particular from Masoud Asadzadeh for setting up and maintaining the VSTTE website. We are thankful to EasyChair for providing an easy and efficient mechanism for submission of papers and management of reviews.

December 2021

Roderick Bloem
Natasha Sharygina

VSTTE 2021 Organization

General Chair

Natarajan Shankar   SRI International, USA

Program Committee Chairs

Roderick Bloem   Graz University of Technology, Austria
Natasha Sharygina   USI Lugano, Switzerland

Program Committee

Christel Baier	TU Dresden, Germany
Nikolaj Bjørner	Microsoft Research, USA
Roderick Bloem	TU Graz, Austria
Borzoo Bonakdarpour	Michigan State University, USA
Supratik Chakraborty	IIT Bombay, India
Hana Chockler	King's College London, UK
Grigory Fedyukovich	Florida State University, USA
Jean-Christophe Filliâtre	CNRS, France
Bernd Finkbeiner	CISPA Helmholtz Center for Information Security, Germany
Carlo A. Furia	USI Lugano, Switzerland
Ganesh Gopalakrishnan	University of Utah, USA
Orna Grumberg	Technion, Israel
Swen Jacobs	CISPA Helmholtz Center for Information Security, Germany
Rajeev Joshi	AWS, USA
Peter Müller	ETH Zurich, Switzerland
Kedar Namjoshi	Bell Labs, USA
Aina Niemetz	Stanford University, USA
Natasha Sharygina	USI Lugano, Switzerland
Sharon Shoham	Tel Aviv University, Israel
Yakir Vizel	Technion, Israel
Chao Wang	University of Southern California, USA
Thomas Wies	NYU, USA
Valentin Wüstholz	ConsenSys Diligence, Germany

NSV 2021 Preface

This volume contains the contributed papers presented at the 14th International Workshop on Numerical Software Verification (NSV 2021), which was held virtually during July 18–19, 2021. NSV 2021 was co-located with the 33rd International Conference on Computer-Aided Verification (CAV 2021).

Numerical computations are ubiquitous in digital systems: supervision, prediction, simulation, and signal processing rely heavily on numerical calculus to achieve desired goals. Design and verification of numerical algorithms has a unique set of challenges, which set it apart from the rest of software verification. To achieve the verification and validation of global properties, numerical techniques need to precisely represent local behaviors of each component. The implementation of numerical techniques on modern hardware adds another layer of approximation because of the use of finite representations of infinite precision numbers that usually lack basic arithmetic properties, such as commutativity and associativity. Finally, the development and analysis of cyber-physical systems (CPS), which involve interacting continuous and discrete components, pose a further challenge. It is hence imperative to develop logical and mathematical techniques for the reasoning about programmability and reliability. The NSV workshop is dedicated to the development of such techniques.

This edition of NSV had strong emphasis on the challenges of the verification of cyber-physical systems with machine learning components. This topic was featured both in invited presentations and in contributed papers.

A highlight of NSV 2021 was the presence of high-profile invited speakers from computer science and from control theory, who gave the following talks:

- Stanley Bak (Stony Brook University, USA):
  "Verifying Neural Networks and Cyber-Physical Systems using Reachability"
- Eva Darulova (Max Planck Institute for Software Systems, Germany):
  "Soundly Approximating Numerical Kernels & Beyond"
- Sanjit A. Seshia (University of California, Berkeley, USA):
  "Verified AI-Based Autonomy: A Numerical Software Perspective"
- Yu Wang (Duke University, USA):
  "Statistical Verification of Hyperproperties for Cyber-Physical Systems"
- Bai Xue (State Key Laboratory of Computer Science, Institute of Software, Chinese Academy of Sciences, China):
  "Convex Computations for Reach Sets"

Regarding the contributed papers, NSV 2021 received three submissions, each of which received three or four reviews, and all of the submissions were accepted. We would like to thank the CAV 2021 organizers, in particular, the workshop chair Arie

Gurfinkel, for their support and the organization of the video conferencing and messaging system, and the NSV Steering Committee, in particular Sergiy Bogomolov, for giving us the opportunity to organize NSV 2021.

December 2021   Rayna Dimitrova
                                                                   Chuchu Fan

NSV 2021 Organization

Program Committee Chairs

Rayna Dimitrova   CISPA Helmholtz Center for Information Security, Germany

Chuchu Fan   Massachusetts Institute of Technology, USA

Steering Committee

Sergiy Bogomolov   Newcastle University, UK

Radu Grosu   TU Vienna, Austria

Matthieu Martel   Université de Perpignan, France

Pavithra Prabhakar   Kansas State University, USA

Sriram Sankaranarayanan   UC Boulder, USA

Program Committee

Houssam Abbas   Oregon State University, USA

Jyotirmoy Deshmukh   University of Southern California, USA

Bruno Dutertre   SRI International, USA

Sicun Gao   University of California, San Diego, USA

Mirco Giacobbe   University of Oxford, UK

Taylor T. Johnson   Vanderbilt University, USA

Soonho Kong   Toyota Research Institute, USA

Laura Nenzi   University of Trieste, Italy

Nicola Paoletti   Royal Holloway, University of London, UK

Yasser Shoukry   University of California, Irvine, USA

Miriam García Soto   IST Austria, Austria

Sadegh Soudjani   Newcastle University, UK

Hoang-Dung Tran   Vanderbilt University, USA

Tichakorn (Nok) Wongpiromsarn   Iowa State University, USA

Paolo Zuliani   Newcastle University, UK

Contents

VSTTE 2021

Quantitative Monitoring of Software

Thomas A. Henzinger[✉]

IST Austria, Klosterneuburg, Austria
tah@ist.ac.at

Abstract. We present a formal framework for the online black-box monitoring of software using monitors with quantitative verdict functions. Quantitative verdict functions have several advantages. First, quantitative monitors can be approximate, i.e., the value of the verdict function does not need to correspond exactly to the value of the property under observation. Second, quantitative monitors can be quantified universally, i.e., *for every* possible observed behavior, the monitor tries to make the best effort to estimate the value of the property under observation. Third, quantitative monitors can watch boolean as well as quantitative properties, such as average response time. Fourth, quantitative monitors can use non-finite-state resources, such as counters. As a consequence, quantitative monitors can be compared according to how many resources they use (e.g., the number of counters) and how precisely they approximate the property under observation. This allows for a rich spectrum of cost-precision trade-offs in monitoring software.

The formal framework for quantitative monitoring which is presented in this invited talk was defined jointly with N. Ege Saraç at LICS 2021. This work was supported in part by the Wittgenstein Award Z211-N23 of the Austrian Science Fund.

Keyword: Runtime verification

1 Why Software Monitoring Should Become Ubiquitous

We advocate the wide-spread use of software monitoring. There are two mega-trends in computing that support this appeal.

First, computing hardware is becoming ever more parallel. This mega-trend manifests itself in many-core processors and GPUs, computer clusters and data centers, cloud connectivity and the internet-of-things. It is time that some fraction of the newly available computing resources are used to achieve better quality assurance for software rather than better performance. In other words, why not dedicate some cores of a many-core processor to watch what the other cores do? Similarly, why no dedicate some machines of a cluster to watch what the other machines do? The choice seems obvious, not only because software quality needs more attention relative to performance, but also because it is becoming increasingly difficult to harness all available hardware parallelism exclusively for performance (after all, parallel programming is hard!).

© Springer Nature Switzerland AG 2022
R. Bloem et al. (Eds.): NSV 2021/VSTTE 2021, LNCS 13124, pp. 3–6, 2022.
https://doi.org/10.1007/978-3-030-95561-8_1

Second, software is becoming ever more difficult to verify statically. In formal verification, we moved from verifying the algorithm to verifying the software stack, but since there are no more isolated computers, now it is really about verifying the cloud. In addition, software is increasingly built from learned-by-a-machine components, such as neural networks, in addition to traditional designed-by-a-human components. As a result, the static verification gap has not been narrowing, but may be widening, i.e., software complexity is growing faster than our verification capabilities. In this situation, a valuable compromise is offered by runtime methods such as monitoring, especially if they are coupled with active measures such as shielding, exception handling, or dynamic program repair. They offer achievable quality assurance for the observed behavior of a system, rather than (often unachievable) guarantees for all possible behaviors of the system.

In order for wide-spread software monitoring to become accepted, it must satisfy three criteria. First, monitors must be real-time and low-overhead, so that the results of the monitor become available immediately, but the performance of the system is not affected significantly. Second, monitors are ideally written by third parties, so that they can be trusted. This means that monitors usually cannot rely on instrumenting the code that is being monitored. Third, monitors should be best-effort; they are not limited to issuing conclusive results. While the first two criteria lead us to focus on *online black-box* monitoring, the third criterion leads us to advocate *quantitative* monitoring.

2   Why Software Monitoring Should be Quantitative

In runtime verification, the most common monitoring frameworks are boolean and existential [1]: (i) an infinite behavior either satisfies or violates a desired property; (ii) if a property is monitorable, then a monitor should issue a conclusive verdict (positive or negative) at least *for some* behaviors, after observing a finite prefix of the behavior. For example, one of the most widely used definitions of monitoring combines universal and existential quantifiers: a property is Pnueli-Zaks monitorable if every finite prefix has some possible finite extension after which the monitor can issue a conclusive verdict [2]. There are, however, few interesting properties that would allow a conclusive verdict by a monitor *for all* possible behaviors, after observing a finite prefix.

In quantitative monitoring, we replace the boolean domain for property values and verdict values by a quantitative domain, which is equipped with a partial order. This has several advantages. First, we can monitor not only boolean properties but also quantitative properties of behaviors, such as maximal or average response time, power consumption, or the mode (i.e., the most common event) of a behavior. Second, we can insist on a fully universal view of monitoring, moving beyond "conclusive versus inconclusive verdicts" to "best possible estimates": a quantitative monitor should on all possible observed behaviors, at all times, issue a verdict value that provides a best estimate of the property value. As a consequence, we can compare monitors according to their precision and speed, asking questions such as "how close do the verdict values of a monitor come to the property value," or "how quickly do the verdict values of a monitor converge" (if indeed they do). Third, we can move naturally beyond finite-state monitors, allowing monitors to keep track of unbounded information about the part of the behavior observed so far, e.g., by using counter registers or registers with more general operations. One of the registers is then designated to contain, at all times, the current verdict value. While the use of register automata quickly leads to undecidable problems in static verification, in online monitoring, the main limitation is that the monitor can perform only a bounded computation (e.g., a bounded number of register operations) after each atomic observation. As a consequence, we can compare monitors also according to their resource use, asking questions such as "how many counter registers does a monitor need." As usual, resources can often be traded against precision and speed, allowing, for example, a more precise monitor if more registers are available. Any of these issues can be studied only in a quantitative setting for monitoring.

We have begun to develop such a quantitative framework for monitoring. In [3], we studied the resource needs of register monitors. In [4], we showed how monitors can predict future property values under probabilistic assumptions. In [5], we showed how the classical boolean view of monitoring can be embedded and generalized in a quantitative setting.

3   Quantitative Monitoring as Engineering Paradigm for Trusted Software

The nature of software makes it difficult to improve the quality of software by traditional engineering practices. In most engineering disciplines, a margin of safety or failure tolerance can be built into a system by "overengineering": if a bridge requires a certain amount of steel in the concrete, extra steel can be added for extra safety; if a vessel requires a communication bus between the cockpit and the actuators, a triple redundant bus can be added for failure tolerance. In contrast, code usually does not get better by adding more of it. Monitoring, however, can be seen as a principled way to improve software quality by adding more software.

Many useful engineering practices are based on underlying continuities that support quantitative degrees of approximation and improvement, relative to a design goal. In static verification, quantitative formalisms have been motivated in this vein, as a means to move beyond the classical boolean view of software correctness [6]. In practice, among all "incorrect" software implementations of a requirements specification, some come closer to realizing the intent of the specification than others. To capture this observation formally, the distance between systems and specifications needs to be measured by a quantitative metric. While efforts in defining such metrics have so far met with limited success, there are natural metrics for measuring the distance, for a given behavior of the system, between the actual verdict function generated by a monitor, and the desired verdict function for a specified property. This is because distances between trace-like objects (behaviors) are easier to define and measure than distances between graph-like objects (systems). A given monitor can then be replaced by a more precise monitor, or one that handles more faults. In this way, quantitative monitoring can be seen as a step towards a continuous theory of software improvement.

Acknowledgment. I thank Ege Saraç for commenting on a draft of this text.

References

1. Bartocci, E., Falcone, Y., Francalanza, A., Reger, G.: Introduction to runtime verification. In: Bartocci, E., Falcone, Y. (eds.) Lectures on Runtime Verification. LNCS, vol. 10457, pp. 1–33. Springer, Cham (2018). https://doi.org/10.1007/978-3-319-75632-5_1
2. Pnueli, A., Zaks, A.: PSL model checking and run-time verification via testers. In: Misra, J., Nipkow, T., Sekerinski, E. (eds.) FM 2006. LNCS, vol. 4085, pp. 573–586. Springer, Heidelberg (2006). https://doi.org/10.1007/11813040_38
3. Ferrère, T., Henzinger, T.A., Saraç, N.E.: A theory of register monitors. In: Logic in Computer Science. ACM/IEEE (2018)
4. Ferrère, T., Henzinger, T.A., Kragl, B.: Monitoring event frequencies. In: Computer Science Logic. LIPIcs, vol. 152. Schloss Dagstuhl (2020)
5. Henzinger, T.A., Saraç, N.E.: Quantitative and approximate monitoring. In: Logic in Computer Science. ACM/IEEE (2021)
6. Henzinger, T.A.: Quantitative reactive modeling and verification. Comput. Sci. Res. Dev. **28**, 331–344 (2013). https://doi.org/10.1007/s00450-013-0251-7

Making Proofs of Floating-Point Programs Accessible to Regular Developers

Claire Dross$^{(\boxtimes)}$ and Johannes Kanig

AdaCore, 75009 Paris, France
dross@adacore.com

Abstract. Formal verification of floating-point computations remains a challenge for the software engineer. Automated, specialized tools can handle floating-point computations well, but struggle with other types of data or memory reasoning. Specialized tools based on proof assistants are very powerful, but require a high degree of expertise. General-purpose tools for deductive verification of programs have added support for floating-point computations in recent years, but often the proved properties are limited to verifying ranges or absence of special values such as NaN or Infinity. Proofs of more complex properties, such as bounds on rounding errors, are generally reserved to experts and often require the use of either a proof assistant or a specialized solver as a backend.

In this article, we show how generic deductive verification tools based on general-purpose SMT solvers can be used to verify different kinds of properties on floating point computations up to bounds on rounding errors. The demonstration is done on a computation of a weighted average using floating-point numbers, using an approach which is heavily based on auto-active verification. We use the general-purpose tool SPARK for formal verification of Ada programs based on the SMT solvers Alt-Ergo, CVC4, and Z3 but it can in principle be carried out in other similar languages and tools such as Frama-C or KeY.

Keywords: Deductive verification · Numerical computation · Numerical precision

1 Introduction

Floating-point computations are at the heart of many critical systems. However, reasoning on floating-point numbers is generally agreed to be counterintuitive. For example, most usual properties on arithmetic operations, such as associativity, no longer hold because of rounding errors [21]. Therefore, floating-point reasoning is an area where tool-assisted verification is welcome.

Deductive verification of programs has improved significantly over the years, and many popular programming languages have their own tool (Java [2,10,17],

© Springer Nature Switzerland AG 2022
R. Bloem et al. (Eds.): NSV 2021/VSTTE 2021, LNCS 13124, pp. 7–24, 2022.
https://doi.org/10.1007/978-3-030-95561-8_2

C [12,17], Rust [3,19], Ada [20]...). Still, floating-point computations remain a challenge in this area. On the one hand, formal verification tools specialized in floating-point computations and error bounds [13,14] generally can only verify the properties they were designed for and cannot take into account separate considerations, such as data-structures, or pointer manipulation. On the other hand, even if some general purpose verification tools support floating-point arithmetic (Frama-C [12], SPARK [16], KeY [1]), they offer less automation in this domain, and the verified properties generally remain limited to ranges and absence of special values, though more precise properties have been considered in the context of the combination of a deductive verification tool with an automated solver specialized in floating-point reasoning (for example using the solver Gappa inside Frama-C [6,7]).

In this article, we want to demonstrate that properties such as error bounds are within reach for deductive verification tools in what we believe is the most common set-up: a generic deductive verification tool with general-purpose SMT solvers as a backend. We use the SPARK tool [20] for the formal verification of a subset of the Ada language [4] with the SMT solvers Alt-Ergo, CVC4, and Z3 as a backend, but the approach could in principle be carried out in other systems.

It is expected that a certain amount of user interaction will be necessary for the verification, especially as we go further in the complexity of the properties we are trying to verify. We choose to stick to auto-active verification only, as opposed to, for example, going to a proof assistant, so that we remain in the range of what a software developer might be expected to do. However we take advantage of the lemma library of SPARK containing lemmas which are themselves verified using the Coq proof assistant. The lemma library is publicly available with the source code of SPARK[1].

After a quick presentation of SPARK, this paper focuses on explaining how to verify increasingly complex properties on floating-point computations while remaining in a classical developer set-up. In Sect. 3, we stick to the verification of absence of special values and bounds on program outputs, like is done in most industrial uses of deductive verification tools. Section 4 goes further and considers bounds on the rounding error of a computation based only on basic arithmetic operations. This work takes advantage of the recently added Ada library for infinite precision arithmetic operations on rational numbers. In Sect. 5, we consider extending this reasoning to operations which do not benefit from a precise support in the verification tool (and/or return irrational values). We take square root as an example.

2   SPARK Ada

SPARK is an environment for the verification of Ada programs used in critical software development. The SPARK language subset and toolset for static verification has been applied for many years in on-board aircraft systems, control systems, cryptographic systems, and rail systems. The SPARK toolset can prove

---

[1] https://github.com/AdaCore/spark2014/tree/master/include.

the absence of run-time errors such as arithmetic and buffer overflow, division by zero, and pointer manipulation. SPARK verification is modular at the subprogram[2] level, so each subprogram is verified independently from its calling context. As a consequence, annotations on subprograms are usually required. In SPARK, this is achieved with contracts - mainly pre- and postconditions. The SPARK tool checks the correctness of the user-provided contracts as well as the absence of run-time errors.

To avoid having to learn a separate language for annotations, all annotations in SPARK, including assertions and pre- and postconditions, use the syntax and semantics of regular Ada boolean expressions. As a consequence, they are executable and can be checked at runtime using a compiler switch. However, the annotation language is somewhat restricted compared to a non-executable logic language. For example, one cannot quantify over arbitrary data, only ranges, enumerations or contents of containers.

Under the hood, SPARK translates the Ada program into a WhyML program suitable for processing by the Why3 tool [5]. Why3 then generates logical formulas, called proof obligations, whose validity implies the correctness of the program. Automatic theorem provers are then used to discharge these proof obligations. SPARK ships with three built-in SMT solvers CVC4, Z3, and Alt-Ergo. For floating-point variables and basic arithmetic operations, SPARK assumes conformance to the IEEE 754 floating-point standard, which allows the tool to take advantage of the recent built-in floating-point support in SMT solvers [23].

The running example used throughout the article is presented in Fig. 1. It is a function doing the weighted average of an array of floating-point numbers. It uses single precision floating-point values (type `Float` in SPARK), but similar results have been obtained with double precision floats without more proof efforts. The example uses recursive functions to make it shorter. However the implementation can easily be rewritten as a loop, while keeping the current definition as a specification.

3 Proof of Integrity of Floating-Point Operations

3.1 Floating Point Support in SPARK

SPARK supports basic floating-point operations natively and assumes IEEE 754 semantics for them. However, the special value NaN, as well as positive and negative infinity, are excluded. Generating such a value in a floating-point computation is considered to be an error, and will result in an unproved check. In practice, this amounts to checking that we never divide by zero and that computations do not overflow. Because of these semantics, SPARK reports failed overflow checks on our running example, one on each arithmetic operation.

One possible way to deal with these potential overflows is to replace problematic operations by saturating operations, which never overflow but yield potentially incorrect results. This is an easy solution that may be appropriate for

---

[2] Ada uses the term *subprogram* to denote functions (which return a value) and procedures (which do not).

```
package Libst with SPARK_Mode is
   Max_Index : constant := 100;
   -- Number of elements in an array of values
   subtype Extended_Index is Natural range 0 .. Max_Index;
   subtype Index is Positive range 1 .. Max_Index;

   type Value_Array is array (Index) of Float;
   type Weight_Array is array (Index) of Float;

   -- Definition of the weighted average on an array of values using floating
   -- point computation.

   function Sum_Weight_Rec
     (Weights : Weight_Array; I : Extended_Index) return Float
   is (if I = 0 then 0.0 else Sum_Weight_Rec (Weights, I - 1) + Weights (I));
   function Sum_Weight (Weights : Weight_Array) return Float is
     (Sum_Weight_Rec (Weights, Max_Index));
   -- Sum of an array of weights

   function Weighted_Sum_Rec
     (Weights : Weight_Array;
      Values  : Value_Array;
      I       : Extended_Index) return Float
   is (if I = 0 then 0.0
       else Weighted_Sum_Rec (Weights, Values, I - 1) + Weights (I) * Values (I));
   function Weighted_Average
     (Weights : Weight_Array; Values : Value_Array) return Float
   is
     (Weighted_Sum_Rec (Weights, Values, Max_Index) / Sum_Weight (Weights))
   with Pre => Sum_Weight (Weights) /= 0.0;
   -- Weighted average of an array of values .
end Libst;
```

Fig. 1. SPARK function computing the weighted average of values in an array

certain use cases, but it changes the algorithm if the saturation happens in practice. In this paper, we instead select bounds for the inputs and intermediate variables such that overflows never occur, and attempt to formally verify their absence.

3.2   Bounds for Floating-Point Types

In general, large negative and positive floating-point inputs need to be excluded to avoid overflows. In the presence of division, it might also be necessary to exclude values that are too close to zero, as the division might overflow in that case. The bounds for the input values can come from the application context (for example, a variable representing an angle can be limited to the range between 0 and 360°), or might be dictated by the needs of the verification of the algorithms.

Ada (and SPARK), in addition to the built-in Float and Long_Float (double precision) types, supports the definition of user-defined subtypes. These subtypes can specify a more restrictive range using the range keyword, or restrict the set of allowed values using a Predicate (or both). It is generally good practice to document application-specific ranges using subtypes when possible, instead of using the built-in types everywhere.

In our example, we choose to bound values so as to specify our algorithm in a more elegant way. We want to express the maximal weighted sum using

a product Max_Value × Max_Index. For this multiplication to be equal to a
sequence of additions, all the intermediate values should be in the range in which
each integer value is representable exactly as a floating-point value. This range
is bounded by 2^{24}, so the largest value we allow is 2^{24}/Max_Index.

We arbitrarily choose to restrict weights to the range between 0 and 1. It is
a common enough use-case for applications of the weighted average. However,
excluding zero from the sum of the weights for the division is not enough to
guarantee the program integrity - if we divide by a very small value, we might
get an overflow. That's why we also exclude very small non-zero values from
the range of the weights. As a reasonable bound[3], we use 2^{-63}. We still allow
individual weights to be zero. The range of weights is thus non-contiguous and
is expressed through a predicate stating that a weight is either zero, or is in the
range from Min_Weight to 1.

```
Max_Exact_Integer_Computation : constant := 2.0 ** 24;
--  Upper bound of the interval on which integer computations are exact
Float_Sqrt : constant Float := 2.0 ** 63;
--  Safe bound for multiplication

Max_Value : constant :=
  Float'Floor (Max_Exact_Integer_Computation/Float (Max_Index));
--  Biggest integer value for which the sum is guaranteed to be exact
subtype Value is Float range -Max_Value .. Max_Value;
type Value_Array is array (Index) of Value;

Min_Weight : constant := 1.0/Float_Sqrt;
--  Avoid values too close to zero to prevent overflow on divisions
subtype Weight is Float range 0.0 .. 1.0 with
  Predicate ⇒ Weight in 0.0 | Min_Weight .. 1.0;
type Weight_Array is array (Index) of Weight;
```

3.3   Proving the Absence of Overflows

As deductive verification is modular on a per-subprogram basis, it is necessary
to annotate all our subprograms with bounds for their floating-point inputs
and outputs. This can be done in two different ways. It is possible to create
new bounded subtypes like the ones we introduced for values and weights for
intermediate values in the computation. However, as SPARK does not support
dependent types, this only works if the bounds do not depend on other input-
s/outputs of the subprogram. Another alternative is to specify the bounds in the
contract (pre- and postcondition) of the subprogram.

In our example, we define a new bounded type for the result of Sum_Weight.
Since weights are always less than 1, the sum of the weights is less than the number of elements in the array. As we need to divide by this sum in the computation
of our weighted average, we also need to provide a lower bound for this sum when
it is not zero. As for the weights, we can say that the sum is either 0 (if all the
weights are 0) or at least Min_Weight (it would be exactly Min_Weight if a
single weight has value Min_Weight and all others have value 0).

---

[3] It is the bound used for lemmas about division in the lemma library of SPARK
(more about the lemma library later in this article).

```
subtype Sum_Of_Weights is Float range 0.0 .. Float (Max_Index) with
  Predicate ⇒ Sum_Of_Weights in 0.0 | Min_Weight .. Float (Max_Index);

function Sum_Weight (Weights : Weight_Array) return Sum_Of_Weights is
  (Sum_Weight_Rec (Weights, Max_Index));
-- Sum of an array of weights
```

Given the recursive definition of Sum_Weight_Rec, using Sum_Of_Weights as a subtype for its result is not enough, as assuming the predicate for the return value of the recursive call would not be sufficient to prove the predicate for the result of the addition. Instead, we add a postcondition to Sum_Weight_Rec which bounds the computation depending on the current index.

```
function Sum_Weight_Rec
  (Weights : Weight_Array; I : Extended_Index) return Float
is (if I = 0 then 0.0 else Sum_Weight_Rec (Weights, I - 1) + Weights (I))
with Post ⇒ Sum_Weight_Rec'Result in 0.0 | Min_Weight .. Float (I);
```

The functions Weighted_Average and Weighted_Sum_Rec can be annotated in a similar way. The function Weighted_Sum_Rec is constrained via a postcondition while Weighted_Average has a constrained return type:

```
function Weighted_Sum_Rec
  (Weights : Weight_Array;
   Values  : Value_Array;
   I       : Extended_Index) return Float
is  (if I = 0 then 0.0
     else Weighted_Sum_Rec (Weights, Values, I - 1) + Weights (I) * Values (I))
with
  Post ⇒ Weighted_Sum_Rec'Result in
   -(Max_Value * Float (I)) .. Max_Value * Float (I);

Max_Sum_Of_Values : constant := Max_Value * Float (Max_Index)/Min_Weight;
subtype Sum_Of_Values is Float range -Max_Sum_Of_Values .. Max_Sum_Of_Values;
function Weighted_Average
  (Weights : Weight_Array; Values : Value_Array) return Sum_Of_Values
is
  (Weighted_Sum_Rec (Weights, Values, Max_Index)/Sum_Weight (Weights))
with Pre ⇒ Sum_Weight (Weights) ≠ 0.0;
-- Weighted average of an array of values
```

Note that the bounds used in the Sum_Of_Values subtype for the result of Weighted_Average are far from the bounds of the mathematical computation (which is known to stay between −Max_Value and Max_Value). Better bounds can be obtained by distributing the division over the addition to compute $w_1/$Sum_Weight $* v_1 + \ldots$. The fact that each weight is smaller than their sum could then be used to reduce Max_Sum_Of_Values to Max_Value $*$ Float(Max_Index). However, as we don't need this improved bound to prove the absence of overflows here, we have decided against changing the formulation.

With these annotations, the tool should theoretically have enough information to verify our program. As it is, the postconditions of Sum_Weight_Rec and Weighted_Sum_Rec remain unproved. This is because reasoning about floating-point computation is a well known challenge, both for programmers and for verification tools. If we want SPARK to automatically verify our subprograms, we will have to help it, using auto-active verification through ghost code.

Bounding Floating-Point Operations: Leino and Moskal coined the term of auto-active verification [18] as a middle ground between fully automatic verification with no user input, and fully interactive verification as with a proof assistant. The idea is to add extra annotations and code to a program purely for the sake of verification. Auto-active verification can come in many forms. The most basic example is adding assertions that can help "cut" a difficult proof into two easier proofs. SPARK supports the notion of ghost code, where variables and subprograms can be marked as ghost [15]. The compiler checks that such code cannot influence the functional behavior of non-ghost code, and strips such code from the program during compilation when runtime assertion checking is disabled.

In SPARK, there is no built-in way to name or parameterize assertions to create reusable lemmas or axioms. An alternative way to share assertions is to use ghost procedures. The premises of the lemma we want to parameterize should be put as preconditions, whereas its conclusion should be used as a postcondition:

```
procedure Lemma (Param1 : T1; Param2 : T2, ...)
with Pre ⇒ Premise1 and then Premise2 and then ...,
     Post ⇒ Conclusion,
     Global ⇒ null,
     Ghost;
```

As SPARK handles subprograms modularly, it will check that the postcondition of Lemma follows from its precondition in any context during its verification. When the procedure is called, it will check the precondition - the premises, and assume the postcondition - the conclusion. As a convention, such *lemma procedures* or simply *lemmas* have the prefix Lemma_ in their name, are marked as ghost, and have no global effects.

The body (implementation) of a lemma procedure may contain any code or ghost code that helps to establish the postcondition, such as calls to other lemma procedures, or even loops to establish an inductive proof. In simple cases the body of the lemma procedure may be empty, because the provers can prove the postcondition from the precondition directly. Note that it is often the case that provers can prove a lemma's postcondition directly, but would not be able to prove an equivalent assertion in the middle of a large subprogram, due to the presence of a large, mostly irrelevant context.

SPARK comes with a *lemma library* that among other things offers basic lemmas to deduce bounds on the result of floating-point operations. Some of these lemmas are proved automatically by the SMT solvers, like the lemma Lemma_Add_Is_Monotonic below[4]. Others are proved using a proof assistant, like the similar Lemma_Mult_Is_Monotonic for multiplication.

```
procedure Lemma_Add_Is_Monotonic
   (Val1 : Float;
    Val2 : Float;
    Val3 : Float)
with
   Global ⇒ null,
   Pre ⇒
```

---

[4] Lemma Lemma_Add_Is_Monotonic takes inputs between Float'First/2.0 and Float'Last/2.0 to statically ensure absence of overflows in the addition.

```
  (Val1 in Float'First/2.0 .. Float'Last/2.0) and then
  (Val2 in Float'First/2.0 .. Float'Last/2.0) and then
  (Val3 in Float'First/2.0 .. Float'Last/2.0) and then
   Val1 ≤ Val2,
Post ⇒ Val1 + Val3 ≤ Val2 + Val3;
```

Coming back to our example, we use a call to Lemma_Add_Is_Monotonic in the proof of Sum_Weight to bound the result of the addition by the sum of the bounds:

```
Lemma_Add_Is_Monotonic
    (Sum_Weight_Rec (Weights, I - 1), Float (I - 1), Weights (I));
```

Precise Bounds on Integers: To prove the integrity of floating-point computations, it might be necessary to know that the computation is exact in special cases. In our examples, the bounds we have deduced earlier on our floating-point computations are not enough to prove the postconditions as they are stated. Indeed, in the postconditions, we have chosen to use a multiplication instead of a sequence of additions, which is not equivalent in general with floating-point numbers because of rounding errors. However, the floating-point computations are sometimes known to be exact, in particular for computations on integers if the values are small enough to fall in a range where all integer values are representable. It is the case in our example, both for the summation from 1 to Max_Index in Sum_Weight and for the additions on Max_Value in the post-condition of Weighted_Average (Max_Value has been chosen for that).

To help SPARK deduce that the computations are exact in our example, we introduce specific lemmas. The lemma Lemma_Add_Exact_On_Index states that floating-point addition is exact on integers in the range of the index type.

```
procedure Lemma_Add_Exact_On_Index (I, J : Natural) with
  Ghost,
  Pre  ⇒ I ≤ Max_Index and J ≤ Max_Index,
  Post ⇒ Float (I) + Float (J) = Float (I + J);
-- Floating-point addition is exact on indexes
```

These lemmas bring the remaining missing pieces for the proof of our example. However, to be able to call them in the bodies of our recursive functions, we need to turn them into regular functions with a proper body. The Subprogram_Variant annotation is unrelated. It is used to prove termination of recursive functions.

```
function Sum_Weight_Rec
  (Weights : Weight_Array;
   I       : Extended_Index) return Float
with
  Subprogram_Variant ⇒ (Decreases ⇒ I),
  Post ⇒ Sum_Weight_Rec'Result =
    (if I = 0 then 0.0 else Sum_Weight_Rec (Weights, I - 1) + Weights (I))
    and then Sum_Weight_Rec'Result in 0.0 | Min_Weight .. Float (I);

function Sum_Weight_Rec
  (Weights : Weight_Array;
   I       : Extended_Index) return Float is
begin
  if I = 0 then
    return 0.0;
```

```
  else
     Lemma_Add_Is_Monotonic
       (Sum_Weight_Rec (Weights, I - 1), Float (I - 1), Weights (I));
     Lemma_Add_Exact_On_Index (I - 1, 1);
     return Sum_Weight_Rec (Weights, I - 1) + Weights (I);
  end if;
end Sum_Weight_Rec;
```

4   Functional Correctness

To go further in the verification process, functional contracts should be added to specify the expected behavior of the program. In general, functional contracts can take various forms. On simple programs doing only floating-point computations, it is interesting to compare the floating-point result with the result using exact computations on real numbers. Aside from the direct interest of having an upper bound on the rounding error in the computation, such a specification allows us to lift properties that are known to hold for the real computation. As an example, the bounds given for Weighted_Average in the previous section are obviously greatly over-approximated. On real numbers, the weighted average of an array of values is known to stay in the bounds of the provided values. This is not true for the floating-point computation, even with a well behaved bound like Max_Value, because of the rounding errors. Bounding the rounding error in the computation of the weighted average would allow us to tighten these bounds efficiently.

4.1   The Big_Real Library

To write specifications describing rounding errors, contracts need to use operations with unlimited precision. As assertions in SPARK are executable, it is not possible to directly use an axiomatic definition of real numbers as can be done for example for Why3 [5] or Frama-C [12]. However, in the upcoming release of Ada (scheduled for 2022) new libraries for infinite precision integers and rational numbers have been added[5]. To specify our example, rational numbers are enough. In the next section, we discuss how the approach can be extended to irrational computations.

The Ada library for infinite precision rational numbers defines a type named (rather counterintuitively) Big_Real as the quotient of two infinite precision integers. It provides the usual operations on rational numbers, as well as conversion functions from floating-point and integer types. This library benefits from built-in support in the SPARK tool. In the generation of proof obligations, objects of type Big_Real are translated as mathematical real numbers and their operations are the corresponding real operations. This allows SPARK to benefit from the native support from the underlying solvers.

---

[5] http://ada-auth.org/standards/2xrm/html/RM-A-5-7.html.

4.2   Specifying the Rounding Error of Floating-Point Computations

Contracts are expressed in terms of specification functions doing computations on rational numbers. These functions are in a package marked as Ghost, so that they will be eliminated if the code is compiled with assertions disabled. It avoids linking the Big_Reals library into production code.

```
function R_Weighted_Sum_Rec
  (Weights : Weight_Array;
   Values  : Value_Array;
   I        : Extended_Index) return Big_Real
is
  (if I = 0 then 0.0
   else R_Weighted_Sum_Rec (Weights, Values, I - 1)
     + To_Big_Real (Weights (I)) * To_Big_Real (Values (I)))
with Subprogram_Variant => (Decreases => I);

function R_Weighted_Average
  (Weights : Weight_Array; Values : Value_Array) return Big_Real
is
  (R_Weighted_Sum_Rec (Weights, Values, Max_Index)/R_Sum_Weight (Weights))
with Pre => R_Sum_Weight (Weights) /= 0.0;
-- Weighted average of an array of values
```

The rounding error performed during the computation is expressed as the difference between the floating-point function and the infinite precision one. The postcondition on the floating-point function could theoretically be extended with an estimation of the rounding error. In our example, we prefer to use separate lemmas. The procedure Error_For_Average below gives an upper bound on the rounding error in the computation of the weighted average. It is called explicitly whenever we need to approximate this bound in our verification.

```
procedure Lemma_Error_For_Average
  (Weights : Weight_Array; Values : Value_Array)
with
  Pre  => R_Sum_Weight (Weights) /= 0.0,
  Post => abs (To_Big_Real (Weighted_Average (Weights, Values)) -
               R_Weighted_Average (Weights, Values)) <= ???;
-- Error bound on the computation of Weighted_Average
```

Evaluating the Error Bound: The first step in the specification process is to determine a bound for the rounding error in the computation. There are tools that can be used to predict it [13,14]. In SPARK, there is no such facility, so the bound needs to be computed manually from the individual operations done in the code. Note that this manual effort of deconstruction is also useful in the next step to help the verification tool. Here this is done through ghost code, but a similar reasoning could be expected if a proof assistant were used.

The basic steps to estimate the error bound are rather automatic. The IEEE 754 standard specifies that rounding on binary operations is always done to the closest floating-point number. As a result, the rounding error is less than half of the difference between two consecutive floating-point values. As the difference between two consecutive floating-point values varies depending on the value of the floating-point, the rounding error is generally bounded relative to the result of the operation. Standard floating-point numbers are spaced logarithmically, so this bound is a constant named Epsilon multiplied by the result of the operation. On 32-bit floating-point numbers, Epsilon is 2^{-24}, that is, roughly 10^{-7}. Subnormal numbers are linearly spaced, so the error on them is at most half of the smallest subnormal number [21].

In our example, the relative error for the function Sum_Weight is bounded by Max_Index × Epsilon. Indeed, the rounding error for each addition but the first (with 0) is proportional to the partial sum at the point of the addition, which is less than the complete sum[6].

```
procedure Lemma_Error_For_Sum_Weight (Weights : Weight_Array)
with Post ⇒
   abs (To_Big_Real (Sum_Weight (Weights)) - R_Sum_Weight (Weights))
   ≤ 1.0E-5 * R_Sum_Weight (Weights);
-- Error bound on the computation of Sum_Weight
```

In the computation of Weighted_Average, the values can be both negative and positive, so we cannot exclude subnormal numbers[7]. Thus, the error bound will have two parts, a relative part for standard numbers, and an absolute one for subnormals. The relative error bound is expressed in terms of the weighted average of the absolute value of the values.

```
procedure Lemma_Error_For_Average
   (Weights : Weight_Array; Values : Value_Array)
with
   Pre ⇒ R_Sum_Weight (Weights) ≠ 0.0,
   Post ⇒ abs (To_Big_Real (Weighted_Average (Weights, Values)) -
                R_Weighted_Average (Weights, Values))
   ≤ 1.01E-45 + 2.03E-43/R_Sum_Weight (Weights)
            + 2.05E-5 * R_Weighted_Average_Abs (Weights, Values);
-- Error bound on the computation of Weighted_Average
```

The error bound is composed of three parts. The first one comes from the absolute error on the division, the second is the absolute error on the computation of the sum of values (100 additions and 100 multiplications), and the third is the sum of the relative errors on the sum of weights and the sum of values (roughly 1.0E−5 for the sum of weights, see above, and the same for the values, plus a bit more for the division itself).

Lifting Properties from the Real Computation: Aside from the direct interest in having an upper bound on the rounding error in the computation, this specification allows us to lift properties that are known to hold for the real computation. For example, it is well-known that the weighted average of an array of real values ranging from -Max_Value to Max_Value is also between -Max_Value and Max_Value. Using this fact, we might want to compute a better bound for

---

[6] Note that we use 10^{-7} as an approximation of Epsilon here. A more precise approximation could be considered, like 6×10^{-8}, but, from our experiments, it causes proofs of error bounds on basic operations to become out of reach of the automated SMT solvers used behind SPARK.

[7] Theoretically, as addition on standard numbers can only give standard numbers and addition on subnormals is exact, the absolute part of the bound should not be necessary here. However, this reasoning is currently out of reach of the underlying SMT solvers.

the result of Weighted_Average than the current one (Max_Sum_Of_Values is larger than 1.5e26 against 1.7e5 for Max_Value). The expected property is proved on the real computation, and then lifted to the floating-point computation using the approximation of error bounds.

The error bound provided by the lemma Lemma_Error_For_Average is maximal when the denominator is close to Min_Weight and the weighted average is close to Max_Value. In this case, the significant part is the relative error on the weighted average. It evaluates to less than 3.5 as an absolute value. This allows us to prove the following lemma, providing notably more precise bounds for the computation.

```
procedure Lemma_Precise_Bounds_For_Average
  (Weights : Weight_Array; Values : Value_Array)
with
  Pre  => Sum_Weight (Weights) /= 0.0,
  Post => Weighted_Average (Weights, Values)
     in - (Max_Value + 3.5) .. Max_Value + 3.5;
-- Precise bounds for Weighted_Average obtained through error bound computation
```

Note that this bound is not optimal, as we have approximated the error bounds in the computations. In particular, we are losing nearly a factor two on the approximation of Epsilon. However, some testing shows that the optimal bound is at least Max_Value + 1.3, so it is not too far off either.

Proving that the Error Bounds Are Correct: Correctly predicting the error bounds is not enough for SPARK to verify them. As in Sect. 3, reasoning about floating-point computations is difficult for the underlying solvers, and it is even worse when considering a combination of floating-point and real numbers. As before, it is possible to help the tool using auto-active verification. The key is to work in small steps, factoring out each proof step in a lemma.

As a basis, shared lemmas are introduced to bound the rounding error performed by a single floating-point operation. If the result is a subnormal number, the error is less than half of the smallest positive subnormal number. If it is a standard number, it can be bounded linearly using the Epsilon constant.

```
procedure Lemma_Bound_Error_Add (X, Y : Floats_For_Add) with
  Post => abs (To_Big_Real (X + Y) - (To_Big_Real (X) + To_Big_Real (Y))) <=
    (if abs (To_Big_Real (X) + To_Big_Real (Y)) >= First_Norm
     then Epsilon * abs (To_Big_Real (X) + To_Big_Real (Y))
     else Error_Denorm);
```

Complex computations are split into parts, each part accounting for an individual error factor. For example, the computation of Weighted_Average is made of three parts: the computation of the weighted sum in the numerator, the computation of the sum of the weights in the denominator, and the division itself. For the tool to be able to put the parts together, the global error needs to be expressible as a sum of the various parts. The following code gives a possible partition of the computation of Weighted_Average:

```
Num_F : constant Float := Weighted_Sum_Rec (Weights, Values, Max_Index);
Den_F : constant Float := Sum_Weight (Weights);
Num_R : constant Big_Real := R_Weighted_Sum_Rec (Weights, Values, Max_Index);
Den_R : constant Big_Real := R_Sum_Weight (Weights);
```

```
abs (To_Big_Real (Num_F/Den_F) - Num_R/Den_R) ≤
   -- Error on the division
   abs (To_Big_Real (Num_F/Den_F) - (To_Big_Real (Num_F)/To_Big_Real (Den_F)))
   -- Error on the computation of the numerator
 + abs (To_Big_Real (Num_F)/To_Big_Real (Den_F) - Num_R/To_Big_Real (Den_F))
   -- Error on the computation of the denominator
 + abs (Num_R/To_Big_Real (Den_F) - Num_R/Den_R)
```

As can be seen in the example, the parts are not necessarily direct applications of one of the basic lemmas, or one of the lemmas introduced for previous computations. For·the second term of the addition, the lemma introduced for Weighted_Sum_Rec will bound the difference between Num_F and Num_R. The effect of dividing each term by To_Big_Real (Den_F) must still be accounted for separately. New lemmas can be introduced for that. The premises are the simple error we are trying to compute, and the errors on other terms mentioned in the expression. The conclusion is the error on the considered operation. It should be expressed in terms of the real computation only.

```
-- Lemma to compute the part of the error in Weighted_Average coming from the
-- computation of the numerator.
procedure Lemma_EB_For_Sum
   (Num_F                 : Floats_For_Mul;
    Den_F                 : Floats_For_Div;
    Num_R, Den_R, Num_A : Big_Real)
with
   Pre ⇒ Den_F > 0.0 and Den_R > 0.0 and Num_A ≥ abs (Num_R)
      -- Error on the computation of the numerator
      and abs (To_Big_Real (Num_F) - Num_R) ≤ 2.01E-43 + 1.01E-5 * Num_A
      -- Error on the computation of the denominator
      and abs (To_Big_Real (Den_F) - Den_R) ≤ 1.0E-5 * Den_R,

   -- Error accounting for the error on the computation of the numerator
   Post ⇒ abs (To_Big_Real (Num_F)/To_Big_Real (Den_F) - Num_R/To_Big_Real (Den_F))
      ≤ 2.02E-43/Den_R + 1.02E-5 * Num_A/Den_R;
```

The statement and auto-active proof of the lemmas providing the error bounds on the computations involved in the evaluation of the weighted average amount to a bit less than 400 lines of ghost code, while the initial (unproved) implementation was 25 lines of code and its real counterpart is 34 lines of code.

4.3   Prover Performance

Encoding. The SPARK tool translates Ada code to Why3, which then generates proof obligations for various provers. The three provers CVC4, Z3 and Alt-Ergo are available in SPARK by default and have been used in our work. CVC4 and Z3 use the SMT-LIB encoding of Why3. This means that floating-point variables and operations are encoded using the corresponding SMT-LIB operations [16]. For Alt-Ergo, its native input is used, together with an axiomatization based on arithmetic operations on reals, following by rounding [11].

Experimental Results. Figure 2 contains the experimental results. All three provers are necessary to fully prove the example. If one of the provers was not available, some additional effort, with additional lemmas and assertions, and possibly longer prover timeouts, could also lead to full proofs.

Prover	**Alt-Ergo** 2.3.0	**CVC4** 1.8	**Z3** 4.8.10	Total
Runtime Checks	453 (0)	470 (10)	437(0)	540
Assert, Lemmas, Pre/Post	70 (10)	45 (2)	51(2)	79

Fig. 2. Results of provers on the Weighted Average example on 619 proof obligations. A timeout of 60 s was used. A cell contains the number of proved VCs, and the number of VCs only this prover could prove in parentheses. The last column contains the total number of VCs in each category. The results were obtained on an AMD Ryzen 3950x with 64 GB of RAM.

One can see that, while CVC4 is strong on runtime checks (mostly array accesses and checks on bounds of integer and floating-point operations on the example), Alt-Ergo is the strongest prover when it comes to lemma procedures, assertions and pre- and postconditions. Alt-Ergo also uniquely proves the most VCs in this category. This probably comes from the fact that Alt-Ergo is the only prover whose support for floating-point arithmetic is not based on bitlevel reasoning, but on an axiomatization using real numbers and rounding, which helps on our example, since it involves both real and floating point computations.

5   Going Beyond Basic Arithmetic Operations

The method applied in the previous section works on computations involving only basic arithmetic operations. However, it is not enough in general. For example, the computation of the standard error of our average computation would require the use of square root. Our method can be extended to handle other operations, but it necessitates some additional preparatory steps.

5.1   Approximating Irrational Computations

The first issue is the lack of a real infinite precision counterpart for the considered floating-point operation. Since SPARK only supports infinite precision rational numbers, and not real numbers, if the operation returns an irrational value, then it is not possible to write a specification function to represent the operation with infinite precision. Fortunately, since we are only interested in the error bounds, it is enough to provide a function giving a good enough approximation of the result as a rational value. Here, we define a function that approximates the square root of a rational number with a given precision. The precision is chosen to be negligible with respect to the rounding errors on the floating-point type.

```
Sqrt_Bound : constant := 1.0E-8;
-- Small enough value to be absorbed by the over-approximation on Epsilon
Sq_Bound   : constant := 1.999 * Sqrt_Bound;
-- Approximation of the minimum bound on the square to ensure Sqrt_Bound

function R_Sqrt (X : Big_Real) return Big_Real with
  Pre  ⇒ X ≥ 0.0,
  Post ⇒ R_Sqrt'Result ≥ 0.0
    and then abs (X - R_Sqrt'Result * R_Sqrt'Result)
      ≤ Sq_Bound * R_Sqrt'Result * R_Sqrt'Result;
-- Approximation of sqrt on real numbers
```

Coming up with a specification for the rational function might be difficult for transcendental functions. A possibility would be to provide only some properties of the function through axioms (that is, lemma procedures without a body, or whose body is not verified). This would not permit us to benefit from native support in the underlying solvers however. This might not be a big deal, as support for transcendental functions is poor in most solvers. This could be alleviated if needed by providing specialized support for most common transcendental functions in the SPARK tool as it is done for the Big_Reals library.

5.2 Axiomatizing Floating-Point Operations

The second issue is the absence of support in the SPARK tool for complex operations on floating-point values. The usual functions on floating-point types (square root, exponentiation, logarithm, trigonometric functions...) are provided as a library. Some of these functions are annotated with a minimal contract providing some bounds on their result, but nothing more precise is known about them by the tool. For example, here is the contract provided for Sqrt.

```
function Sqrt (X : Float) return Float with
  Pre  ⇒ X ≥ 0.0,
  Post ⇒ Sqrt'Result ≥ 0.0
    and then (if X = 0.0 then Sqrt'Result = 0.0)
    and then (if X = 1.0 then Sqrt'Result = 1.0)
    and then (if X ≥ Float'Succ (0.0) then Sqrt'Result > 0.0);
```

The reason for this minimal support is that the language does not necessarily enforce compliance to the IEEE 754 standard for these functions on all platforms. When additional information is needed, it can be supplied through axioms. On a safety critical project, particular care should be taken that these axioms are indeed valid on the chosen architecture. Here are some examples of axioms that could be provided for the Sqrt function on 32-bit integers:

```
procedure Axiom_Bound_Error_Sqrt (X : Float) with
  Pre  ⇒ X ≥ 0.0,
  Post ⇒ abs (To_Big_Real (Sqrt (X)) - R_Sqrt (To_Big_Real (X))) ≤
    (if Sqrt (To_Big_Real (X)) ≥ First_Norm
     then Epsilon * R_Sqrt (To_Big_Real (X)) else Error_Denorm);

procedure Axiom_Sqrt_Is_Monotonic (X, Y : Float) with
  Pre  ⇒ X ≥ 0.0 and Y ≥ X,
  Post ⇒ Sqrt (Y) ≥ Sqrt (X);

procedure Axiom_Sqrt_Exact_Integer (X : Integer) with
  Pre  ⇒ X in 0 .. 4096,
  Post ⇒ Sqrt (Float (X) ** 2) = Float (X);
```

The first axiom gives an over approximation of the error bound with respect to the approximation of square root on rational numbers. The following two are variants of the lemmas used on basic arithmetic operations to verify program integrity in Sect. 3. The first states that square root is monotonic while the second expresses that Sqrt is exact on the square of a small enough integer. Using these axioms, we have proven correct an implementation of the euclidean norm of a vector which could be used to compute the standard error of our weighted average[8]. It uses a method similar to the one from Sects. 3 and 4.

6   Related Work

Historically, most deductive verification tools interpreted floating-point numbers as real numbers. Following the addition of floating-point support in SMT solvers [9,11], some verification tools changed to a sound handling, even if it meant a decrease in provability. This is the case for Frama-C and SPARK [16], as well as KeY [1] more recently.

Even with built-in support in SMT solvers, verifying floating-point computations remains a challenge. As a result, most verification efforts on floating-point computations rely on either specialized tools or proof assistants to reason about error bounds. For example, the static analyzer Fluctuat [14] is used in an industrial context to automatically estimate the propagation of error bounds in C programs. Specialized libraries are also available inside proof assistants. The Flocq [8] library offers a formalization to reason about floating- and fixed-point computations in Coq. As a middle ground between both approaches, Gappa [13] is a proof assistant targeting specifically verification of floating-point computation, with automated evaluation and propagation of rounding errors.

Verification efforts using standard deductive verification tools largely do not go beyond absence of special values. It is still possible to use a standard verification tool in combination with either a specialized tool or a proof assistant. For example, Gappa was used as a backend for the Frama-C tool to successfully verify an average computation on C code [6,7]. In the opposite direction, a Point-in-Polygon algorithm was verified by first generating lemmas about stable tests using the specialized tool PRECiSA and then reusing them inside Frama-C to prove the program [22].

7   Conclusion

We have demonstrated that it is possible to use general purpose verification tools like SPARK to verify advanced properties of (simple) floating-point programs. Absence of overflows is achievable through bounds propagation. Precise specifications can be written in terms of the equivalent real computation and error bounds, but proving them correct is more involved and requires user interaction currently. The situation could improve in the future, either following improvements in SMT solvers, as support for floating-point in SMT-LIB is fairly recent. Though we believe it stays within the reach of regular developers, our approach does require some expertise, in particular to compute the correct error bounds. It might be possible to use external tools to estimate the bounds and reuse the results, but we have not explored this approach.

---

[8] https://github.com/AdaCore/spark2014/tree/master/testsuite/gnatprove/tests/U129-014_sqrt_error_bounds.

References

1. Abbasi, R., Schiffl, J., Darulova, E., Ulbrich, M., Ahrendt, W.: Deductive verification of floating-point Java programs in KeY. In: TACAS (2), pp. 242–261 (2021)
2. Ahrendt, W., Beckert, B., Bubel, R., Hähnle, R., Schmitt, P.H., Ulbrich, M.: Deductive software verification-the key book. Lecture Notes in Computer Science, vol. 10001. Springer, Cham (2016). https://doi.org/10.1007/978-3-319-49812-6
3. Astrauskas, V., Müller, P., Poli, F., Summers, A.J.: Leveraging rust types for modular specification and verification. Proc. ACM Program. Lang. 3(OOPSLA), 1–30 (2019)
4. Barnes, J.: Programming in Ada 2012. Cambridge University Press, Cambridge (2014)
5. Bobot, F., Filliâtre, J.C., Marché, C., Paskevich, A.: Why3: shepherd your herd of provers. In: Boogie 2011: First International Workshop on Intermediate Verification Languages, pp. 53–64 (2011)
6. Boldo, S.: Formal verification of programs computing the floating-point average. In: Butler, M., Conchon, S., Zaïdi, F. (eds.) ICFEM 2015. LNCS, vol. 9407, pp. 17–32. Springer, Cham (2015). https://doi.org/10.1007/978-3-319-25423-4_2
7. Boldo, S., Marché, C.: Formal verification of numerical programs: from c annotated programs to mechanical proofs. Math. Comput. Sci. 5(4), 377–393 (2011)
8. Boldo, S., Melquiond, G.: Flocq: a unified library for proving floating-point algorithms in Coq. In: 2011 IEEE 20th Symposium on Computer Arithmetic, pp. 243–252. IEEE (2011)
9. Brain, M., Schanda, F., Sun, Y.: Building better bit-blasting for floating-point problems. In: Vojnar, T., Zhang, L. (eds.) TACAS 2019. LNCS, vol. 11427, pp. 79–98. Springer, Cham (2019). https://doi.org/10.1007/978-3-030-17462-0_5
10. Cok, D.R.: OpenJML: JML for Java 7 by extending OpenJDK. In: Bobaru, M., Havelund, K., Holzmann, G.J., Joshi, R. (eds.) NFM 2011. LNCS, vol. 6617, pp. 472–479. Springer, Heidelberg (2011). https://doi.org/10.1007/978-3-642-20398-5_35
11. Conchon, S., Iguernlala, M., Ji, K., Melquiond, G., Fumex, C.: A three-tier strategy for reasoning about floating-point numbers in SMT. In: Majumdar, R., Kunčak, V. (eds.) CAV 2017. LNCS, vol. 10427, pp. 419–435. Springer, Cham (2017). https://doi.org/10.1007/978-3-319-63390-9_22
12. Cuoq, P., Kirchner, F., Kosmatov, N., Prevosto, V., Signoles, J., Yakobowski, B.: Frama-C. In: Eleftherakis, G., Hinchey, M., Holcombe, M. (eds.) SEFM 2012. LNCS, vol. 7504, pp. 233–247. Springer, Heidelberg (2012). https://doi.org/10.1007/978-3-642-33826-7_16
13. De Dinechin, F., Lauter, C., Melquiond, G.: Certifying the floating-point implementation of an elementary function using Gappa. IEEE Trans. Comput. 60(2), 242–253 (2010)
14. Delmas, D., Goubault, E., Putot, S., Souyris, J., Tekkal, K., Védrine, F.: Towards an industrial Use of FLUCTUAT on safety-critical avionics software. In: Alpuente, M., Cook, B., Joubert, C. (eds.) FMICS 2009. LNCS, vol. 5825, pp. 53–69. Springer, Heidelberg (2009). https://doi.org/10.1007/978-3-642-04570-7_6
15. Dross, C., Moy, Y.: Auto-active proof of red-black trees in SPARK. In: Barrett, C., Davies, M., Kahsai, T. (eds.) NFM 2017. LNCS, vol. 10227, pp. 68–83. Springer, Cham (2017). https://doi.org/10.1007/978-3-319-57288-8_5
16. Fumex, C., Marché, C., Moy, Y.: Automating the verification of floating-point programs. In: Paskevich, A., Wies, T. (eds.) VSTTE 2017. LNCS, vol. 10712, pp. 102–119. Springer, Cham (2017). https://doi.org/10.1007/978-3-319-72308-2_7

17. Jacobs, B., Smans, J., Philippaerts, P., Vogels, F., Penninckx, W., Piessens, F.: VeriFast: a powerful, sound, predictable, fast verifier for C and Java. In: Bobaru, M., Havelund, K., Holzmann, G.J., Joshi, R. (eds.) NFM 2011. LNCS, vol. 6617, pp. 41–55. Springer, Heidelberg (2011). https://doi.org/10.1007/978-3-642-20398-5_4

18. Leino, K.R.M., Moskal, M.: Usable auto-active verification. In: Usable Verification Workshop (2010)

19. Matsushita, Y., Tsukada, T., Kobayashi, N.: RustHorn: CHC-based verification for rust programs. In: European Symposium on Programming, pp. 484–514. Springer, Cham (2020)

20. McCormick, J.W., Chapin, P.C.: Building High Integrity Applications with SPARK. Cambridge University Press, Cambridge (2015)

21. Monniaux, D.: The pitfalls of verifying floating-point computations. ACM Trans. Program. Lang. Syst. (TOPLAS) 30(3), 1–41 (2008)

22. Moscato, M.M., Titolo, L., Feliú, M.A., Muñoz, C.A.: Provably correct floating-point implementation of a point-in-polygon algorithm. In: ter Beek, M.H., McIver, A., Oliveira, J.N. (eds.) FM 2019. LNCS, vol. 11800, pp. 21–37. Springer, Cham (2019). https://doi.org/10.1007/978-3-030-30942-8_3

23. Rümmer, P., Wahl, T.: An SMT-LIB theory of binary floating-point arithmetic. In: International Workshop on Satisfiability Modulo Theories (SMT), p. 151 (2010)

A Calculus for Multi-language
Operational Semantics

Matteo Cimini(✉) (iD)

University of Massachusetts Lowell, Lowell, MA 01854, USA
matteo_cimini@uml.edu

Abstract. We present $\lambda^{\mathcal{L}}$, a statically typed lambda-calculus with languages as first-class citizens. In $\lambda^{\mathcal{L}}$, languages can be defined and used to execute programs and, furthermore, they also can be bound to variables, passed to functions, and returned by functions, among other operations. Moreover, code of different languages can safely interact thanks to pre- and post-conditions that are checked at run-time.

We provide a type system and an operational semantics for $\lambda^{\mathcal{L}}$. We observe that Milner's type safety is too strong a property in this context, as programmers may intentionally execute unsafe languages. We then identify a type safety theorem that is specific to the domain of multi-language programming, and we prove that $\lambda^{\mathcal{L}}$ satisfies this theorem.

Keywords: Multi-language programming · Type systems · Operational semantics

1 Introduction

Different parts of a programming solution should be written with different programming languages. Accordingly, software has been increasingly written combining multiple programming languages, and a number of systems have been created to support multi-language programming. These systems fall under the umbrella name of language workbenches [14], and are sophisticated software tools that empower programmers to define their own languages, and assist them in most aspect of language development and composition.

One of the major questions that arise when designing a language workbench is: What is the status that languages have within the system? In most language workbenches, languages have an ad-hoc treatment, programmers define them in a separate part of the system, and they are composed with specific directives in another part of the system [3,16,17]. Racket [13], SugarJ [10] and SugarHaskell [11], instead, make an attempt to a seamless integration of languages into a host programming language. In this approach, languages are macro-expanded into a plain functional programming language in Racket, into plain Java in SugarJ, and into plain Haskell in SugarHaskell.

R. Bloem et al. (Eds.): NSV 2021/VSTTE 2021, LNCS 13124, pp. 25–42, 2022.
https://doi.org/10.1007/978-3-030-95561-8_3

Cimini has presented a vision paper that proposes an approach based on languages as first-class citizens, implemented in the LANG-N-PLAY programming language [6]. In this approach, language definitions (operational semantics descriptions) are part of a general-purpose programming language with the same status as any other expressions. Languages are elevated to be run-time values and can be bound to variables, passed to functions, returned by functions, inserted into lists, and so on. These are features that are not available in Racket, SugarJ and SugarHaskell, as languages are not first-class citizens in those systems. We notice, however, that these features *are* possible in other systems that can *internally represent* or encode languages, as objects, for example, which then can be passed around and stored. However, in the same way that it is worth formalizing functions as first-class citizens despite the fact that there are languages such as C which can *represent/encode* them, we believe that it is worth formalizing languages as first-class citizens on their own.

The goal of this paper is to provide a small core calculus based on first-class languages, which in turn provides a semantics for multi-language programming. The contributions of this paper are the following.

- We present $\lambda^{\mathcal{L}}$, a typed lambda-calculus with languages as first-class citizens.
- We provide a type system and a dynamic semantics for $\lambda^{\mathcal{L}}$.
- We observe that Milner's type safety is too strong a property in this context, as programmers may intentionally execute unsafe languages. We then identify a type safety theorem that formalizes the idea that programs can only go wrong in the context of programmer-defined languages. We then prove that $\lambda^{\mathcal{L}}$ satisfies this theorem.

It is traditional in the programming languages field to elevate various entities as first-class citizens, such as functions, continuations, objects, and proofs, among others. In keeping with this tradition, this paper provides a formal semantics of languages as first-class citizens.

Ultimately, $\lambda^{\mathcal{L}}$ contributes to providing a solid foundation for multi-language programming.

Closely Related Work. The idea of first-class languages has been previously presented [6], and is not a contribution of this paper. That previous contribution is a short paper (4 pages + references) that briefly describes the approach with LANG-N-PLAY examples. That contribution does not provide a formal semantics and a type safety theorem, which are the contributions of this paper.

Some parts of the implementation of LANG-N-PLAY have been previously described [7]. This latter contribution makes the point that features such as first-class formulae and implicative goals have been a great fit in implementing LANG-N-PLAY. Again, a core calculus for first-class languages, together with a type system, dynamic semantics, and a safety theorem, is novel in this paper.

Roadmap of the Paper. Section 2 presents a formalization of $\lambda^{\mathcal{L}}$: Sect. 2.1 and 2.2 provide the syntax of $\lambda^{\mathcal{L}}$, Sect. 2.3 presents a type system, and Sect. 2.4

presents an operational semantics for $\lambda^{\mathcal{L}}$. Section 3 offers examples of $\lambda^{\mathcal{L}}$ programs. Section 4 provides a type safety result for $\lambda^{\mathcal{L}}$. Section 5 discusses the limitations of our system, and future work. Section 6 discusses related work, and Sect. 7 concludes the paper.

Proofs and the auxiliary definitions that are not in the paper can be found in the online additional material of the paper [8].

2 Formalizing First-Class Languages

We present $\lambda^{\mathcal{L}}$, a formal semantics for a core fragment of LANG-N-PLAY. This calculus is a lambda-calculus with language definitions embedded. $\lambda^{\mathcal{L}}$ provides a syntax for (programmer-defined) language definitions (Sect. 2.1), and a host lambda-calculus ($\lambda^{\mathcal{L}}$ programs, Sect. 2.2).

2.1 Syntax for Language Definitions

The syntax for language definitions is the following, where **cname** $\in$ CATNAME, **X** $\in$ META-VAR, **opname** $\in$ OPNAME, and **pn** $\in$ PREDNAME.

Language	$\mathcal{L}$ ::=	$(\mathbf{G}, \mathbf{I})$
Grammar	$\mathbf{G}$ ::=	$\mathbf{s_1} \cdots \mathbf{s_n}$
Grammar Production	$\mathbf{s}$ ::=	$\mathbf{cname\ X} ::= \mathbf{t_1} \mid \cdots \mid \mathbf{t_n}$
Inference System	$\mathbf{I}$ ::=	$\mathbf{r_1} \cdots \mathbf{r_n}$
Rule	$\mathbf{r}$ ::=	$\dfrac{f_1 \ \cdots \ f_n}{f}$
Formula	$\mathbf{f}$ ::=	$(\mathbf{pn\ t_1} \cdots \mathbf{t_n})$
Term	$\mathbf{t}$ ::=	$\mathbf{X} \mid (\mathbf{opname\ t_1} \cdots \mathbf{t_n}) \mid (\mathbf{X})\mathbf{t} \mid \mathbf{t}[\mathbf{t}/\mathbf{X}].$

We assume a set of grammar category names CATNAME, a set of meta-variables META-VAR, a set of constructor operator names OPNAME, and a set of predicate names PREDNAME. As CATNAME contains the names of the syntactic categories that can be used in grammars, some examples of its elements are Expression, Type, and Value. OPNAME contains elements such as head, unitType, and λ (elements do not have to necessarily be (string) names). PREDNAME contains the predicates that model the various relations of the language being defined. Examples of predicates in PREDNAME are $\vdash$, to model a typing relation, and $\longrightarrow$, to model a reduction relation. Predicates are used to build the formulae that are derivable in an inference system defined by the language.

To facilitate the modeling of our calculus, we assume that terms and formulae are defined in abstract syntax tree style. Therefore, terms have a top level constructor applied to a list of terms. To make an example, the β rule is represented with $(\longrightarrow (\mathbf{app\ (abs(x)e)\ v})\ \mathbf{e[v/x]}))$. We omit drawing the horizontal line in rules with no premises.

$\lambda^{\mathcal{L}}$ provides syntax to specify unary binding $(\mathbf{X})\mathbf{t}$ [5], where the variable $\mathbf{X}$ is bound in the term $\mathbf{t}$. $\lambda^{\mathcal{L}}$ also provides an explicit construct $\mathbf{t[t/X]}$ for the capture-avoiding substitution operartion.

To make an example, the following is a large part of the definition of the simply typed λ-calculus in $\lambda^{\mathcal{L}}$. (The type for integers and the constant for zero only serve as base case so that we can make examples later on).

(
Type T ::= (int) | ($\rightarrow$ **T T**)
Expression e ::= (zero) | (var x) | (app e e) | (abs (x)e)
Value v ::= (zero) | (abs (x)e)
TEnvironment Gamma ::= (emptyTE) | (consTE x T Gamma)
Configuration c ::= (conf e)
Context E ::= □ | (app E e) | (app v E)
TypeChecker _ ::= ($\vdash$ (emptyTE) c T),

$$(\longrightarrow \ (app \ (abs(x)e) \ v) \ e[v/x])$$

$$\frac{(\longrightarrow \ e \ e')}{(\longrightarrow \ (conf \ e) \ (conf \ e'))}$$

$$(\vdash \ \textbf{Gamma} \ (zero) \ (int))$$

$$\frac{(lookup \ \textbf{Gamma} \ x \ \textbf{T})}{(\vdash \ \textbf{Gamma} \ x \ \textbf{T})}$$

$$\frac{(\vdash \ \textbf{Gamma} \ e_1 \ (\rightarrow \ T_1 \ T_2)) \qquad (\vdash \ \textbf{Gamma} \ e_2 \ T_1)}{(\vdash \ \textbf{Gamma} \ (app \ e_1 \ e_2) \ T_2)}$$

$$\frac{(\vdash \ (consTE \ x \ T_1 \ \textbf{Gamma}) \ e \ T_2)}{(\vdash \ \textbf{Gamma} \ (abs \ (x)e) \ T_2)}$$

$$\frac{(\vdash \ \textbf{Gamma} \ e \ T)}{(\vdash \ \textbf{Gamma} \ (conf \ e) \ T)}$$

and the rest of the rules, which define **lookup**.

).

In this language definition, **Type**, **Expression**, **Value**, **TEnvironment**, **Configuration**, **Context**, and **TypeChecker** are in CATNAME, **int**, $\rightarrow$, **zero**, **app**, **abs**, **emptyTE**, **consTE**, □, and **conf** are in OPNAME, $\longrightarrow$ and $\vdash$ are in PREDNAME, and meta-variables such as **e**, **T**, **v**, and so on, are in META-VAR.

We have omitted the inference rules that define the lookup function for the type environment **Gamma**, which can certainly be defined with inference rules.

We call the language definition above *lambda* in the remainder of the paper. As languages may have a state, (which *lambda* does not have), $\lambda^{\mathcal{L}}$ fixes the

convention that the configuration (expression + state) must be declared in the
syntactic category **Configuration**. The constructor **conf** is used for configura-
tions in the following way: $(\textbf{conf } \hat{t_1}\ t_2\ \ldots\ t_n)$, where the first argument $\hat{t_1}$ is
the expression to execute, and the other arguments form the state. The state is
formed with terms and not executable terms, so the state cannot contain program executions. The use of the constructor **var** as in $(\textbf{var x})$ indicates that the
meta-variables **x**, **x1**, **x2**, and so on, are variables of the language being defined.
Also by convention, the syntactic category **TypeChecker** specifies the formula
to call for type checking.

2.2 Syntax for Programs

The syntax of $\lambda^{\mathcal{L}}$ programs is defined as follows. Below, $\mathcal{X} \in \{\textbf{T}, \textbf{U}\}$.

Type	τ	$::= \mathcal{L} \mid \tau \rightarrow \tau \mid \alpha \mid \forall(\alpha <: \mathcal{L}).\tau \mid \diamond$
Expression	e	$::= \textsf{x} \mid \lambda\textsf{x} : \tau.\textsf{e} \mid \textsf{e e}$
(*languages*)		$\mid \mathcal{L} \mid (\textsf{e pn}_1\ \textsf{pn}_2)\mathord{>}^{\mathcal{X}}\ \hat{\textsf{t}} \mid \textsf{e union e}$
(*lang. polymorphism*)		$\mid \Lambda(\alpha <: \mathcal{L}).\textsf{e} \mid \textsf{e } [\mathcal{L}]$
(*embedded values*)		$\mid \textsf{Val t in } \mathcal{L}$
(*errors*)		$\mid \texttt{InteropErrorPre} \mid \texttt{InteropErrorPost}$
Value	v	$::= \mathcal{L} \mid \lambda\textsf{x} : \tau.\textsf{e} \mid \Lambda(\alpha <: \mathcal{L}).\textsf{e} \mid \textsf{Val t in } \mathcal{L}$
Error	err	$::= \texttt{InteropErrorPre} \mid \texttt{InteropErrorPost}$
Executable Term	$\hat{\textsf{t}}$	$::= \textbf{X} \mid (\textsf{opname } \hat{t_1} \cdots \hat{t_n}) \mid (\textbf{X})\hat{\textsf{t}} \mid (\textsf{e pn}_1\ \textsf{pn}_2)\mathord{>}^{\mathcal{X}}\ \hat{\textsf{t}}.$

$\lambda^{\mathcal{L}}$ includes variables, functions and applications. Languages $\mathcal{L}$ (from the
grammar in Sect. 2.1) are also expressions as any others. Notice that languages
are also types. In $\lambda^{\mathcal{L}}$, the type of a language $\mathcal{L}$ is $\mathcal{L}$ itself. This is because we
call the type checker of $\mathcal{L}$ before executing a program. However, as languages
can be built via unions and functions, they may not be syntactically explicit,
and so we keep track of the intended language with a type.

Program Executions. The expressions $(\textsf{e pn}_1\ \textsf{pn}_2)\mathord{>}^{\textbf{T}}\ \hat{\textsf{t}}$ and $(\textsf{e pn}_1\ \textsf{pn}_2)\mathord{>}^{\textbf{U}}\ \hat{\textsf{t}}$
are *program executions*, **e** is a language, $\textbf{pn}_1$ and $\textbf{pn}_2$ are predicate names for
pre- and post-conditions, respectively, and $\hat{\textsf{t}}$ is the program to be executed (which
we will explain shortly). The program execution tagged with **T** type checks $\hat{\textsf{t}}$
at compile-time using the type checker defined in the language **e**. The program
execution tagged with **U** does not. We use the distinction **T** versus **U** to model
the fact that a program $\hat{\textsf{t}}$ is type checked only at the beginning, and it is not
type checked after each step that it takes afterwards. After the first step, a
program execution always becomes **U**-tagged. A term $\hat{\textsf{t}}$ is an *executable term*,
which can be a term t without substitution notation[1], and which can contain
other program executions inside. Nested program executions, each with its own
language, invoke the switch from a language to another.

---

[1] Substitution operations such as $e[v/x]$ are used in reduction rules, and not in the
plain programs that programmers write.

As a simple example of a program execution, consider the $\lambda^{\mathcal{L}}$ program

$$(lambda \text{ \textbf{true} \textbf{true}})>^{\text{T}} (\textbf{conf} (\textbf{app} (\textbf{abs} (\textbf{x})\textbf{x}) (\textbf{zero}))).$$

At compile-time, $\lambda^{\mathcal{L}}$ extracts the type checker defined in $lambda$ (the inference rules in Sect. 2.1), and type checks (**conf** (**app** (**abs** (**x**)**x**) (**zero**))) successfully with it. If we had $(lambda \text{ \textbf{true} \textbf{true}})>^{\text{T}}$ (**conf** (**app** (**zero**) (**zero**))), the type checker of $lambda$ would fail, and so $\lambda^{\mathcal{L}}$ would reject the $\lambda^{\mathcal{L}}$ program.

At run-time, the pre-condition is checked on the program to be executed. In $(\textbf{e} \text{ \textbf{pn}}_1 \text{ \textbf{pn}}_2)>^{\text{T}} \hat{t}$, we have that $\textbf{pn}_1$ and $\textbf{pn}_2$ are the predicate names for the pre- and post-condition checks. These predicates are defined in the inference rules of the language. $\lambda^{\mathcal{L}}$ fixes the convention that these predicates take in input a configuration. Notice that since the pre- and post-conditions are defined with inference rules, programmers may also end up writing undecidable checks. Above, we assume that the predicate **true** always holds. In our example, the inference system of $lambda$ is interrogated for the formula (**true** (**conf** (**app** (**abs** (**x**)**x**) (**zero**)))). Afterwards, $\lambda^{\mathcal{L}}$ extracts the reduction semantics relation from $lambda$, and uses it to compute a step. The program above reduces to $(lambda \text{ \textbf{true} \textbf{true}})>^{\text{U}}$ (**conf** (**zero**)).

Union and Functions. The $\lambda^{\mathcal{L}}$ calculus also includes the union operation on languages. The union operator simply adds new grammar items and inference rules to a language. For example, let us call the following piece of language *nan*:

$$($$
$$\textbf{Expression e} ::= (\textbf{NaN})$$
$$\textbf{Value v} ::= (\textbf{NaN}),$$

$$(\vdash \textbf{Gamma (NaN) (int)})$$
$$).$$

We have that $lambda$ **union** *nan* returns a language which is $lambda$ where **NaN** (Not a Number) is added to the grammars **Expression** and **Value**, and that also contains the typing rule for **NaN**. In the remainder of the paper, we call this resulting language *lambdaNan*, that is, *lambdaNan = lambda* **union** *nan*.

The union operator is rather rudimental in that it does not check whether the additions make sense. For example, we may merge two languages with typing rules of different shapes. As we are formalizing a core language, we are not concerned with sophisticated correctness checks at this stage.

$\lambda^{\mathcal{L}}$ can also define functions over languages. For example, we can define a function that takes a language and adds *nan* to it. $\lambda^{\mathcal{L}}$ does so with the abstraction $\lambda\textbf{x} : lambda.$ **x** **union** *nan*.

Bounded Polymorphism. The function $\lambda\textbf{x} : lambda.$ **x** **union** *nan*. is of little use, as it works only for one language as argument: *lambda*. What we would like to express is a function that adds *nan* to any language that has integers. $\lambda^{\mathcal{L}}$ can express that with bounded polymorphism à la System $F_{<:}$. Language abstraction $\Lambda(\alpha <: \mathcal{L}).\mathbf{e}$ means that the expression $\mathbf{e}$ is polymorphic over languages that contain the language $\mathcal{L}$. We say that α is a *language variable*. Language application $\mathbf{e}\ [\mathcal{L}]$ instantiates a language abstraction with $\mathcal{L}$. In our example, we would write $\Lambda(\alpha <: (\mathbf{Type\ T}::=\text{int})).\lambda x : \alpha.\ x\ \text{union}\ nan$. If we passed a language without integers, our type system would reject the program. (Standard mechanism of System $F_{<:}$).

Results of Programs. Val t in $\mathcal{L}$ is an *embedded value* and means that t is a finished computation for the language $\mathcal{L}$. More precisely, we have that the expression in **conf** in t is a value of $\mathcal{L}$. After executing each step of a program execution, $\lambda^{\mathcal{L}}$ checks whether we have reached a value. For example, after we end up with $(lambda\ \mathbf{true\ true})\text{>}^{\mathrm{U}}$ (**conf** (**zero**)) in the example above, $\lambda^{\mathcal{L}}$ extracts the grammar **Value** from *lambda*, and checks whether (**zero**) can be derived with this grammar. If that is not the case, $\lambda^{\mathcal{L}}$ strives to compute more steps. If (**zero**) is a value of *lambda*, as it is the case, then $\lambda^{\mathcal{L}}$ returns the embedded value Val (**conf** (**zero**)) in *lambda* as a result. As (**zero**) may return in the context of a parent program execution, $\lambda^{\mathcal{L}}$ checks that the post-condition on (**conf** (**zero**)) holds.

$\lambda^{\mathcal{L}}$ can throw errors InteropErrorPre and InteropErrorPost when pre- and post-conditions checks fail at run-time. Pre- and post-conditions for language interoperability are not a novelty introduced by $\lambda^{\mathcal{L}}$. Readers may think of analogous checks that Racket can do with contracts, for example. Ultimately, the evaluation of a $\lambda^{\mathcal{L}}$ program can lead to Val t in $\mathcal{L}$, InteropErrorPre, InteropErrorPost, or to a stuck or non terminating execution.

On Our Language Conventions. As the reader may have noticed, $\lambda^{\mathcal{L}}$ adopts a number of conventions, which we describe in this paper as we encounter them. For the sake of reference, the online additional material of the paper [8] collects these conventions in one section.

2.3   Type System

Figure 1 shows the type system for $\lambda^{\mathcal{L}}$. The main typing judgement is $\Gamma \vdash \mathbf{e} : \tau$, which says that the expression $\mathbf{e}$ has type τ under the assumptions in Γ. The type environment Γ assigns types to variables, and collects subtyping information of the form $\alpha <: \mathcal{L}$.

The typing rules for variables, functions, applications and errors (which can be typed at any type) are standard, and are omitted from Fig. 1. They are repeated in the additional material [8]. Rules (T-LANG-ABS) and (T-LANG-APP) are adaptations of the standard rules of System $F_{<:}$. The subtyping relations are also defined in Fig. 1. The crux of subtyping is that a language $\mathcal{L}_1$ is a subtype of another language $\mathcal{L}_2$ if $\mathcal{L}_1$ contains $\mathcal{L}_2$.

(T-LAN) assigns the language itself as the type of a language.

(T-EXEC-T) type checks program executions $(\mathbf{e}\ \mathbf{pn_1}\ \mathbf{pn_2})\text{>}^{\mathrm{T}}\ \hat{t}$. Here, $\mathbf{e}$ must be of language type. Next, we need to check that $\hat{t}$ is well-typed in the language

Type Environment $\Gamma ::= \emptyset \mid \Gamma, x : \tau \mid \Gamma, \alpha <: \mathcal{L}$

$$\boxed{\Gamma \vdash e : \tau}$$

(T-EXEC-T)

$$\Gamma \vdash e : \mathcal{L}$$
$$\text{type-check-formula}(\mathcal{L}) = (\text{pn } t_1 \cdots t_n \text{ c } T)$$
$$[\![\mathcal{L} \cup_{snx} \{!(\text{pn } X_1 \cdots X_n ((X_e \ X_{pn1} \ X_{pn2})>^T X_t) \ T)!\}]\!]^{lp} \models (\text{pn } t_1 \cdots t_n \ \hat{t} \ T)$$
$$\Gamma \vdash_{trm} \hat{t}$$
$$\overline{\Gamma \vdash (e \ pn_1 \ pn_2)>^T \hat{t} : \diamond}$$

(T-EXEC-U)

$$\frac{\Gamma \vdash e : \mathcal{L}}{\Gamma \vdash (e \ pn_1 \ pn_2)>^U \hat{t} : \diamond}$$

(T-UNION)

$$\frac{\Gamma \vdash e_1 : \mathcal{L}_1 \quad \Gamma \vdash e_2 : \mathcal{L}_2}{\Gamma \vdash e_1 \text{ union } e_2 : \mathcal{L}_1 \cup_{snx} \mathcal{L}_2}$$

(T-EMB-VAL)

$$\frac{\text{grammar}(\mathcal{L}) = G \quad v \Rightarrow^*_G |t|}{\Gamma \vdash \text{Val } t \text{ in } \mathcal{L} : \diamond}$$

(T-LAN)

$$\frac{}{\Gamma \vdash \mathcal{L} : \mathcal{L}}$$

(T-LANG-ABS)

$$\frac{\Gamma, \alpha <: \mathcal{L} \vdash e : \tau}{\Gamma \vdash \Lambda(\alpha <: \mathcal{L}).e : \forall(\alpha <: \mathcal{L}).\tau}$$

(T-LANG-APP)

$$\frac{\Gamma \vdash e : \forall(\alpha <: \mathcal{L}_1).\tau \quad \Gamma \vdash \mathcal{L}_2 <: \mathcal{L}_1}{\Gamma \vdash e \ [\mathcal{L}_2] : \tau[\mathcal{L}_2/\alpha]}$$

$$\boxed{\Gamma \vdash_{trm} \hat{t}}$$

(T-TERM)

$$\frac{\Gamma \vdash_{trm} \hat{t_1} \quad \cdots \quad \Gamma \vdash_{trm} \hat{t_n}}{\Gamma \vdash_{trm} (\text{opname } \hat{t_1} \cdots \hat{t_n})}$$

(T-TERM-EXEC)

$$\frac{\Gamma \vdash (e \ pn_1 \ pn_2)>^{\mathcal{X}} \hat{t} : \diamond}{\Gamma \vdash_{trm} (e \ pn_1 \ pn_2)>^{\mathcal{X}} \hat{t}} \quad \mathcal{X} \in \{T, U\}$$

$$\boxed{\Gamma \vdash \mathcal{L}_1 <: \mathcal{L}_2, \text{ and related subtyping relations}}$$

(S-VAR)

$$\frac{\alpha <: \mathcal{L}_1 \in \Gamma \quad \Gamma \vdash \mathcal{L}_1 <: \mathcal{L}_2}{\Gamma \vdash \alpha <: \mathcal{L}_2}$$

(S-LANG)

$$\frac{G_1 <: G_2 \quad I_1 <: I_2}{\Gamma \vdash (G_1, I_2) <: (G_2, I_2)}$$

(S-GRAMMAR-WIDTH)

$$\frac{n \geq m}{s_i <: s_i' \quad \forall i. \ 0 \leq i \leq n}$$
$$\overline{\Gamma \vdash s_1 \cdots s_n <: s_1' \cdots s_m'}$$

(S-RULES-WIDTH)

$$\frac{n \geq m}{r_i <: r_i' \quad \forall i. \ 0 \leq i \leq n}$$
$$\overline{\Gamma \vdash r_1 \cdots r_n <: r_1' \cdots r_m'}$$

(S-ITEMS-WIDTH)

$$\frac{n \geq m}{\Gamma \vdash \text{cname } X ::= t_1 \mid \cdots \mid t_n <: \text{cname } X ::= t_1 \mid \cdots \mid t_m}$$

Fig. 1. Type system for $\lambda^{\mathcal{L}}$

of **e** (which is $\mathcal{L}$). To do so, we use the meta-operation `type-check-formula(`$\mathcal{L}$`)`, whose definition can be found in the online additional material [8]. This operation retrieves the formula that the language $\mathcal{L}$ specifies for type checking. This function tells us that our type checking call is of the form (**pn** $t_1 \cdots t_n$ **c T**). By convention, $\lambda^{\mathcal{L}}$ fixes that the last argument is always the output type and the second last argument is the configuration in input to be type checked. The formula we need to check is then (**pn** $t_1 \cdots t_n$ $\hat{t}$ **T**), where we placed $\hat{t}$ at the correct position. However, we encounter a problem here because $\hat{t}$ may not exclusively contain operators of $\mathcal{L}$, as it may contain nested program executions. The program execution construct is unrecognized by the type checker of $\mathcal{L}$. To solve this problem, we augment the type checker of $\mathcal{L}$ with a typing rule that always succeeds to type check program executions. We do so with $\mathcal{L} \cup_{\mathsf{snx}} \{!(\mathbf{pn}\ X_1 \cdots X_n\ ((X_e\ X_{\mathrm{pn1}}\ X_{\mathrm{pn2}}) >^T X_t)\ T)!\}$, where all variables are free to be instantiated with anything, and so we have that program executions are always well-typed. The union $\cup_{\mathsf{snx}}$ is the meta-operation that is counterpart to the $\lambda^{\mathcal{L}}$ syntactic operation **union**. This operation simply adds new grammar items and inference rules to a language. Its definition is straightforward, and can be found in the online additional material [8].

At this point, we have another problem. The type system of $\mathcal{L}$ is a syntactic description. Instead, we are supposed to use it as an inference rule system to check whether a typing formula can be derived. To achieve that, we translate the language into a higher-order logic program, and we use the provability relation of logic programs to check whether (**pn** $t_1 \cdots t_n$ $\hat{t}$ **T**) is derivable. The translation of our language definitions into logic programs is easy, and can be found in the online additional material [8]. The provability relation $\models$ comes directly from the semantics of logic programs [19].

Although we ignore nested program executions in $\hat{t}$ when we type check $\hat{t}$ in $\mathcal{L}$, we still need to handle them. Indeed, a nested (**e**' $\mathbf{pn}'_1\ \mathbf{pn}'_2$) > $\hat{t}'$ in $\hat{t}$ needs to see whether **e**' type checks $\hat{t}'$. Intuitively, we need to apply the very (T-EXEC-T) rule to that subterm. We do so with $\Gamma \vdash_{\mathsf{trm}} \hat{t}$, which traverses executable terms, and applies the main typing judgement $\vdash$ to program executions.

Ultimately, we assign the type $\diamond$ to program executions, which simply says that the program execution is well-typed.

(T-EXEC-U) is analogous to (T-EXEC-T) but it does not type check $\hat{t}$.

(T-UNION) type checks the union operation. The type assigned to this operation is $\mathcal{L}_1 \cup_{\mathsf{snx}} \mathcal{L}_2$, which performs the union previously described.

(T-EMB-VAL) type checks **Val t in** $\mathcal{L}$. The meta-operation `grammar(`$\mathcal{L}$`)` returns the formal grammar of $\mathcal{L}$. That is, the description of the grammar is translated into the formal tuple (V, Σ, R, S) of context-free grammars. We then use the standard derivation relation to check that $|t|$ can be derived from the grammar category of **v**, that is, the values of $\mathcal{L}$. The operation $|t|$ extracts the expression argument of **conf**. The definition of `grammar(`$\mathcal{L}$`)` and $|t|$ are straightforward, and can be found in the online additional material [8].

Context $E ::= \Box \mid E\ e \mid v\ E \mid (E\ pn_1\ pn_2)>^{\mathcal{X}} \hat{t} \mid E$ union $e \mid v$ union $E \mid E\ [\mathcal{L}]$

(R-BETA)   (R-LANG-PASS)

$\lambda x : \tau . e\ v \longrightarrow e[v/x]$ $(\Lambda(\alpha <: \mathcal{L}_1).e)\ [\mathcal{L}_2] \longrightarrow e[\mathcal{L}_2/\alpha]$

(R-PRE-SUCCESS)
$$\frac{[\![\mathcal{L}]\!]^{lp} \models (pn_1\ \hat{t})}{(\mathcal{L}\ pn_1\ pn_2)>^T \hat{t} \longrightarrow (\mathcal{L}\ pn_1\ pn_2)>^U \hat{t}}$$

(R-PRE-ERROR)
$$\frac{[\![\mathcal{L}]\!]^{lp} \not\models (pn_1\ \hat{t})}{(\mathcal{L}\ pn_1\ pn_2)>^T \hat{t} \longrightarrow \texttt{InteropErrorPre}}$$

(R-EXEC)
$$\frac{[\![\mathcal{L}]\!]^{lp} \models (\hat{t} \longrightarrow \hat{t}')}{(\mathcal{L}\ pn_1\ pn_2)>^U \hat{t} \longrightarrow (\mathcal{L}\ pn_1\ pn_2)>^U \hat{t}'}$$

(R-EXEC-SUCCESS)
$$\frac{\texttt{grammar}(\mathcal{L}) = G \quad v \Rightarrow^*_G \hat{t} \quad [\![\mathcal{L}]\!]^{lp} \models (pn_2\ \hat{t})}{(\mathcal{L}\ pn_1\ pn_2)>^U \hat{t} \longrightarrow \texttt{Val}\ \hat{t}\ \texttt{in}\ \mathcal{L}}$$

(R-EXEC-POST-ERROR)
$$\frac{\texttt{grammar}(\mathcal{L}) = G \quad v \Rightarrow^*_G t \quad [\![\mathcal{L}]\!]^{lp} \not\models (pn_2\ \hat{t})}{(\mathcal{L}\ pn_1\ pn_2)>^U \hat{t} \longrightarrow \texttt{InteropErrorPost}}$$

(R-SWITCH)
$$\frac{\begin{array}{c}[\![\mathcal{L}]\!]^{lp} \models \hat{t_1} = E[(e\ pn_3\ pn_4)>^{\mathcal{X}} (conf\ \hat{t_1^?}\ t_2'\ \dots\ t_n')] \\ (e\ pn_3\ pn_4)>^{\mathcal{X}} (conf\ \hat{t_1^?}\ t_2\ \dots\ t_n) \longrightarrow e' \\ \texttt{config-split}(e') = (t_1^{?\prime\prime}, t_2''\ \dots\ t_n'')\end{array}}{(\mathcal{L}\ pn_1\ pn_2)>^U (conf\ \hat{t_1}\ t_2\ \dots\ t_n) \longrightarrow (\mathcal{L}\ pn_1\ pn_2)>^U (conf\ E[t_1^{?\prime\prime}]\ t_2''\ \dots\ t_n'')}$$

(R-SWITCH-ERROR)
$$\frac{\begin{array}{c}[\![\mathcal{L}]\!]^{lp} \models \hat{t_1} = E[(e\ pn_3\ pn_4)>^{\mathcal{X}} (conf\ \hat{t_1^?}\ t_2'\ \dots\ t_n')] \\ (e\ pn_3\ pn_4)>^{\mathcal{X}} (conf\ \hat{t_1^?}\ t_2\ \dots\ t_n) \longrightarrow \texttt{err}\end{array}}{(\mathcal{L}\ pn_1\ pn_2)>^U (conf\ \hat{t_1}\ t_2\ \dots\ t_n) \longrightarrow \texttt{err}}$$

(R-UNION)   (CTX)   (CTX-ERR)

$\mathcal{L}_1$ union $\mathcal{L}_2 \longrightarrow \mathcal{L}_1 \cup_{\textsf{snx}} \mathcal{L}_2$ $\dfrac{e \longrightarrow e'}{E[e] \longrightarrow E[e']}$ $\dfrac{E \neq \Box}{E[\texttt{err}] \longrightarrow \texttt{err}}$

Fig. 2. Reduction semantics of $\lambda^{\mathcal{L}}$. In this figure, we have $\mathcal{X} \in \{T, U\}$.

2.4   Reduction Semantics

Figure 2 shows the reduction semantics of $\lambda^{\mathcal{L}}$. We adopt a small-step operational semantics style with evaluation contexts, which are defined in Fig. 2, as well. The reduction relation has a standard form $\mathbf{e} \longrightarrow \mathbf{e}$.

Rule (R-BETA) is standard, and rule (R-LANG-PASS) is the type application of System $F_{<:}$, adapted to passing languages. Here, the substitution $\mathbf{e}[\mathcal{L}/\alpha]$ replaces α with $\mathcal{L}$ in $\mathbf{e}$.

Rules (R-PRE-SUCCESS) and (R-PRE-ERROR) apply before starting to execute $(\mathcal{L}\ \mathbf{pn_1}\ \mathbf{pn_2})\mathbf{>^T}\ \hat{\mathbf{t}}$. The language is translated into a logic program, and we use the provability relation to check whether the pre-condition $(\mathbf{pn_1}\ \hat{\mathbf{t}})$ holds. If it holds then the program execution turns to $\mathbf{U}$-tagged. If it does not hold then we throw the error `InteropErrorPre`.

(R-EXEC) executes programs according to the reduction semantics of a given language. It applies to $\mathbf{U}$-tagged program executions. The language is translated into a logic program, and we use the provability relation to compute a step.

Rules (R-EXEC-SUCCESS) and (R-EXEC-POST-ERROR) apply when a program execution is finished. We detect that the computation is finished by extracting the grammar of the language, which we do with $\mathtt{grammar}(\mathcal{L})$, and then by using it to check that $\mathbf{t}$ can be derived with the grammar **Value**. If that is the case, the computation is finished, therefore we check the post-condition. We do so by translating the language into a logic program, and using the provability relation to check whether $(\mathbf{pn_2}\ \hat{\mathbf{t}})$ holds. If it holds then rule (R-EXEC-SUCCESS) applies, and we return an embedded value. If it does not hold then rule (R-EXEC-POST-ERROR) applies, and we throw the error `InteropErrorPost`.

Rule (R-SWITCH) handles the case in which a program execution is stuck because one of its subterms is a program execution, as well. Let us consider the program execution $(\mathcal{L}\ \mathbf{pn_1}\ \mathbf{pn_2})\mathbf{>^U}\ (\mathbf{conf}\ \hat{\mathbf{t_1}}\ \mathbf{t_2}\ \dots\ \mathbf{t_n})$. When the focus of the evaluation contexts of $\hat{\mathbf{t_1}}$ points to another program execution, then $\hat{\mathbf{t_1}}$ is stuck because program executions are not recognized by the operational semantics of $\mathcal{L}$. We detect this scenario by translating the language into a logic program and using the provability relation to derive that $\hat{\mathbf{t_1}}$ can be decomposed in an evaluation context with the focus on a program execution $(\mathbf{e}\ \mathbf{pn_3}\ \mathbf{pn_4})\mathbf{>^{\mathcal{X}}}\ (\mathbf{conf}\ \hat{\mathbf{t_1'}}\ \mathbf{t_2'}\ \dots\ \mathbf{t_n'})$. At this point, we need to execute this nested program execution. To do so, rule (R-SWITCH) computes the reduction $(\mathbf{e}\ \mathbf{pn_3}\ \mathbf{pn_4})\mathbf{>^{\mathcal{X}}}\ (\mathbf{conf}\ \hat{\mathbf{t_1'}}\ \mathbf{t_2}\ \dots\ \mathbf{t_n}) \longrightarrow \mathbf{e'}$, where the program $\hat{\mathbf{t_1'}}$ of the nested program execution is executed in the context of the state $\mathbf{t_2}\ \dots\ \mathbf{t_n}$ of the parent. At this point, there are three cases: 1) the step above produced $\mathbf{e'} = (\mathbf{e''}\ \mathbf{pn_3}\ \mathbf{pn_4})\mathbf{>^{\mathcal{X}}}\ (\mathbf{conf}\ \hat{\mathbf{t_1''}}\ \mathbf{t_2''}\ \dots\ \mathbf{t_n''})$, which means that the nested program execution is not finished, 2) $\mathbf{e'} = \mathtt{Val}\ (\mathbf{conf}\ \hat{\mathbf{t_1''}}\ \mathbf{t_2''}\ \dots\ \mathbf{t_n''})$ in $\mathcal{L}$, or 3) $\mathbf{e'} = \mathbf{err}$. Case 3) is handled by rule (R-SWITCH-ERROR), described below. (R-SWITCH) handles cases 1) and 2) in the following way. We use the meta-operation `config-split(e')` to split the configuration $\mathbf{e'}$. We define it as

$$\text{config-split}(\mathbf{e}) = (\mathbf{e}, t_2'' \ \dots \ t_n'')$$
$$where \ \mathbf{e} = (\mathbf{e}' \ pn_3 \ pn_4) >^{\mathcal{X}} \ (\text{conf} \ \hat{t_1''} \ t_2'' \ \dots \ t_n'')$$
$$\text{config-split}(\text{Val} \ (\text{conf} \ \hat{t_1''} \ t_2'' \ \dots \ t_n'') \ \text{in} \ \mathcal{L}) = (\hat{t_1''}, t_2'' \ \dots \ t_n'').$$

Suppose we are in case 1). We need to keep computing the nested program execution. The very rule (R-SWITCH) is responsible for executing that. We therefore prepare the ground for (R-SWITCH) to do that at the next step. We place $(\mathbf{e}'' \ pn_3 \ pn_4) >^{\mathcal{X}} \ (\text{conf} \ \hat{t_1''} \ t_2'' \ \dots \ t_n'')$ in the context, so that (R-SWITCH) will pick *that* up. We then copy the new state $t_2' \ \dots \ t_n'$ in the state of the parent because that state is inherited by the nested program execution.

Suppose we are in case 2). We place $\hat{t_1''}$ in the context, which is the final value just computed. Then, the control can go back to the parent program execution. As the nested program execution has modified the state, which is now $t_2' \ \dots \ t_n'$, we copy it in the state of the parent.

Rule (R-SWITCH-ERROR) handles case 3). This is the case in which a nested program execution results in an error **err** (whether it be `InteropErrorPre` or `InteropErrorPost`). In this case, we return the error.

Rule (R-UNION) performs the union of two languages using the operation that we have described previously.

Finally, (CTX) and (CTX-ERR) are the standard rules for evaluation contexts.

3   Examples

In this section, we provide some examples of $\lambda^{\mathcal{L}}$ programs. Due to lack of space, we show only examples that are related to multi-language programming, and we present simple, yet illustrative, examples. Additional examples can be found in the online additional material of the paper [8].

Example with Post-conditions. Consider augmenting *lambdaNan* with the predicate **noNan** defined by (**noNan** (conf (**zero**))). That is, **noNan** holds when a value is not **Nan**. Consider the $\lambda^{\mathcal{L}}$ program

(*lambda* **true true**)$>^{\mathbf{T}}$
(**conf** (**app** (**abs** (x).x) ((*lambdaNan* **true noNan**)$>^{\mathbf{T}}$ (**conf** (**NaN**)))))).

Here, we use the language *lambda* to compute a function application. However, the argument of the function is computed by invoking *lambdaNan*. This latter language has more values than *lambda*, as **NaN** is not recognized by *lambda*. Therefore, we set the post-condition **noNan** to check that the value computed with *lambdaNan*, which will cross to *lambda*, is not **NaN**.

At compile-time, the whole configuration is type checked with the type checker of *lambda* thanks to rule (T-EXEC-T). The problematic subterm for *lambda* is (*lambdaNan* **true noNan**)$>^{\mathbf{T}}$ (**conf** (**NaN**)). However, this subterm is well-typed because (T-EXEC-T) augments the type checker of *lambda* with the typing rule $\vdash ((\mathbf{X_e} \ \mathbf{X_{pn1}} \ \mathbf{X_{pn2}}) >^{\mathbf{T})} \ \mathbf{X_t} \ \mathbf{T}$.

We also need to check that **(conf (NaN))** is well-typed in *lambdaNan*, which $\vdash_{\mathsf{trm}}$ *(lambdaNan* **true noNan)**>$^{\mathbf{T}}$ **(conf (NaN))** checks, as it ultimately applies (T-EXEC-T) to such nested program execution.

At run-time, rule (R-SWITCH-ERROR) picks the nested program execution *(⟨lambdaNan* **true noNan)**>$^{\mathbf{T}}$ **(conf (NaN))**) and evaluates it using (R-EXEC-POST-ERROR) because **(NaN)** can be derived by the grammar of values of *lambdaNan*, and the post-condition **(noNan (conf (NaN)))** does not hold. Therefore, we throw `InteropErrorPost`, which is then taken by (R-SWITCH-ERROR) and propagated to the overall step.

As a second example, let us suppose that the argument of the function provides instead a value that is recognizable by *lambda*. For example, let us suppose that the argument is *(lambdaNan* **true noNan)**>$^{\mathbf{T}}$ **(conf (zero))**. The computation proceeds as previously, but rule (R-SWITCH) evaluates this subterm with (R-EXEC-SUCCESS) because the post-condition **(noNan (conf (zero)))** holds. Then, the step returns `Val` **(conf (zero))** in *lambdaNan*, which is going to place **(zero)** as the argument of the function in the *lambda* execution. Therefore, we end up with

$$\textit{(lambda } \textbf{true true)}\mathtt{>}^{\mathbf{T}} \textbf{ (conf (app (abs(x).x) (zero)))},$$

which can continue computing in *lambda*.

Example with Pre-conditions. Consider the language *increment*, where the state is an integer, and expressions can only do two operations: 1) **increment**, which increments the state, 2) and **(seq e e)**, which composes instructions in sequence. As types do not play a role, we make this language untyped. In our setting, this means that all configurations are well-typed. We also equip *increment* with a pre-condition predicate **okState** that checks that the integer state is a value that is recognizable by *increment*. The language *increment* is

```
(
Type T ::= (top)
Integer n ::= = (zero) | (succ n)
Expression e ::= = n | (increment) | (seq e e)
Context E ::= = (seq E e)
Value v ::= = n
Configuration c ::= = (conf e n)
TypeChecker _ ::= = ⊢ c T,
(⊢ c T)
(⟶ (conf (increment) n) (conf (succ n) (succ n)))
(⟶ (conf seq v e) n) (conf e n))
(okState (conf e (zero)))
(okState (conf e (succ n)))
).
```

Let us also define the language *nullify*, which includes *increment*, and adds the ability to nullify the state with the operation **nullify**, which turns the state into **NaN**. That is, *nullify = increment* **union**

(
Integer n ::= = (NaN)
Expression e ::= = (nullify),
(⟶ (conf (nullify) n) (conf (NaN) (NaN)))
).

Let us consider the $\lambda^{\mathcal{L}}$ program

(*nullify* true true)>T
    (conf (seq (nullify)
              ((*increment* okState true)>^{T} (conf (increment) (zero))))
         (zero)).

We start in the context of the language *nullify*, and we execute the first instruction, which is a **nullify** operation in the initial state **(zero)**. Then, we switch to the language *increment*. The pre-condition **okState** checks that the state is not **NaN**, otherwise we would end up trying to increment **NaN**.

At run-time, the **nullify** operation is executed, and the state becomes **NaN**. Next, the program switches to *increment*. Rule (R-SWITCH-ERROR) applies, and picks up (*increment* **okState true**)>^{T} (conf (increment) (zero)) where, regardless of the state **(zero)** indicated, the state computed by the parent execution in *nullify* is copied into *increment*. The configuration that we execute is then **(conf (increment) (NaN))**. At this point, rule (R-PRE-ERROR) detects that the pre-condition **(okState (conf (increment) (NaN)))** does not hold. The resulting step throws the error `InteropErrorPre`.

4   Meta-theory

Milner's type safety is too strong a property in the context of $\lambda^{\mathcal{L}}$ because it does not take into account that programmer-defined languages can be unsafe, either by mistake or by design. For example, a language designer may intentionally omit checking out-of-bounds accesses on arrays at run-time, so to run code more efficiently. Providing a bad array index, then, causes the program to simply get stuck in the middle of a computation, hence type safety is jeopardized.

Therefore, Milner's type safety simply does not hold for $\lambda^{\mathcal{L}}$, and we cannot use it to test whether $\lambda^{\mathcal{L}}$ is well-designed. We therefore prove a weaker type safety theorem that says that:

> *Well-typed multi-language programs can only go wrong on programmer-defined languages.*

We have proved that $\lambda^{\mathcal{L}}$ satisfies this theorem using the standard syntactic approach of Wright and Felleisen [24]. This approach is based on the progress theorem, and the subject reduction theorem.

Theorem 1 (Progress Theorem). *if* $\Gamma \vdash e : \tau$ *then*

- $e = v$, *for some value* v, *or*
- $e = err$, *for some error* err, *or*
- $e \longrightarrow e'$, *or*
- $e = E[(\mathcal{L}\ pn_1\ pn_2)>^U\ \hat{t}]$ *and* $(\mathcal{L}\ pn_1\ pn_2)>^U\ \hat{t} \not\longrightarrow$.

Since we have a small-step semantics formulation, the expression may be stuck because there is a nested subexpression which cannot take a step. Hence, the use of $E[(\mathcal{L}\ pn_1\ pn_2)>^U\ \hat{t}]$ in the theorem.

Theorem 2 (Subject Reduction). *if* $\Gamma \vdash e : \tau$ *and* $e \longrightarrow e'$ *then* $\Gamma \vdash e' : \tau$.

Theorem 3 (Type Safety). *if* $\Gamma \vdash e : \tau$ *and* $e \longrightarrow^* e'$ *then*

- $e' = v$, *for some value* v, *or*
- $e' = err$, *for some error* err, *or*
- $e' \longrightarrow e''$, *or*
- $e' = E[(\mathcal{L}\ pn_1\ pn_2)>^U\ \hat{t}]$ *and* $(\mathcal{L}\ pn_1\ pn_2)>^U\ \hat{t} \not\longrightarrow$.

The proofs of Theorem 1, 2 and 3 can be found in the online additional material of the paper [8].

5   Limitations and Future Work

$\lambda^{\mathcal{L}}$ programs can define languages through operational semantics, which is an effective approach to the semantics of languages. $\lambda^{\mathcal{L}}$ comes with some restrictions, however. The shape of typing relations must be such to have one output of type kind. Some languages with effects or typestate, however, have typing relations that return multiple outputs. Also, $\lambda^{\mathcal{L}}$ imposes configurations to be formed with one expression that is evaluated, and a state which cannot be evaluated. Depending on the language at hand, this may be an inconvenience for language designers. In the future, we plan to relax these restrictions.

Our type system does not prevent language designers from writing unsafe languages. In the future, we plan to integrate approaches to language analysis that aim at statically determining whether a language definition is sound [2, 9,15,23]. Similarly, programmers are responsible to write meaningful pre- and post-conditions. The wrong checks may have programs get stuck regardless.

The union of languages is merely syntactical, and programmers are responsible for making sure that two sets of rules work well when merged. As $\lambda^{\mathcal{L}}$ is meant to be a simple core calculus, we have formalized a raw union operation. In the future, we would like to explore more sophisticated union mechanisms that also work for languages with different shapes of typing relations, or that adopt different variable handling styles such as substitution versus environment.

$\lambda^{\mathcal{L}}$ handles a simple form of variable binding that is unary binding [5]. In the future, we would like to extend $\lambda^{\mathcal{L}}$ with more sophisticated binding specification tools such as scopes as types [1] or nominal techniques.

6   Related Work

There are several tools for the specification of programming languages. These are tools such as the K framework [21], PLT Redex [12], and also proof assistants such as Coq, to name a few (it is impossible to name all of them). Although these tools are equipped with a formal semantics, such semantics does not address multi-language interoperability as a primitive feature.

Racket [13] provides special syntax and sophisticated DSLs such as TurnStyle for handling languages [4]. However, languages are macro-expanded into a host programming language. Racket does have a formal semantics but that is the semantics of a functional programming language with macros and contracts. In contrast, $\lambda^{\mathcal{L}}$ offers a semantics that explicitly involves languages as first-class. This aspect of $\lambda^{\mathcal{L}}$ also distinguishes $\lambda^{\mathcal{L}}$ from other systems such as SugarJ [10] and SugarHaskell [11], which are based on macro-expansion.

Some remarkable works provide an operational semantics for multi-language programming, together with guarantees of safe code interoperability [18,20,22]. However, these works do that for two specific languages which have been chosen beforehand. $\lambda^{\mathcal{L}}$ presents a more challenging scenario because programmers can define their own languages, which can be as complex as they wish. Furthermore, languages can also be created at run-time via unions and functions. It would be interesting to investigate generalizations of such works in the context of $\lambda^{\mathcal{L}}$.

7   Conclusion

We have presented $\lambda^{\mathcal{L}}$, a typed λ-calculus with languages as first-class citizens. We have provided a type system and an operational semantics for $\lambda^{\mathcal{L}}$. We have identified a variant of Milner's type safety that is appropriate for $\lambda^{\mathcal{L}}$, and we have proved that $\lambda^{\mathcal{L}}$ satisfies this property.

It is traditional in the programming languages field to elevate various entities as first-class citizens, such as functions, continuations, objects, and proofs, among others. This paper contributes to that line, and provides a formal semantics of languages as first-class citizens. We believe that $\lambda^{\mathcal{L}}$ contributes to providing a solid foundation for multi-language programming.

References

1. van Antwerpen, H., Bach Poulsen, C., Rouvoet, A., Visser, E.: Scopes as types. Proc. ACM Program. Lang. (PACMPL) **2**(OOPSLA) (2018). https://doi.org/10. 1145/3276484
2. Bach Poulsen, C., Rouvoet, A., Tolmach, A., Krebbers, R., Visser, E.: Intrinsically-typed definitional interpreters for imperative languages. Proc. ACM Program. Lang. (PACMPL) **2**(POPL) (2017). https://doi.org/10.1145/3158104
3. Bousse, E., Degueule, T., Vojtisek, D., Mayerhofer, T., Deantoni, J., Combemale, B.: Execution framework of the GEMOC studio (tool demo). In: Proceedings of the 2016 ACM SIGPLAN International Conference on Software Language Engineering, SLE 2016, pp. 84–89. Association for Computing Machinery, New York (2016). https://doi.org/10.1145/2997364.2997384

4. Chang, S., Knauth, A., Greenman, B.: Type systems as macros. In: Proceedings of the 44th ACM SIGPLAN Symposium on Principles of Programming Languages, POPL 2017, pp. 694–705. Association for Computing Machinery, New York (2017). https://doi.org/10.1145/3009837.3009886
5. Cheney, J.: Toward a general theory of names: binding and scope. In: Proceedings of the 3rd ACM SIGPLAN Workshop on Mechanized Reasoning about Languages with Variable Binding, MERLIN 2005, pp. 33–40. Association for Computing Machinery, New York (2005). https://doi.org/10.1145/1088454.1088459
6. Cimini, M.: Languages as first-class citizens (vision paper). In: Proceedings of the 11th ACM SIGPLAN International Conference on Software Language Engineering, SLE 2018, pp. 65–69. Association for Computing Machinery, New York (2018). https://doi.org/10.1145/3276604.3276983
7. Cimini, M.: On the effectiveness of higher-order logic programming in language-oriented programming. In: Nakano, K., Sagonas, K. (eds.) FLOPS 2020. LNCS, vol. 12073, pp. 106–123. Springer, Cham (2020). https://doi.org/10.1007/978-3-030-59025-3_7
8. Cimini, M.: A calculus for multi-language operational semantics (additional material) (2021). http://www.cimini.info/MultiLangCalculus/additionalMaterial.pdf
9. Cimini, M., Miller, D., Siek, J.G.: Extrinsically typed operational semantics for functional languages. In: Proceedings of the 13th ACM SIGPLAN International Conference on Software Language Engineering, SLE 2020, Virtual Event, USA, 16–17 November 2020, pp. 108–125. Association for Computing Machinery, New York (2020). https://doi.org/10.1145/3426425.3426936
10. Erdweg, S., Rendel, T., Kästner, C., Ostermann, K.: SugarJ: library-based syntactic language extensibility. In: Proceedings of the 2011 ACM International Conference on Object Oriented Programming Systems Languages and Applications, OOPSLA 2011, pp. 391–406. Association for Computing Machinery, New York (2011). https://doi.org/10.1145/2048066.2048099
11. Erdweg, S., Rieger, F., Rendel, T., Ostermann, K.: Layout-sensitive language extensibility with SugarHaskell. In: Proceedings of the 5th ACM SIGPLAN Symposium on Haskell, Haskell 2012, Copenhagen, Denmark, 13 September 2012, pp. 149–160 (2012). https://doi.org/10.1145/2364506.2364526
12. Felleisen, M., Findler, R.B., Flatt, M.: Semantics Engineering with PLT Redex, 1st edn. The MIT Press, Cambridge (2009)
13. Flatt, M.: PLT: reference: racket. Technical report PLT-TR-2010-1, PLT Design Inc. (2010). https://racket-lang.org/tr1/
14. Fowler, M.: Language workbenches: the killer-app for domain specific languages? (2005). http://www.martinfowler.com/articles/languageWorkbench.html
15. Grewe, S., Erdweg, S., Wittmann, P., Mezini, M.: Type systems for the masses: deriving soundness proofs and efficient checkers. In: 2015 ACM International Symposium on New Ideas, New Paradigms, and Reflections on Programming and Software (Onward!), Onward! 2015, pp. 137–150. ACM, New York (2015). https://doi.org/10.1145/2814228.2814239
16. Klint, P., van der Storm, T., Vinju, J.J.: RASCAL: a domain specific language for source code analysis and manipulation. In: Ninth IEEE International Working Conference on Source Code Analysis and Manipulation, SCAM 2009, Edmonton, Alberta, Canada, 20–21 September 2009, pp. 168–177 (2009). https://doi.org/10.1109/SCAM.2009.28
17. Krahn, H., Rumpe, B., Völkel, S.: MontiCore: a framework for compositional development of domain specific languages. Int. J. Softw. Tools Technol. Transf. **12**(5), 353–372 (2010). https://doi.org/10.1007/s10009-010-0142-1

18. Matthews, J., Findler, R.B.: Operational semantics for multi-language programs. In: Proceedings of the 34th Annual ACM SIGPLAN-SIGACT Symposium on Principles of Programming Languages, POPL 2007, pp. 3–10. Association for Computing Machinery, New York (2007). https://doi.org/10.1145/1190216.1190220
19. Miller, D., Nadathur, G.: Programming with Higher-Order Logic, 1st edn. Cambridge University Press, Cambridge (2012)
20. Patterson, D., Perconti, J., Dimoulas, C., Ahmed, A.: FunTAL: reasonably mixing a functional language with assembly. In: Proceedings of the 38th ACM SIGPLAN Conference on Programming Language Design and Implementation, PLDI 2017, Barcelona, Spain, 18–23 June 2017, pp. 495–509. ACM (2017). https://doi.org/10.1145/3062341.3062347
21. Rosu, G., Serbanuta, T.: An overview of the K semantic framework. J. Log. Algebraic Methods Program. **79**(6), 397–434 (2010). https://doi.org/10.1016/j.jlap.2010.03.012
22. Scherer, G., New, M.S., Rioux, N., Ahmed, A.: Fabulous interoperability for ML and a linear language. In: Proceedings of Foundations of Software Science and Computation Structures - 21st International Conference, FOSSACS 2018, Held as Part of the European Joint Conferences on Theory and Practice of Software, ETAPS 2018, Thessaloniki, Greece, 14–20 April 2018, pp. 146–162 (2018). https://doi.org/10.1007/978-3-319-89366-2_8
23. Schürmann, C.: Automating the meta theory of deductive systems. Ph.D. thesis, Department of Computer Science, Carnegie Mellon University, August 2000. http://reports-archive.adm.cs.cmu.edu/anon/2000/abstracts/00-146.html. Available as Technical Report CMU-CS-00-146
24. Wright, A., Felleisen, M.: A syntactic approach to type soundness. Inf. Comput. **115**(1), 38–94 (1994). https://doi.org/10.1006/inco.1994.1093

Partial Order Reduction for Timed Actors

Maryam Bagheri[1]([✉])[iD], Marjan Sirjani[2][iD], Ehsan Khamespanah[3][iD],
Hossein Hojjat[3,4][iD], and Ali Movaghar[1][iD]

[1] Sharif University of Technology, Tehran, Iran
mbagheri@ce.sharif.edu
[2] Mälardalen University, Västeras, Sweden
[3] University of Tehran, Tehran, Iran
[4] Tehran Institute for Advanced Studies, Tehran, Iran

Abstract. We propose a compositional approach for the Partial Order
Reduction (POR) in the state space generation of asynchronous timed
actors. We define the concept of *independent actors* as the actors that
do not send messages to a common actor. The approach avoids exploring
unnecessary interleaving of executions of independent actors. It performs
on a component-based model where actors from different components,
except for the actors on borders, are independent. To alleviate the effect
of the cross-border messages, we enforce a *delay condition*, ensuring that
an actor introduces a delay in its execution before sending a message
across the border of its component. Within each time unit, our technique
generates the state space of each individual component by taking its
received messages into account. It then composes the state spaces of all
components. We prove that our POR approach preserves the properties
defined on timed states (states where the only outgoing transition shows
the progress of time). We generate the state space of a case study in the
domain of air traffic control systems based on the proposed POR. The
results on our benchmarks illustrate that our POR method, on average,
reduces the time and memory consumption by 76 and 34%, respectively.

Keywords: Actor model · Partial order reduction · Composition ·
Verification

1 Introduction

Actor [1,14] is a mathematical model of concurrent computations. As units of
computation, actors have single threads of execution and communicate via asynchronous message passing. Different variants of actors are emerged to form the
concurrent model of modern programming languages, e.g. Erlang [26], Scala [12],
Akka [2], Lingua Franca [16], and simulation and verification tools, e.g. Ptolemy
[20] and Afra [21]. In the interleaving semantics of actors, the executions of
actors are interleaved with each other. State space explosion is a fundamental
problem in the model checking of actors. Interleaving of actor executions results
in a huge state space and henceforth exponential growth in the verification time.

© Springer Nature Switzerland AG 2022
R. Bloem et al. (Eds.): NSV 2021/VSTTE 2021, LNCS 13124, pp. 43–60, 2022.
https://doi.org/10.1007/978-3-030-95561-8_4

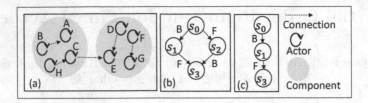

Fig. 1. (a): An actor model with two components. Connections show how actors communicate. (b): Different interleavings of executions of two independent actors B and F. State space of (b) is reduced to (c) using POR.

Partial Order Reduction (POR) [10,18] is a well-known technique to tackle the state space explosion problem. While generating the state space, POR avoids the exploration of unnecessary interleaving of independent transitions.

In this paper, we propose a compositional approach for POR of timed actors. We describe our approach on Timed Rebeca [22,24]. Actors in Timed Rebeca can model the computation time or the communication delays in time-critical systems. Standard semantics of Timed Rebeca is based on the Timed Transition System (TTS) [15]. TTS has instantaneous transitions over which the time does not progress (the so-called discrete transitions) and the timed transitions that model the progress of time. In this semantics, there is a notion of logical time that is a global time synchronized between the actors. The instantaneous transitions model executions of the actors and are interleaved if more than one actor is executed at each logical time. The time progresses if no instantaneous transition is enabled. We call a state whose outgoing transition is a timed transition a timed state.

Our POR method works on an actor model where actors are grouped together as components. We define the concept of *independent actors* as the actors that do not send messages to a common actor. Actors from different components, except for the actors on the borders of the components, are independent. We show that we can abstract the interleaved executions of independent actors within one time unit while preserving all the properties on the timed states. Dependent actors sending messages to a common actor within the same logical time are the cause of different ordering of messages in the message queue of the common actor and hence different future execution paths. The set of actors in a component are dependent. The actors sitting on the border of a component may communicate via cross-border messages to actors in other components. For such cross-border messages, we enforce a *delay condition* in this paper. The delay condition forces an actor to introduce a delay in its execution before sending a cross-border message. This way, we can avoid the interleaved executions of actors from different components in the current logical time and postpone any simultaneous arrival of messages to a common actor on borders to the next logical time. We introduce *interface components* to send such messages in the next logical time. Our method performs two operations at each logical time to generate the state space: first, builds the state space of each component, and second, composes the state spaces. We call the TTS built using our method the Compositionally-built TTS (C-TTS). Figure 1(a) shows an actor model with two components where the independent actors B and F are triggered at a logical time. As Fig. 1(b) shows, two sequences of transitions $s_0 \xrightarrow{B} s_1 \xrightarrow{F} s_3$ and $s_0 \xrightarrow{F} s_2 \xrightarrow{B} s_3$ are different interleavings of executions of B and F, both reaching the state s_3. With respect to the system properties, only one of these interleavings is necessary. Using our method, each final state in the state space of a component at the current logical time, e.g., s_1, is the initial state to generate the state space of a second component at the current logical time (Fig. 1(c)). Each final state in the state space of the second component at the current logical time is the initial state to generate the state space of a third one, and so on, no matter how the components are ordered to generate their state spaces.

An actor can send a message across the boundary of its component, and this message can interfere with another message if both messages are sent to a common actor at the same logical time. Our POR method is only applicable if an actor introduces a delay in its execution before sending a message across the border of its component. This way, there is no need to interleave executions of independent actors from different components. Let actor H in Fig. 1(a) sends a message to actor C at a logical time. In response, C is triggered but does not send a message to E at the current logical time, and it can only send a message to E in the next logical time (or later). However, in the next logical time, the message sent by C to E may interfere with a message sent to E by D (which belongs to the same component as E). Our method is aware of communications of actors over different components. For each component, we define an interface component that simulates the behaviors of the environment of the component by sending messages to the component while generating its state space.

We prove that our method preserves the properties over timed states. We reduce TTS (built by the standard semantics) and C-TTS by abstracting and removing all instantaneous transitions, and prove that the reduced transition systems are isomorphic. To investigate the efficiency of our method, we use a case study from the air traffic control systems.

Related Work. To apply standard POR techniques to timed automata, [6] proposes a new symbolic local-time semantics for a network of timed automata. The paper [11] adopts this semantics and proposes a new POR method in which the structure of the model guides the calculation of the ample set. In [17], the author proposes a POR method for timed automata, where the method preserves linear-time temporal logic properties. The authors of [13] introduce an abstraction to relax some timing constraints of the system, and then define a variant of the stubborn set method for reducing the state space. Compared to our method, none of the above approaches are compositional. In [25], there is a compositional POR method for hierarchical concurrent processes. The ample set of a process in the orchestration language *Orc* is obtained by composing ample sets of its subprocesses. Compared to [25], our method, instead of dynamically calculating the ample sets, uses the static structure of the model to remove the unnecessary interleavings.

There are several approaches for formal specification and analysis of actor models, i.e., Real-time Maude [27] is used for specifying and statistical model checking of composite actors [9], and McErlang [8] is a model checker for the Erlang programming language. The compositional verification of Rebeca is proposed in [24], but it does not perform on timed actors. To the best of our knowledge, none of them proposes a compositional approach for POR of timed actors in generating the state space.

Contributions. The contributions of the paper are as follows:

1. We propose a compositional approach for POR of timed actors. Using independent actors and the assumption of delay conditions for cross-border message passing, this approach reduces the time and memory consumption in generating state spaces by removing redundant interleavings in executions of actors.
2. We prove that our POR method preserves properties over timed states. The proof reduces TTS and C-TTS and shows that their reduced versions are isomorphic.

Our method performs on a component-based actor model, so, in the case of having a flat model, we need to organize actors into several groups of ideally independent actors, or use actors that have a delay before sending a message to determine the borders between different components. As future work, we plan to perform static analysis of models for grouping actors as components.

2   Background: Timed Rebeca

Timed Rebeca is a timed version of Rebeca [24] created as an imperative interpretation of the actor model [7]. In Timed Rebeca, communication is asynchronous, and actors have message bags to store their incoming messages that are tagged with their arrival times. Each actor takes a message with the least arrival time from its bag and executes the corresponding method, called message server. In message servers, an actor can send messages to its known actors and change values of its state variables. The actor executes the method in an atomic and non-preemptive way. Each actor can use the keyword *delay* to model passing of time during the execution of the method. In Timed Rebeca, the keywords *delay* and *after* are used to enforce the increase of logical time. To simplify the description of the method, we only consider *delay*.

In the standard semantics of Timed Rebeca, the logical time is a global time synchronized between actors. The only notion of time in our method is the logical time, so hereafter, we use the term "time" and "logical time" interchangeably. To simplify the description of the method, we assume that actors in this paper only have one message server, so, we present the simplified standard semantics of Timed Rebeca in this section.

Formal Specification of Timed Rebeca. A Timed Rebeca model $\mathcal{M} = \|_{j \in AId}$ a_j consists of actors $\{a_j | j \in AId\}$ concurrently executing, where AId is the set of the identifiers of all actors. An actor a_j is defined as a tuple (V_j, msv_j, K_j), where V_j is the set of all state variables of a_j, msv_j is the message server of a_j, and K_j is the set of all known actors of a_j.

Simplified Standard Semantics of Timed Rebeca. The standard semantics of $\mathcal{M}$ is the TTS $T = (S, s_0, Act, \rightarrow, AP, L)$, where S is the set of states, s_0 is the initial state, Act is the set of actions, $\rightarrow \subseteq S \times (Act \cup \mathbb{R}_{\geq 0}) \times S$ is the transition relation, AP is the set of atomic propositions, and $L : S \rightarrow 2^{AP}$ is a labeling function associating a set of atomic propositions with each state. The state $s \in S$ consists of the local states of all actors along with the current time of the state. The local state of an actor a_j is $s_{a_j} = (v_j, B_j, res_j, pc_j)$, where v_j is the valuation of the state variables, B_j is the message bag storing a finite sequence of messages, $res_j \in \mathbb{R}_{\geq 0}$ is the resuming time, and $pc_j \in (\mathbb{N} \cup \{0\})$ is the program counter referring to the next statement after completing the execution of *delay*. In the message $m_k = (vals_k, ar_k)$ with the unique identifier k, $vals_k$ is a sequence of values and ar_k is the arrival time. Let S_{a_j} be the set of all states of the actor a_j. The set S is defined as $\mathbb{R}_{\geq 0} \times \prod_{j \in AId} S_{a_j}$, where $\prod$ is the Cartesian product. So, the state $s \in S$ is $(now_s, Atrs_s)$, where now_s is the current time in s and $Atrs_s$ contains the states of all actors. In s_0, each actor a_j has an initial message in its bag, and res_j, pc_j, and now_{s_0} are zero.

The set of actions is defined as $Act = Msg \cup \{\tau_j | j \in AId\}$, where Msg is the set of all messages. The transition relation $\rightarrow$ contains the following transitions that are related to taking a message and triggering an actor, resuming the execution of an actor, and progressing the time.

$1 - $ ***Message taking transition.*** (s, m_k, s'), $m_k \in Msg$, iff in the state s there is an actor a_j such that $m_k = (vals_k, ar_k)$ is a message in B_j, $ar_k \leq now_s$, and res_j is zero. The state s' results from the state s through the atomic execution of two activities: m_k is removed from B_j, and the message server of a_j is executed. The latter may change the local state of a_j and send messages that are tagged with the arrival time now_s and are stored in bags of the receiver actors. If a_j executes *delay*, the execution of the actor is suspended, the sum of now_s and the introduced delay value is stored in res_j, and pc_j is set to the location of the statement after the executed *delay*.

$2 - $ ***Internal transition.*** (s, τ_j, s') iff in the state s there is an actor a_j such that $res_j > 0$ and $res_j = now_s$. The state s' results from s by resuming the execution of the message server of a_j from the location referred to by pc_j. This case may add messages to actors' bags and change the state of a_j. Besides, res_j and pc_j are set to zero unless *delay* is executed.

$3 - $ ***Time progress transition.*** (s, d, s'), $d \in \mathbb{R}_{\geq 0}$, iff there is an actor a_j such that $res_j \neq 0$, and for each actor a_k, either B_k is empty or $res_k > now_s$. The state s' results from s through progressing the time. The time progresses to the smallest time of all resuming times that are greater than zero. The amount of the time progress is denoted by d.

The *message taking* and *internal* transitions are instantaneous transitions over which the time does not progress. These transitions have priority over the *time progress* transition; the third transition is only enabled when no transitions from the other two types are enabled. The *time progress* transition is also called a timed transition. An actor may show different behaviors depending on the order in which the messages are taken from its bag.

Timed Rebeca Extended with Components. Our POR method performs on a component-based Timed Rebeca model which consists of a set CO of components $\{co_i | i \in CID\}$, where CID is the set of all component identifiers. A component $co_i = \|_{j \in AId_i} a_j$ encapsulates a set of actors $\{a_j | j \in AId_i\}$, where AId_i is the set of identifiers of all actors in co_i, and $AId = \bigcup_{i \in CID} AId_i$. A local state of co_i consists of the local states of its actors and is an instance of $S_{co_i} = \prod_{j \in AId_i} S_{a_j}$. So, the state $s \in S$ is an instance of $\mathbb{R}_{\geq 0} \times \prod_{i \in CID} S_{co_i}$ and is defined as $(now_s, CAtrs_s)$, where now_s is the current time in s and $CAtrs_s$ contains the states of all components.

3   Overview of the Proposed POR Method

At each logical time, our POR method iterates over the components. To avoid exploring interleavings of executions of *independent actors* from different components, it generates the set of reachable states of each component using the *message taking* and *internal* transitions, and composes the sets of reachable states. Using the *time progress* transition, the time progresses, and the same procedure repeats for the newly generated states. Our method should be aware of the messages sent to the component while generating its state space. The order in which these messages are sent to the component may affect the reachable state. Below, we define *interface components* that are responsible for sending such messages to the components. We also describe the *delay condition* making our method applicable and explain the method using an example.

Modeling Interface Components. An actor of a component may send messages across the component's border. An actor with this ability is called a *boundary actor*. All actors of a component except for the boundary actors are called *internal actors*. The message sent by a boundary actor across the border of its component interferes with another message if both messages are sent at the same time to the same actor. The order in which these messages are taken from the bag of the receiver actor affects the system state. So we need to consider the interleavings of executions of actors of a component and its neighboring actors. A neighboring actor of a component co_i is a boundary actor of co_j, if this actor can directly communicate with an actor in co_i. To make the components independent while considering the mentioned interleavings, our method defines an *interface component* for each component. An interface component of co_i, denoted by $co_{int,i}$, contains a set of actors called interface neighboring actors. Corresponding to each neighboring actor a_j of co_i, an interface neighboring actor with the same behaviors as a_j is defined in $co_{int,i}$. Instead of neighboring actors, interface neighboring actors in $co_{int,i}$ are triggered or resume their executions to send messages to co_i. To generate the state space of co_i in isolation, executions of actors of co_i and $co_{int,i}$ are interleaved with each other.

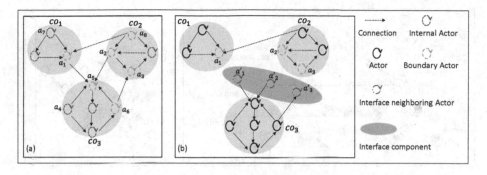

Fig. 2. (a): Three components co_1, co_2, co_3. (b): Interface component of co_3.

Figure 2(a) shows an actor model with three components co_1, co_2, and co_3. The internal and boundary actors of each component are respectively shown in blue (dotted rounded arrow) and red (dashed rounded arrow). The actors a_1, a_2, and a_3 are neighboring actors of co_3. Let actors a_1, a_2, a_3, a_4, and a_6 in Fig. 2(a) send messages to actor a_5 at the current time. The order in which these actors send their messages is important. The interface component of co_3, shown in Fig. 2(b), contains the interface neighboring actors of co_3, i.e. actors a_1', a_2', and a_3' that respectively correspond to actors a_1, a_2, and a_3. The same as the neighboring actors, interface neighboring actors can communicate with boundary actors of co_3.

The Delay Condition. When an actor of a component co_i sends a message to a boundary actor of co_i, in response, the boundary actor is triggered and may send a message across the component's border. Therefore, an internal actor may be the source of interferences between messages. In such a case, interleaving executions of internal actors of two components has to be considered. For instance, let actors a_1 and a_2 in Fig. 2(a), by respectively taking a message from actors a_7 and a_8 at the current time, be triggered, and in response, send a message to actor a_5. Actor a_5 may receive the message of actor a_1 first if actor a_7 is triggered first, and may receive the message of actor a_2 first if actor a_8 is triggered first. Therefore, interleaving executions of actors a_8 and a_7 is important. To reduce interferences between messages and have independent transitions, we consider that a boundary actor is not able to send a message across the border of its component unless it has introduced a delay greater than zero before sending the message. So, actors a_1 and a_2 do not send a message to actor a_5 at the same time they receive a message. Using this condition, interleaving the executions of internal actors of two components (independent actors) is not needed. This condition is not out of touch with reality, because this delay can be the communication delay or the computation time.

We describe the POR method using Fig. 3. The right side shows three components and the left side shows how the state space of the model is generated. We divide each state into three parts, where each part denotes the local state of a component and its interface component. We show the new local state of each

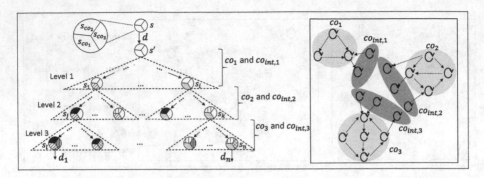

Fig. 3. The left side shows how the state space of the model of the right side is generated using the compositional approach. The interface component of co_i is denoted by $co_{int,i}$.

component with a different color. Since the state of an interface component does not contribute to verifying a property, we remove it from the figure. Let the state s be a timed state at which the time progresses. At the current time of the state s', the method generates the state space of co_1, considering the messages sent to it by $co_{int,1}$. In this case, the local states of co_2 and co_3 do not change. The new local states of co_1 are shown with different colors in states $\{s_1, \cdots, s_i\}$.

Each state of $\{s_1, \cdots, s_i\}$ is an initial state from which the state space of co_2, considering $co_{int,2}$, is generated. The method generates the state space of co_2 only once and copies the built state space for each state $s_v \in \{s_1, \cdots, s_i\}$. Then, the method updates states of the state space copied for s_v such that the local states of all components except for co_2 are set to their values in s_v. For instance, the most left triangle in the second level of Fig. 3 shows that only the local state of co_2 has changed, while the local states of co_1 and co_3 have the same values as the state s_1. Similarly, for each state of $\{s_j, \cdots, s_k\}$, the state space of co_3 is created. Finally, the time progresses at each state of $\{s_l, \cdots, s_n\}$, and the same procedure repeats. In the next section, we present the algorithm of the method.

4   The POR Algorithm

Figure 4 shows the high-level pseudo-code of our POR method. The function *porMethod* progresses the time and invokes *createInStateSpace* to generate the state space at the current time. The function *createInStateSpace* invokes *executeCOM* to generate the state space of a component considering its interface component. For instance, *porMethod* progresses the time in s in Fig. 3 and then invokes *createInStateSpace*. This function generates the whole state space from s' to $s_l, \cdots, s_n$ in three iterations. It generates each level of Fig. 3 in one iteration where it invokes *executeCOM* only once to generate a triangle and copies and updates the triangle several times.

Let $queue_{timed}$ in *porMethod* be a queue of timed states. The algorithm uses the *deQueue* function to take the head of $queue_{timed}$ (line 6) and calls *timeProg* (line 7). The *timeProg* function progresses the time and returns s' and d as the

1 Function *porMethod* (CO, s_0)
   Input: CO set of components whose boundary actors follow the delay
         condition, s_0 the initial state
   Output: S, T sets of states & transitions
2 $(S_{timed}, newS, newT) \leftarrow createInStateSpace(CO, s_0)$
3 $queue_{timed} \leftarrow \langle S_{timed} \rangle$
4 $S \leftarrow \{s_0\} \cup newS, T \leftarrow newT$
5 while $queue_{timed} \neq \emptyset$ **do**
6 $s \leftarrow deQueue(queue_{timed})$
7 $(s', d) \leftarrow timeProg(s)$
8 $S \leftarrow S \cup \{s'\}, T \leftarrow T \cup \{(s, d, s')\}$
9 $(S_{timed}, newS, newT) \leftarrow createInStateSpace(CO, s')$
10 $queue_{timed} \leftarrow \langle queue_{timed} | S_{timed} \rangle$
11 $S \leftarrow S \cup newS, T \leftarrow T \cup newT$
13 return (S, T)
14 Function *createInStateSpace* (CO, s)
   Input: CO set of components, s a state
   Output: $S_{frontier}, S$ sets of states, T set of transitions
15 $S_{frontier} \leftarrow \{s\}, S \leftarrow \emptyset, T \leftarrow \emptyset$
16 $updateIntComp(s, CO)$
17 foreach $co \in CO$ **do**
18 $(st, trans, finalSt) \leftarrow executeCOM(co, s)$
19 $leavesOfaCom \leftarrow \emptyset$
20   **while** $S_{frontier} \neq \emptyset$ **do**
21 $s' \leftarrow take(S_{frontier})$
22 $(newS, newTr, newFS) \leftarrow updateSts(CO, co, s', st, trans, finalSt)$
23 $leavesOfaCom \leftarrow leavesOfaCom \cup newFS$
24 $T \leftarrow T \cup newTr, S \leftarrow S \cup (newS \cup newFS)$
25 $S_{frontier} \leftarrow leavesOfaCom$
27 return $(S_{frontier}, S, T)$
28 Function *executeCOM* (co, s)
   Input: co a component, s a state
   Output: S_{in}, T sets of states & transitions, *leavesOfCom* final states of the
         state space of co
29 $leavesOfCom \leftarrow \emptyset, S_{in} \leftarrow \emptyset, T \leftarrow \emptyset$
30 $enabledActors \leftarrow getEnabledActors(s, co)$
31 if $enabledActors = \emptyset$ **then**
32   **return** $(\emptyset, \emptyset, \{s\})$
33 while $enabledActors \neq \emptyset$ **do**
34 $(aid, msg) \leftarrow take(enabledActors)$
35 $s' \leftarrow trigger(s, aid, msg)$
36   **if** $msg = null$ **then**
37 $T \leftarrow T \cup \{(s, \tau_{aid}, s')\}$
38   **else**
39 $T \leftarrow T \cup \{(s, msg, s')\}$
40 $(newS, newTr, newFS) \leftarrow executeCOM(co, s')$
41 $leavesOfCom \leftarrow leavesOfCom \cup newFS$
42 $T \leftarrow T \cup newTr$
43   **if** $newFS \neq \{s'\}$ **then**
44 $S_{in} \leftarrow S_{in} \cup newS \cup \{s'\}$
46 return $(S_{in}, T, leavesOfCom)$

Fig. 4. State-space generation by the compositional approach

new state and the amount of the time progress based on which the state space is updated (line 8). Then, the algorithm invokes *createInStateSpace* to generate the state space at the current time (line 9). This function returns the set of timed states (leaves), the set of states, and the set of transitions of the state space. The timed states are added to the end of $queue_{timed}$ (line 10), over which *porMethod* repeats the same process (line 5). Based on the semantics described in Sect. 2, the initial state s_0 is not a timed state. The function handles s_0 as a separate case; without progressing the time, uses *createInStateSpace* to generates the state space at time zero (line 2).

Let $S_{frontier}$, including the given state s in *createInStateSpace* (line 15), stores final states of state spaces generated for a component from different initial states. For instance, it stores states $\{s_1, \cdots, s_i\}$ in the first level or states $\{s_j, \cdots, s_k\}$ in the second level of Fig. 3. Assume a_{id} is a neighboring actor and a'_{id} is the interface neighboring actor corresponding to a_{id}, where id is an arbitrary index. The algorithm first uses the function *updateIntComp(s, CO)* to update states of interface components of all components (line 16). Using this function, the local state of each interface neighboring actor, i.e. a'_{id}, is updated to the local state of the corresponding neighboring actor, i.e. a_{id}, in s. The variables, the resuming time, and the program counter of the interface neighboring actor a'_{id} are respectively set to values of the variables, the resuming time, and the program counter of the corresponding neighboring actor a_{id} in s. Then, the algorithm iterates over components (lines 17 to 25) and performs as follows. For each component co, it uses the function *executeCOM* to generate the state space of co from the given base state s (line 18). This function returns the states of the state space that are not final states, the transitions, and the final states of the state space. The algorithm then iterates over $S_{frontier}$ (lines 20 to 24). It uses the *take* function to take a state s' from $S_{frontier}$ (line 21) and uses the function *updateSts* to make a copy from the generated state space and update the states of the copy one based on s' (line 22); except for the state of the component co, states of all components are set to their values in s'. The final states (leaves) of the copied state space are stored in *leavesOfaCom* (line 23), and all created states and transitions are stored (line 24). When for each state of $S_{frontier}$ as an initial state, the state space of co is built, $S_{frontier}$ is updated to *leavesOfaCom* (line 25). The final states of the state spaces of the last component are timed states that are returned.

The function *executeCOM* in Fig. 4 has a recursive algorithm that uses depth first search to generate the state space of a given component from a given state considering only the *message taking* and *internal* transitions. This function interleaves executions of actors and the interface neighboring actors of the component. The function *getEnabledActors* returns a set of tuples (aid, msg) where aid is the identifier of an actor or an interface neighboring actor of the component and msg is a message or a null value (line 30). This function returns (aid, msg) with $msg \neq null$ if actor a_{aid} can take the message msg from its bag in the state s (the *message taking* transition) and returns (aid, msg) with $msg = null$ if a_{aid} can resume its execution in s (the *internal* transition). The algorithm then iteratively takes a tuple (line 34). The algorithm triggers the actor or resumes

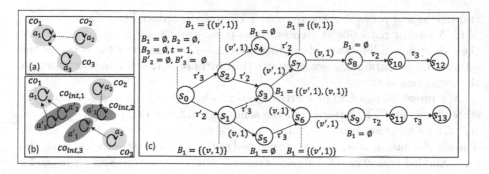

Fig. 5. (a),(b): Three components and their interface components. (c): State space in $t = 1$. B_j, B'_j bags of a_j and a'_j, respectively.

its execution using the function *trigger* (line 35). As a result, a new state is generated, and a transition is added to the set of transitions (lines 36 to 39). Then, the algorithm is executed for the new state (line 40). It stores the final states of the state space of the component (line 41) and the states that are not final states (line 44) in two disjoint sets. Finally, the transitions and the states of the state space of the component are returned (line 46). It is worthy to mention that messages sent by a component co_i to a component co_j are not stored, because these messages are generated for co_j using $co_{int,j}$.

We use the example in Fig. 5 to describe our approach. Figure 5(a) shows an actor model with three components, Fig. 5(b) shows the interface component of each component, and Fig. 5(c) shows the state space of the model for time $t = 1$. We assume that a_2 and a_3 resume their executions at time $t = 1$ and respectively send v and v' as the sequences of values to actor a_1. For $j = 1, 2, 3$, we use B_j and B'_j to denote the bag of actor a_j and the bag of the interface neighboring actor a'_j, respectively. We also use τ_j and τ'_j to denote the internal transitions over which a_j and a'_j resume their executions, respectively. The actor a_1 takes a message and performs a computation. The algorithm generates the state spaces of co_1, co_2, and co_3 in order. To generate the state space of co_1, instead of actors a_2 and a_3, actors a'_2 and a'_3 resume their executions to send messages to actor a_1. The time in all states is 1. To have a simple figure, we do not label the states with state variables of the actors. The label of each state only shows how the bag of an actor is changed when the actor is triggered or the execution of another actor is resumed. For instance, over the transition from s_0 to s_2, B_1 changes to $\{(v', 1)\}$ and the bags of other actors remain unchanged. The actors a_2 and a_3 are respectively triggered in the states s_9 and s_{11} (s_8 and s_{10}) and values of their state variables are stored.

5   Correctness Proof

We prove that our POR method preserves the properties with state formulas over timed states. We reduce TTS and C-TTS by removing all instantaneous transitions and prove that the reduced TTS and the reduced C-TTS are isomorphic. A similar reduction is used (with no proof) in [23] by Sirjani et al., where they show how a hardware platform can be used to hide from the observer the interleaved execution of a set of events (instantaneous transitions) occurring at the same logical time.

We prove that our POR method preserves deadlock: if there is a deadlock state, TTS and C-TTS reach it at the same logical time. Let $T = (S, s_0, Act, \rightarrow, AP, L)$ be the transition system of a component-based timed Rebeca model. The set S contains two sets of states: timed states and instantaneous states. The only enabled transition of a timed state is a timed transition and all outgoing transitions from an instantaneous state are instantaneous transitions.

Definition 1. *(Timed state) $s \in S$ in a given T is a timed state if there exists a state $s' \in S$ and a value $d \in \mathbb{R}_{>0}$ such that $(s, d, s') \in \rightarrow$.* $\square$

Definition 2. *(Instantaneous state) $s \in S$ in a given T is an instantaneous state if there exists a state $s' \in S$ and an action $act \in Act$ such that $(s, act, s') \in \rightarrow$.* $\square$

According to the standard semantics in Sect. 2, the sets of timed states and instantaneous states are disjoint since a timed transition is enabled in the state which does not have an enabled instantaneous transition. The set S contains a deadlock state if deadlock happens in the system. A state with no outgoing transition is a deadlock state.

Definition 3. *(Deadlock state) $s \in S$ in T is a deadlock state if there is no state $s' \in S$ and $l \in (Act \cup \mathbb{R}_{>0})$ such that $(s, l, s') \in \rightarrow$.* $\square$

To simplify the proofs of this section, we add a dummy state to the set S and define a dummy transition as a timed transition with an infinite value between a deadlock state and the dummy state. If $s \xrightarrow{d} s'$ is a dummy transition where s is a deadlock state, s' is the dummy state, and d is infinite. The dummy state has no outgoing transition. Let $T_{TTS} = (S_1, s_0, Act, \rightarrow_1, AP, L)$ and $T_{CTTS} = (S_2, s_0, Act, \rightarrow_2, AP, L)$ be respectively TTS and C-TTS of a component-based Timed Rebeca model. We use $(v_j^s, B_j^s, res_j^s, pc_j^s)$ to denote the local state of the actor a_j in a state s.

Definition 4. *(Relation between a State of TTS and a State of C-TTS). A state $s \in S_1$ and a state $s' \in S_2$ are in the relation $\mathcal{R} \subseteq S_1 \times S_2$ if and only if s and s' are equal, which means:*

- *$now_s = now_{s'}$,*
- *$\forall i \in CID, \forall j \in AId_i, v_j^s = v_j^{s'}, B_j^s = B_j^{s'}, res_j^s = res_j^{s'}, and\ pc_j^s = pc_j^{s'}.$* $\square$

Let $e = s_1 \xrightarrow{l_1} s_2 \xrightarrow{l_2} \cdots s_{n-1} \xrightarrow{l_{n-1}} s_n$ be an execution path from a given state s_1 to a reachable state s_n, where for all $x \in [1, n-1]$, $l_x \in (Act \cup \mathbb{R}_{>0})$. Having the relation $\mathcal{R}$ between two states s and s', i.e. $(s, s') \in \mathcal{R}$, we are able to prove that all executions from s and s' reach the same set of timed states. Note that by defining a dummy transition, a deadlock state is also a timed state.

Lemma 1. *Let $(s_1, s_1') \in \mathcal{R}$ and for all $x \in [1, n-1]$, $act_x \in Act$ and for all $y \in [1, n'-1]$, $act_y' \in Act$. For each execution $e = s_1 \xrightarrow{act_1} s_2 \xrightarrow{act_2} \cdots \xrightarrow{act_{n-1}} s_n \xrightarrow{d} t$ in T_{TTS}, there is an execution $e' = s_1' \xrightarrow{act_1'} s_2' \xrightarrow{act_2'} \cdots \xrightarrow{act_{n'-1}'} s_{n'}' \xrightarrow{d} t'$ in T_{CTTS} such that $(s_n, s_{n'}') \in \mathcal{R}$, and vice versa.*

Proof. This proof consists of two parts:

***Part1*: For each execution e in T_{TTS} there is an execution e' in T_{CTTS} such that $(s_n, s_{n'}') \in \mathcal{R}$.** Let $BA_{co_i} = \{a_j | \ j \in AId_i \ \wedge \ \exists z \in K_j \cdot \exists i' \in CID \cdot (i \neq i' \ \wedge \ z \in AId_{i'})\}$ be the set of boundary actors of the component co_i. Assume that a boundary actor a_j is triggered at the current time of s_1, i.e., $\exists x \in [1, n-1] \cdot act_x = m_k \ \wedge \ m_k \in B_j^{s_x} \wedge a_j \in BA_{co_i}$. Based on the input of the function *porMethod* in Fig. 4, a_j follows the delay condition and does not send a cross-border message at the current time, and hence, interleaving executions of internal actors of different components does not affect the reachable timed state. Let $seq_{co_i,e}$ contains the messages and the orders in which those massages are taken from the bags of actors of the component co_i over e, i.e., if $seq_{co_i,e} = \langle m_{k_1,1}, m_{k_2,2}, \cdots, m_{k_w,w} \rangle$, then $\forall j, z \in [1, w] \cdot z > j \cdot \exists act_x, act_{x'} \cdot x, x' \in [1, n-1] \wedge act_x = m_{k_j,j} \wedge act_{x'} = m_{k_z,z} \wedge x' > x \wedge m_{k_j,j} \in B_b^{s_x} \wedge m_{k_z,z} \in B_p^{s_{x'}} \wedge b, p \in AId_i$.

Similarly, $seq_{co_i,e'}$ can be defined for an execution e' in T_{CTTS}. If for the execution e in T_{TTS} there exists an execution e' in T_{CTTS} such that for all $i \in CID$, $seq_{co_i,e} = seq_{co_i,e'}$, then e' reaches a state $s_{n'}'$ where $(s_n, s_{n'}') \in \mathcal{R}$. This is because the messages and the orders in which these messages are taken from the bags affects the reachable system states. We use proof by contradiction to show that there is such an execution. Assume that $(s_1, s_1') \in \mathcal{R}$ but there is no execution e' with the mentioned condition. This means that for all executions e' in T_{CTTS}, $seq_{co_i,e} \neq seq_{co_i,e'}$ for some co_i. In our POR method, *createInStateSpace* generates the reachable states of all components at each logical time. It first uses the function *updateIntComp* to update the local state of each interface neighboring actor of each component to the local state of the corresponding neighboring actor of the component. The set of neighboring actors of co_i is $\{a_j | \exists i' \in CID \cdot (i \neq i' \wedge a_j \in BA_{co_{i'}} \ \wedge \ \exists z \in AId_i \cdot (z \in K_j \vee j \in K_z)\}$. The function *createInStateSpace* then invokes *executeCOM* to generate the reachable states of each component. The function *executeCOM* selects an actor from the set of enabled actors (line 34) and triggers the actor or resumes its execution. The set of enabled actors (line 30) includes actors of the component and its interface neighboring actors, where these actors can be triggered or resume their executions at the current time. Therefore, our POR method besides interleaving executions of actors of each component, interleaves executions of neighboring actors (through interface neighboring actors) and actors of a component. So the only case in which none of the executions e' corresponds to e, i.e. $seq_{co_i,e} \neq seq_{co_i,e'}$, is that $(s_1, s_1') \notin \mathcal{R}$, that contradicts the assumption.

***Part2*: For each execution e' in T_{CTTS} there is an execution e in T_{TTS} such that $(s_n, s_{n'}') \in \mathcal{R}$.** As mentioned before, an interleaving of executions of actors is considered in the generation of C-TTS; however, all interleavings of

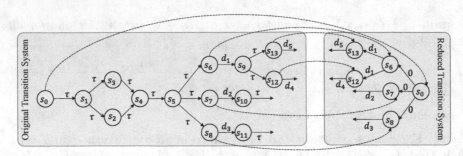

Fig. 6. The left side shows a timed transition system in which all instantaneous transitions are τ transitions and the right side shows its reduced version. The dotted arrows show the mappings between states.

executions of actors are considered in the generation of TTS. So, all reachable timed states in C-TTS can be found in TTS.   □

To show that our POR method preserves the properties over timed states, we reduce TTS and C-TTS by changing the instantaneous transitions to τ transitions and removing the τ transitions. We define $Act_\tau = \{\tau\}$ and use $T_\tau = (S, s_0, Act_\tau, \rightarrow_\tau, AP, L)$ to denote a transition system in which all instantaneous transitions are changed to τ transitions.

Definition 5. *(Reduced Transition System) For $T_\tau = (S, s_0, Act_\tau, \rightarrow_\tau, AP, L)$, its reduced transition system is $T' = (S', s_0, \emptyset, \rightarrow', AP, L)$, where:*

- *$S' \subseteq S$ that contains all timed states and the state s_0,*
- *For all $s, s' \in (S' \setminus \{s_0\})$, $(s, d, s') \in \rightarrow'$ if and only if there exists an execution $s \xrightarrow{d} s_1 \xrightarrow{\tau} \ldots s_n \xrightarrow{\tau} s'$ in T_τ, where $s_1, \cdots, s_n$ are not timed states,*
- *For all $s' \in (S' \setminus \{s_0\})$, $(s_0, 0, s') \in \rightarrow'$ if and only if there exists an execution $s_0 \xrightarrow{\tau} s_1 \ldots s_n \xrightarrow{\tau} s'$ in T_τ, where $s_1, \cdots, s_n$ are not timed states.*   □

There is a transition between two states of T' if and only if those are consecutive timed states or are the initial state and its following timed states in T_τ (or T). The reduced version of a transition system is shown in Fig. 6. In the following theorem, we prove that the reduced TTS and the reduced C-TTS have the same sets of states and transitions and so are isomorphic.

Theorem 1. *The reduced TTS and the reduced C-TTS are isomorphic.*

Proof. Let $T'_{TTS} = (S'_1, s_0, Act, \rightarrow'_1, AP, L)$ and $T'_{CTTS} = (S'_2, s_0, Act, \rightarrow'_2, AP, L)$ be respectively the reduced versions of TTS and C-TTS. We have $(s_0, s_0) \in \mathcal{R}$. Now, let $(s_1, s_2) \in \mathcal{R}$ and $s_1 \xrightarrow{d}_1 t_1$. Based on Lemma 1, all executions from s_1 and s_2 reach the same set of timed states in TTS and C-TTS. Based on Definition 5, the set of states in the reduced TTS and the reduced C-TTS includes timed states. Therefore, there is $t_2 \in S'_2$ such that $s_2 \xrightarrow{d}_2 t_2$ and $(t_1, t_2) \in \mathcal{R}$. Therefore, T'_{TTS} and T'_{CTTS} have the same sets of states and transitions, and hence, are isomorphic.

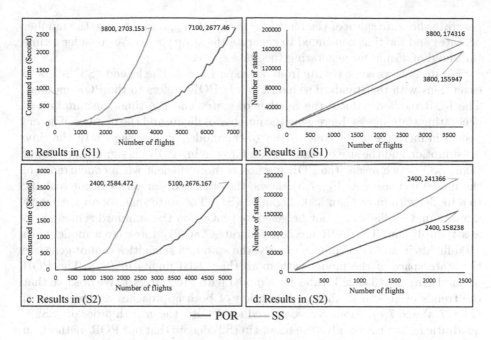

Fig. 7. The number of states and time consumption of model checking in (S1) and (S2), where "SS" stands for the standard semantics and "POR" for the POR method.

6   Experimental Results

In this section, we report our experiments on a benchmark in the domain of air traffic control systems (ATCs) [3–5] to compare the model checking time and memory consumption of using the standard semantics and the proposed POR method. We model an ATC application with four components. Each component consists of $n^2/4$ actors modeling the traveling routes in the ATC application and might consist of several actors modeling the source and destination airports. Similar to [3], we use Ptolemy II as our implementation platform to generate the state space based on both approaches. Our source codes are available in [19].

We consider three scenarios in our experiments: (S1) and (S2) that respectively use a low-concurrency model with $n = 10$ and $n = 18$, and (S3) that uses a high-concurrency model with $n = 18$. We generate a batch p of flight plans for 10000 aircraft in each scenario, where aircraft are modeled as messages passed between the actors. We partition the batch p into smaller batches $p_i, 1 \leq i \leq 100$, where p_1 contains the first 100 flight plans of p, p_2 contains the first 200 flight plans of p, and so on. By increasing the number of aircraft, the concurrency contained in the model increases. Similarly, by increasing n, the number of actors involved in the analysis and subsequently the concurrency of the model increase. Compared to (S1) and (S2), the flight plans in (S3) are selected in a way that many actors can send or receive messages corresponding to the aircraft at the same time, which lead to a high-concurrency model. We use both approaches to generate the state space of the model for each batch p_i and measure the number of states and the time consumed to generate the state space. We consider a time threshold of 45 min for generating the state space.

Figure 7 shows some results from our experiments. The legend "SS" refers to executions with the standard semantics and "POR" refers to the POR method. The POR method reduces the number of states and the time consumption of generating state spaces. Increasing the number of flights and the number of actors results in increases in the concurrency of the model, and subsequently, the time consumption and the size of state spaces. Growth in "POR" is significantly lower than "SS", which means the POR method is more efficient when concurrency of the model increases. As Fig. 7(a) shows, the standard semantics is not scalable to a model with more than 3800 flights in (S1). The state space of a model with more than 3800 flights cannot be generated based on the standard semantics in less than 45 min. The POR method generates 286427 states for a model with 7100 flights in around 45 min. Similarly, the standard semantics cannot generate the state space of the model with more than 2400 flights in (S2). The POR method generates 333,283 states for a model with 5100 aircraft. We observe that the trends of growth in time consumption of both approaches are exponential (Figs. 7(a) and 7(c)). However, compared to "POR", the growth order of "SS" is quadratic for our case study. The results in (S2) denote that our POR method, on average, reduces the time and memory consumption by 76 and 34%, respectively. The POR method removes unnecessary execution paths. Since several execution paths may pass through a common state, the number of transitions removed is more than the number of states removed. As the time consumption mostly relates to creation of the transitions, the reduction in the time consumption is more than the reduction in the memory consumption.

The scenario (S3) examines a model with highly concurrent actors. The standard semantics is not scalable to more than 13 flights: it generates 15,280,638 states for the model with 13 flights in 45 min. The POR method scales to the model with 220 flights. It generates 412,377 states for the model with 220 flights in 45 min.

7   Conclusion

We proposed a compositional method for POR of timed actors. Instead of interleaving executions of actors of all components to generate the state space, our method iterates over components at each logical time, generates the set of reachable states of each component, and composes the sets of reachable states. By considering the communications of actors over different components, our method interleaves executions of actors and neighboring actors of each component to generate the set of reachable states. We proved that our POR method preserves the properties of our interest.

References

1. Agha, G.: Actors: A Model of Concurrent Computation in Distributed Systems. MIT Press, Cambridge, MA, USA (1986)
2. Akka library (2021). http://akka.io
3. Bagheri, M., Sirjani, M., Khamespanah, E., Baier, C., Movaghar, A.: Magnifier: a compositional analysis approach for autonomous traffic control. IEEE Trans. Softw. Eng. 1 (2021). https://doi.org/10.1109/TSE.2021.3069192
4. Bagheri, M., et al.: Coordinated actors for reliable self-adaptive systems. In: Kouchnarenko, O., Khosravi, R. (eds.) FACS 2016. LNCS, vol. 10231, pp. 241–259. Springer, Cham (2017). https://doi.org/10.1007/978-3-319-57666-4_15
5. Bagheri, M., et al.: Coordinated actor model of self-adaptive track-based traffic control systems. J. Syst. Softw. **143**, 116–139 (2018)
6. Bengtsson, J., Jonsson, B., Lilius, J., Yi, W.: Partial order reductions for timed systems. In: Sangiorgi, D., de Simone, R. (eds.) CONCUR 1998. LNCS, vol. 1466, pp. 485–500. Springer, Heidelberg (1998). https://doi.org/10.1007/BFb0055643
7. Boer, F.D., et al.: A survey of active object languages. ACM Comput. Surv. **50**(5) (2017). https://doi.org/10.1145/3122848
8. Earle, C.B., Fredlund, L.Å.: Verification of timed erlang programs using McErlang. In: Giese, H., Rosu, G. (eds.) FMOODS/FORTE -2012. LNCS, vol. 7273, pp. 251–267. Springer, Heidelberg (2012). https://doi.org/10.1007/978-3-642-30793-5_16
9. Eckhardt, J., Mühlbauer, T., Meseguer, J., Wirsing, M.: Statistical model checking for composite actor systems. In: Martí-Oliet, N., Palomino, M. (eds.) WADT 2012. LNCS, vol. 7841, pp. 143–160. Springer, Heidelberg (2013). https://doi.org/10.1007/978-3-642-37635-1_9
10. Godefroid, P.: Using partial orders to improve automatic verification methods. In: Clarke, E.M., Kurshan, R.P. (eds.) CAV 1990. LNCS, vol. 531, pp. 176–185. Springer, Heidelberg (1991). https://doi.org/10.1007/BFb0023731
11. Håkansson, J., Pettersson, P.: Partial order reduction for verification of real-time components. In: Raskin, J.-F., Thiagarajan, P.S. (eds.) FORMATS 2007. LNCS, vol. 4763, pp. 211–226. Springer, Heidelberg (2007). https://doi.org/10.1007/978-3-540-75454-1_16
12. Haller, P., Odersky, M.: Scala actors: unifying thread-based and event-based programming. Theor. Comput. Sci. **410**(2), 202–220 (2009). distributed Computing Techniques
13. Hansen, H., Lin, S.-W., Liu, Y., Nguyen, T.K., Sun, J.: Diamonds are a girl's best friend: partial order reduction for timed automata with abstractions. In: Biere, A., Bloem, R. (eds.) CAV 2014. LNCS, vol. 8559, pp. 391–406. Springer, Cham (2014). https://doi.org/10.1007/978-3-319-08867-9_26
14. Hewitt, C.: Description and theoretical analysis (using schemata) of planner: A language for proving theorems and manipulating models in a robot. Technical report, Massachusetts Inst of Tech Cambridge ArtificiaL Intelligence Lab (1972)
15. Khamespanah, E., Sirjani, M., Sabahi Kaviani, Z., Khosravi, R., Izadi, M.J.: Timed rebeca schedulability and deadlock freedom analysis using bounded floating time transition system. Sci. Comput. Program. **98**, 184–204 (2015). special Issue on Programming Based on Actors, Agents and Decentralized Control
16. Lohstroh, M., et al.: Reactors: a deterministic model for composable reactive systems. In: Chamberlain, R., Edin Grimheden, M., Taha, W. (eds.) CyPhy/WESE -2019. LNCS, vol. 11971, pp. 59–85. Springer, Cham (2020). https://doi.org/10.1007/978-3-030-41131-2_4

17. Minea, M.: Partial order reduction for model checking of timed automata. In: Baeten, J.C.M., Mauw, S. (eds.) CONCUR 1999. LNCS, vol. 1664, pp. 431–446. Springer, Heidelberg (1999). https://doi.org/10.1007/3-540-48320-9_30

18. Peled, D.: All from one, one for all: on model checking using representatives. In: Courcoubetis, C. (ed.) CAV 1993. LNCS, vol. 697, pp. 409–423. Springer, Heidelberg (1993). https://doi.org/10.1007/3-540-56922-7_34

19. Source codes (2021). https://github.com/maryambagheri1989/POR/

20. Ptolemaeus, C.: System Design, Modeling, and Simulation: Using Ptolemy II. Ptolemy.org, Berkeley, CA, USA (2014)

21. Afra Tool (2021). http://rebeca-lang.org/alltools/Afra

22. Reynisson, A.H., et al.: Modelling and simulation of asynchronous real-time systems using timed rebeca. Sci. Comput. Program. **89**, 41–68 (2014). https://doi.org/10.1016/j.scico.2014.01.008, http://www.sciencedirect.com/science/article/pii/S0167642314000239, special issue on the 10th International Workshop on the Foundations of Coordination Languages and Software Architectures (FOCLASA 2011)

23. Sirjani, M., Lee, E.A., Khamespanah, E.: Model checking software in cyberphysical systems. In: 2020 IEEE 44th Annual Computers, Software, and Applications Conference (COMPSAC), pp. 1017–1026 (2020)

24. Sirjani, M., Movaghar, A., Shali, A., de Boer, F.S.: Modeling and verification of reactive systems using rebeca. Fundam. Inf. **63**(4), 385–410 (2004)

25. Tan, T.H., Liu, Y., Sun, J., Dong, J.S.: Verification of orchestration systems using compositional partial order reduction. In: Qin, S., Qiu, Z. (eds.) ICFEM 2011. LNCS, vol. 6991, pp. 98–114. Springer, Heidelberg (2011). https://doi.org/10.1007/978-3-642-24559-6_9

26. Virding, R., Wikström, C., Williams, M., Armstrong, J.: Concurrent Programming in ERLANG, 2nd (ed.). Prentice Hall International (UK) Ltd., GBR, London (1996)

27. Ölveczky, P.C., Meseguer, J.: Real-time maude 2.1. Electron. Notes Theor. Comput. Sci. **117**, 285–314 (2005). proceedings of the Fifth International Workshop on Rewriting Logic and Its Applications (WRLA 2004)

Uncertainty-Aware Signal Temporal Logic Inference

Nasim Baharisangari[1], Jean-Raphaël Gaglione[2], Daniel Neider[3], Ufuk Topcu[2], and Zhe Xu[1(✉)]

[1] School for Engineering of Matter, Transport and Energy, Arizona State University, Tempe, AZ 85287, USA
{nbaharis,xzhe1}@asu.edu
[2] University of Texas at Austin, Austin, TX 78712TX, USA
{jr.gaglione,utopcu}@utexas.edu
[3] Max Planck Institute for Software Systems, Kaiserslautern, Germany
neider@mpi-sws.org

Abstract. Temporal logic inference is the process of extracting formal descriptions of system behaviors from data in the form of temporal logic formulas. The existing temporal logic inference methods mostly neglect uncertainties in the data, which results in the limited applicability of such methods in real-world deployments. In this paper, we first investigate the uncertainties associated with trajectories of a system and represent such uncertainties in the form of *interval trajectories*. We then propose two *uncertainty-aware* signal temporal logic (STL) inference approaches to classify the undesired behaviors and desired behaviors of a system. Instead of classifying finitely many trajectories, we classify infinitely many trajectories within the interval trajectories. In the first approach, we incorporate robust semantics of STL formulas with respect to an interval trajectory to quantify the margin at which an STL formula is satisfied or violated by the interval trajectory. The second approach relies on the first learning algorithm and exploits the decision trees to infer STL formulas to classify behaviors of a given system. The proposed approaches also work for non-separable data by optimizing the *worst-case robustness margin* in inferring an STL formula. Finally, we evaluate the performance of the proposed algorithms and present the obtained numerical results, where the proposed algorithms show reduction in the computation time by up to the factor of 95 on average, while the worst-case robustness margins are improved by up to 330% in comparison with the sampling-based baseline algorithms.

Keywords: Temporal logic inference · Uncertainties · Decision trees

1 Introduction

There is a growing emergence of artificial intelligence (AI) in different fields, such as traffic prediction and transportation [1–3], or image [4] and pattern

© Springer Nature Switzerland AG 2022
R. Bloem et al. (Eds.): NSV 2021/VSTTE 2021, LNCS 13124, pp. 61–85, 2022.
https://doi.org/10.1007/978-3-030-95561-8_5

recognition [5,6]. Competency-awareness is an advantageous capability that can raise the accountability of AI systems [7]. For example, AI systems should be able to explain their behaviors in an interpretable way.

One option to represent system behaviors is to use formal languages such as linear temporal logic (LTL) [8,9]. LTL is an expressive language which is interpretable by humans, and at the same time preserves the rigor of formal logics. However, LTL is used for analyzing discrete programs; hence, LTL falls short when coping with continuous systems such as mixed-signal circuits in *cyber-physical systems* (CPS) [10,11]. Signal temporal logic (STL) is an extension of LTL that tackles this issue. STL is a temporal logic defined over signals [12,13], and branches out LTL in two directions: on top of using atomic predicates, it deploys real-valued variables, and it is defined over time intervals [14].

Recently, inferring the temporal properties of a system from its trajectories has been in the spotlight. We can derive such properties by inferring STL formulas. One way of computing such STL formulas is incorporating *satisfibilty modulo theories* (SMT) solvers such as *Z3 theorem prover* [15]. Such solvers can determine whether an STL formula is satisfiable or not, according to some theories such as *arithmetic theory* [16,17]. Most of the frequently used algorithms for STL inference deploy customized templates for a solver to conform to. These pre-determined templates suffer from applying many limitations to the inference process. First, a template that complies with the behavior of the system is not easy to handcraft. Second, the templates can constrain the structure of an inferred formula; hence, the formulas not compatible with the template are removed from the search space [18–21].

Moreover, the importance of *uncertainties* is well established in several fields such as machine learning (ML) application in weather forecast [22], or deep learning application in facilitating statistical inference [23]. Failure to account for the uncertainties in any system can reduce the reliability of the output as *predictions* in AI systems [24]. Specifically, in AI, uncertainties happen due to different reasons including noise in data or overlap between classes of data [24]. *Uncertainty quantification* techniques in AI systems have been developed to address this matter [25]. Incorporating the quantified *uncertainties* in the process of inferring temporal properties can lead to higher credibility of the predictions. However, most of the current approaches of inferring temporal properties do not account for uncertainties in the inference process.

In this paper, we propose two *uncertainty-aware* STL inference algorithms for inferring the temporal properties of a system in the form of STL formulas. In the proposed algorithms, the uncertainties associated with trajectories describing the evolution of a system are implemented in the form of *interval trajectories*. The second algorithm relies on the first one and uses decisions trees to infer STL formulas. By taking uncertainties into consideration, instead of classifying finitely many trajectories to infer an STL formula that classifies the trajectories, we classify infinitely many trajectories within the interval trajectories.

Besides, the uncertainty-aware STL inference algorithms quantify the margin at which an interval trajectory violates or satisfies an inferred STL formula by incorporating the robust semantics of uncertainty-aware STL formulas (Sect. 3.2). We maximize *worst-case robustness* margin for increasing the robustness of the inferred STL formulas in the presence of uncertainties; thus, we can view our problem as an optimization problem with the objective of maximizing the worst-case robustness margin. Moreover, we introduce a framework in which we employ the optimized robustness to compute the optimal STL formula for non-separable datasets (Sect. 5). We evaluate the performance of the proposed uncertainty-aware STL inference algorithms and present the obtained numerical results. The proposed algorithms show reductions in the computation time by up to the factor of 17 on average, while the worst-case robustness margins are improved by up to 330% in comparison with the sampling-based baseline algorithms. Incorporating decision trees in the second proposed algorithm further expedites the inference with the computation time being 1/95 of the computation time of the sampling-based baseline algorithms with decision trees (Sect. 7).

Related Work: Recently, inferring temporal properties of a system by its temporally evolved trajectories have been in the spotlight [26–28]. Kong *et al.* developed an algorithm for STL inference from trajectories that show the desired behavior and those having the undesired behavior [29]. Kyriakis *et al.* proposed *stochastic temporal logic* (StTL) inference algorithm for characterizing time-varying behaviors of a dynamical stochastic system. Neider *et al.* [18] proposed a framework for learning temporal properties using LTL. Several other frameworks for inferring temporal properties such as [19,21,30–32], etc. have been proposed. Unlike the mentioned works, in this paper, we account for the uncertainty in the inference process.

2 Preliminaries

In this section, we set up definitions and notations used throughout this paper.

Finite Trajectories: We can describe the state of an underlying system by a vector $x = [x^1, x^2, .., x^n]$, where n is a non-negative integer (the superscript i in x^i refers to the i-th dimension). The domain of x is denoted by $\mathbb{X} = \mathbb{X}^1 \times \mathbb{X}^2 \times ... \times \mathbb{X}^n$, where each $\mathbb{X}^i$ is a subset of $\mathbb{R}$. The evolution of the underlying system within a finite time horizon is defined in the discrete-time-domain $\mathbb{T} = \{t_0, t_1, ..., t_J\}$, where J is a non-negative integer. We define a finite *trajectory* describing the evolution of the underlying system as a function $\zeta : \mathbb{T} \to \mathbb{X}$. We use $\zeta_j \triangleq x(t_j)$ to denote the value of ζ at time-step t_j.

Intervals and Interval Trajectories: An *interval*, denoted by $[\underline{a}, \overline{a}]$, is defined as $[\underline{a}, \overline{a}] := \{a \in \mathbb{R}^n | \underline{a}^i \leq a^i \leq \overline{a}^i, \quad i = 1, .., n\}$, where $\underline{a}, \overline{a} \in \mathbb{R}^n$, and $\underline{a}^i \leq \overline{a}^i$ holds true for all i. The superscript i refers to the i-th dimension. For this work, we introduce *interval trajectories*. We define an *interval trajectory* $[\underline{\zeta}, \overline{\zeta}]$ as a set of trajectories such that for any $\zeta \in [\underline{\zeta}, \overline{\zeta}]$, we have $\zeta_j \in [\underline{\zeta_j}, \overline{\zeta_j}]$ for all $t_j \in \mathbb{T}$ [33]. We know that the time length of a trajectory $\zeta \in [\underline{\zeta}, \overline{\zeta}]$ is equal to the time length of an interval trajectory $[\underline{\zeta}, \overline{\zeta}]$; thus, we can denote the time length of an interval trajectory $[\underline{\zeta}, \overline{\zeta}]$ with $|\zeta|$.

3   Signal Temporal Logic and Robust Semantics of Interval Trajectories

3.1   Signal Temporal Logic

We first briefly review the signal temporal logic (STL). We start with the Boolean semantics of STL. The domain $\mathbb{B} = \{True, False\}$ is the Boolean domain. Moreover, we introduce a set $\Pi = \{\pi_1, \pi_2, \ldots, \pi_n\}$ which is a set of predefined *atomic predicates*. Each of these predicates can hold values *True* or *False*. The syntax of STL is defined recursively as follows.

$$\varphi := \top \mid \pi \mid \neg\varphi \mid \varphi_1 \wedge \varphi_2 \mid \varphi_1 \vee \varphi_2 \mid \varphi_1 \mathbf{U}_I \varphi_2$$

where $\top$ stands for the Boolean constant *True*, π is an atomic predicate in the form of an inequality $f(x) > 0$ where f is some real-valued function. $\neg$ (negation), $\wedge$ (conjunction), $\vee$ (disjunction) are standard Boolean connectives, and "$\mathbf{U}$" is the temporal operator "until". We add syntactic sugar, and introduce the temporal operators "$\mathbf{F}$" and "$\mathbf{G}$" representing "eventually" and "always", respectively. I is a time interval of the form $I = [a, b)$, where $a < b$, and they are non-negative integers. We call the set containing all the mentioned operators $C = \{\top, \wedge, \vee, \neg, \rightarrow, \mathbf{F}, \mathbf{G}, \mathbf{U}\}$.

We employ the Boolean semantics of an STL formula in *strong* and *weak* views, as shown in Definitions 1 and 2 below. We denote the length of a trajectory $\zeta \in [\underline{\zeta}, \overline{\zeta}]$ by T [34]. In the strong view, $(\zeta, t_j) \models_S \varphi$ means that trajectory $\zeta \in [\underline{\zeta}, \overline{\zeta}]$ strongly satisfies the formula φ at time-step t_j. $(\zeta, t_j) \not\models_S \varphi$ means that trajectory $\zeta \in [\underline{\zeta}, \overline{\zeta}]$ does not strongly satisfy the formula φ at time-step t_j. Similar interpretations hold for the weak view ($\models_W$ means "weakly satisfies" and $\not\models_W$ means "does not weakly satisfy"). By considering the Boolean semantics of STL formulas in strong and weak views, the strong satisfaction or violation of an STL formula φ by a trajectory at time-step t_j implies the weak satisfaction or violation of the STL formula by the trajectory at time-step t_j. Consequently, we can take either of the views for trajectories with label $l_i = +1$ (representing desired behavior) and trajectories with label $l_i = -1$ (representing undesired behavior) for perfect classification [34]. In this paper, we choose to adopt the strong view for the problem formulations of Sects. 4 and 5.

Definition 1. *The Boolean semantics of an STL formula φ, for a trajectory $\zeta \in [\underline{\zeta}, \overline{\zeta}]$ with the time length of T at time-step t_j in strong view is defined recursively as follows.*

$$(\zeta, t_j) \models_S \pi \ \textit{iff} \ t_j \leq T \ \textit{and} \ f(\zeta_j) > 0$$
$$(\zeta, t_j) \models_S \neg\varphi \ \textit{iff} \ (\zeta, t_j) \not\models_W \varphi,$$
$$(\zeta, t_j) \models_S \varphi_1 \wedge \varphi_2 \ \textit{iff} \ (\zeta, t_j) \models_S \varphi_1 \ \textit{and} \ (\zeta, t_j) \models_S \varphi_2,$$
$$(\zeta, t_j) \models_S \varphi_1 \mathbf{U}_{[a,b)} \varphi_2 \ \textit{iff} \ \exists j' \in [j + a, j + b),$$
$$(\zeta, t_{j'}) \models_S \varphi_2 \ \textit{and} \ \forall j'' \in [j + a, j'), (\zeta, t_{j''}) \models_S \varphi_1.$$

Definition 2. *The Boolean semantics of an STL formula φ, for a trajectory $\zeta \in [\underline{\zeta}, \overline{\zeta}]$ with the time length of T at time-step t_j in weak view is defined recursively as follows.*

$$(\zeta, t_j) \models_W \pi(\zeta, t_j) \models_W \pi \text{ iff either of the 1) or 2) holds:}$$
$$1)\ t_j > T,\ 2)\ t_j \leq T \text{ and } f(\zeta_j) > 0,$$
$$(\zeta, t_j) \models_W \neg \varphi \text{ iff } (\zeta, t_j) \not\models_S \varphi,$$
$$(\zeta, t_j) \models_W \varphi_1 \wedge \varphi_2 \text{ iff } (\zeta, t_j) \models_W \varphi_1 \text{ and}$$
$$(\zeta, t_j) \models_W \varphi_2,$$
$$(\zeta, t_j) \models_W \varphi_1 \mathbf{U}_{[a,b)} \varphi_2 \text{ iff } \exists j' \in [j + a, j + b),$$
$$(\zeta, t_{j'}) \models_W \varphi_2 \text{ and } \forall j'' \in [j + a, j'),\ (\zeta, t_{j''}) \models_W \varphi_1.$$

Syntax DAG: Any STL formula can be represented as a syntax directed acyclic graph, i.e., syntax DAG. In a syntax DAG, the nodes are labeled with atomic predicates or temporal operators that form an STL formula [18]. For instance, Fig. 1a shows the unique syntax DAG of the formula $(\pi_1 \mathbf{U} \pi_2) \wedge \mathbf{G}(\pi_1 \vee \pi_2)$, in which the subformula π_2 is shared. Figure 1b shows arrangement of the identifiers of each node in the syntax DAG ($i \in \{1, .., 7\}$).

(a) Syntax DAG

(b) Identifiers

Size of an STL Formula: If we present an STL formula by a syntax DAG, then each node corresponds to a subformula; thus, the size of an STL formula is equal to the number of the DAG nodes. We denote the size of an STL formula φ by $|\varphi|$ [35].

Fig. 1. Syntax DAG and identifier of syntax DAG of the formula $(\pi_1 \mathbf{U} \pi_2) \wedge \mathbf{G}(\pi_1 \vee \pi_2)$

3.2 Robust Semantics of STL Formulas

Robust semantics quantifies the margin at which a certain trajectory satisfies or violates an STL formula φ at time-step t_j. The robustness margin of a trajectory ζ with respect to an STL formula φ at time-step t_j is given by $r(\zeta, \varphi, t_j)$, where $r(\zeta, \varphi, t_j) \in \mathbb{R}$ can be calculated recursively via the robust semantics [36]. In the following, we assume that the length of the trajectory is sufficiently long such that the robustness margin can be computed in the strong view.

$$r(\zeta, \pi, t_j) = f(\zeta_j),$$
$$r(\zeta, \neg\varphi, t_j) = -r(\zeta, \varphi, t_j),$$
$$r(\zeta, \varphi_1 \wedge \varphi_2, t_j) = \min(r(\zeta, \varphi_1, t_j), r(\zeta, \varphi_2, t_j)),$$
$$r(\zeta, \varphi_1 \mathbf{U}_{[a,b)} \varphi_2, t_j) = \max_{j+a \leq j' < j+b} (\min(r(\zeta, \varphi_2, t_{j'}), \min_{j+a \leq j'' < j'} r(\zeta, \varphi_1, t_{j''}))).$$

We can define the robustness margin of an interval trajectory in two views: *worst-case* and *best-case*. The worst-case view chooses the trajectory with the minimum corresponding robustness within an interval trajectory (Eq. (1)). The best-case view chooses the trajectory with maximum corresponding robustness within an interval trajectory (Eq. (2)); thus, we define the robustness margin of an interval trajectory in two views, as follows.

$$\underline{r}([\underline{\zeta}, \overline{\zeta}], \varphi, t_j) = \min_{\zeta \in [\underline{\zeta}, \overline{\zeta}]} r(\zeta, \varphi, t_j) \tag{1}$$

$$\overline{r}([\underline{\zeta}, \overline{\zeta}], \varphi, t_j) = \max_{\zeta \in [\underline{\zeta}, \overline{\zeta}]} r(\zeta, \varphi, t_j) \tag{2}$$

4   Problem Formulation

In this section, we present the problem formulation of perfectly classifying interval trajectories. Then, we derive sufficient conditions to solve the problem. The existing methods for inferring STL formulas mostly classify finitely many trajectories without considering the uncertainties. For the problem of classifying finitely many trajectories, we define the following.

Definition 3. *Given a labeled set of trajectories* $\mathcal{D} = \{(\zeta^i, l_i)\}_{i=1}^{N_{\mathcal{D}}}$, *where* $l_i = +1$ *represents the desired behavior and* $l_i = -1$ *represents the undesired behavior, an STL formula* φ, *evaluated at time* t_0, *perfectly classifies the desired behaviors and the undesired behaviors if the following condition is satisfied.* $(\zeta^i, t_0) \models_s \varphi$, *if* $l_i = +1$; $(\zeta^i, t_0) \models_s \neg\varphi$, *if* $l_i = -1$.

With Definition 3, the problem of STL inference for classifying finitely many trajectories is as follows.

Problem 1. Given a labeled set of trajectories $\mathcal{D} = \{(\zeta^i, l_i)\}_{i=1}^{N_{\mathcal{D}}}$, compute an STL formula φ such that φ, which is evaluated at time t_0, perfectly classifies the desired behaviors and undesired behaviors, and $|\varphi| \leq N$, where N is a predetermined positive integer.

Definition 3 cannot classify infinitely many trajectories; thus, by considering the uncertainties, and substituting trajectories with interval trajectories, we define the following.

Definition 4. *Given a labeled set of interval trajectories* $\mathcal{D}_{unc} = \{([\underline{\zeta}, \overline{\zeta}]^i, l_i)\}_{i=1}^{N_{\mathcal{D}}}$, $l_i = +1$ *represents the desired behavior and* $l_i = -1$ *represents the undesired behavior, an STL formula* φ, *which is evaluated at time* t_0, *perfectly classifies the desired behaviors and the undesired behaviors if the following condition is satisfied.*
if $l_i = +1$, *then* $\forall \zeta \in [\underline{\zeta}, \overline{\zeta}]^i$, *we have* $(\zeta, t_0) \models_s \varphi$; *if* $l_i = -1$, *then* $\forall \zeta \in [\underline{\zeta}, \overline{\zeta}]^i$, *we have* $(\zeta, t_0) \models_s \neg\varphi$.

Now, we define a problem formulation of classifying infinitely many trajectories within the interval trajectories.

Problem 2. Given a labeled set of interval trajectories $\mathcal{D}_{unc} = \{([\underline{\zeta}, \overline{\zeta}]^i, l_i)\}_{i=1}^{N_{\mathcal{D}}}$, compute an STL formula φ, which is evaluated at time t_0, perfectly classifies the desired behaviors and undesired behaviors, and $|\varphi| \leq N$, where N is a predetermined positive integer.

Definition 5. *We define that two interval trajectories $[\underline{\varsigma}, \overline{\varsigma}]$ and $[\underline{\varsigma}, \overline{\varsigma}]'$ are separable if there exists at least one time-step t_j and one dimension k such that the two intervals $[\underline{\varsigma}_j^k, \overline{\varsigma}_j^k]$ and $[\underline{\varsigma}_j^k, \overline{\varsigma}_j^k]'$ do not intersect, i.e., $[\underline{\varsigma}_j^k, \overline{\varsigma}_j^k] \cap [\underline{\varsigma}_j^k, \overline{\varsigma}_j^k]' = \emptyset$.*

Definition 6. *We define that two finite sets of interval trajectories Z and Z' are separable if all pairs of interval trajectories $[\underline{\varsigma}, \overline{\varsigma}] \in Z$ and $[\underline{\varsigma}, \overline{\varsigma}]' \in Z'$ are separable.*

By extension, we write that a labeled set of interval trajectories $\mathcal{D}_{unc} = \{([\underline{\varsigma}, \overline{\varsigma}]^i, l_i)\}_{i=1}^{N_D}$ is separable if $\{[\underline{\varsigma}, \overline{\varsigma}]^i | l_i = +1\}$ and $\{[\underline{\varsigma}, \overline{\varsigma}]^i | l_i = -1\}$ are separable.

Now, we provide a sufficient condition that allows us to use Definition 4 to classify two interval trajectories.

Theorem 1. *If $[\underline{\varsigma}, \overline{\varsigma}]^i$ with label $l_i = +1$ and $[\underline{\varsigma}, \overline{\varsigma}]^{\tilde{i}}$ with label $l_{\tilde{i}} = -1$ are separable, then there exists at least one STL formula that perfectly classifies these two interval trajectories.*

Now that we have the sufficient condition for the perfect classification of two interval trajectories, we provide the sufficient condition for the case of having multiple interval trajectories.

Theorem 2. *If a given labeled set of interval trajectories $\mathcal{D}_{unc} = \{([\underline{\varsigma}, \overline{\varsigma}]^i, l_i)\}_{i=1}^{N_D}$ is separable, then there exists at least one STL formula φ that perfectly classifies $\mathcal{D}_{unc}$.*

5   STL Inference for Non-separable Interval Trajectories

One source of uncertainty in a dataset is overlap between the interval trajectories satisfying an STL formula φ and interval trajectories violating φ. This type of dataset is called *non-separable* dataset [37]. We deploy robust semantics to set up a method to infer STL formulas for a non-separable dataset with two labeled classes. We define that two interval trajectories are *non-separable* if they are not separable according to Definition 5. Similarly, we define a non-separable labeled dataset if it is not separable according to Definition 6.

Given a set of N_D labeled interval trajectories $\mathcal{D}_{unc} = \{([\underline{\varsigma}, \overline{\varsigma}]^i, l_i)\}_{i=1}^{N_D}$, we define in Eq. (3) a function $\tilde{F}$ that gives the worst-case robustness margin of an interval trajectory $[\underline{\varsigma}, \overline{\varsigma}]^i$ with respect to φ or $\neg\varphi$ if $l_i = +1$ or $l_i = -1$, respectively.

$$\tilde{F}([\underline{\varsigma}, \overline{\varsigma}]^i, l_i, \varphi) := \begin{cases} \underline{r}([\underline{\varsigma}, \overline{\varsigma}]^i, \varphi, t_0), & \text{if } l_i = +1. \\ \underline{r}([\underline{\varsigma}, \overline{\varsigma}]^i, \neg\varphi, t_0), & \text{if } l_i = -1. \end{cases} \tag{3}$$

We then construct in Eq. (4) our objective function F. If we consider the STL formula for perfect classification of $\mathcal{D}_{unc}$: $\bigwedge_{\varsigma \in [\underline{\varsigma}, \overline{\varsigma}]^i, l_i = +1} (\varsigma \models_S \varphi) \wedge \bigwedge_{\varsigma \in [\underline{\varsigma}, \overline{\varsigma}]^i, l_i = -1} (\varsigma \models_S \neg\varphi)$, F would be the worst-case robustness margin of it. Hence, F represents the lower worst-case robustness margin amongst all the interval trajectories.

$$F(\mathcal{D}_{unc}, \varphi) := \min_{i=1,..,N_D} \tilde{F}([\underline{\zeta}, \overline{\zeta}]^i, l_i, \varphi) \tag{4}$$

Problem 3. Given a possibly non-separable set of labeled interval trajectories $\mathcal{D}_{unc} = \{([\underline{\zeta}, \overline{\zeta}]^i, l_i)\}_{i=1}^{N_D}$, compute an STL formula φ that maximizes $F(\mathcal{D}_{unc}, \varphi)$ such that $|\varphi| \leq N$, where N is a predetermined positive integer.

To solve Problem 3, we compute an STL formula φ by maximizing $F(\mathcal{D}_{unc}, \varphi)$, and we set an upper-bound on the size of the φ for interpretability.

Figure 2 shows a simple illustrative example of how we use $\tilde{F}([\underline{\zeta}, \overline{\zeta}]^i, l_i, \varphi)$ for computing such an STL formula. In this example, the inferred STL formula can be in the form of $\varphi := x^1 > c$, where x^1 is the state of a 1-dimensional trajectory.

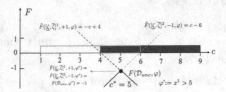

Fig. 2. In this illustrative example we show how we use $F(\mathcal{D}_{unc}, \varphi)$ and $\tilde{F}([\underline{\zeta}, \overline{\zeta}]^i, l_i, \varphi)$ to compute an STL formula for non-separable interval trajectories. We consider a labeled set $\mathcal{D}_{unc}$ composed of two interval trajectories $[\underline{\zeta}, \overline{\zeta}]^1$ and $[\underline{\zeta}, \overline{\zeta}]^2$, and a unique atomic predicate $\pi_1 := f(x) > 0$ with $f(x) = x^1 - c$, where c is an unknown constant. For sake of simplicity, we only consider STL formula φ in the form of π_1 in this example. The first interval trajectory is defined such that $l_1 = +1$ and $[\underline{\zeta}_0^1, \overline{\zeta}_0^1]^1 = [4, 9]$ (filled blue box). The second interval trajectory is defined such that $l_2 = -1$ and $[\underline{\zeta}_0^1, \overline{\zeta}_0^1]^2 = [1, 6]$ (empty red box). The vertical axis represents the objective function F, as well as the underlying functions $\tilde{F}$ for each interval trajectory, and the horizontal axis represents c. In this example, the optimal value for $F(\mathcal{D}_{unc}, \varphi)$ is -1 and is achieved at $\varphi^* = x^1 > c^*$ and $c^* = 5$. (Color figure online)

Lemma 1. *Given a sufficiently long trajectory $\zeta : \mathbb{T} \to \mathbb{X}$ and an STL formula φ, the following statements holds:*

$$r(\zeta, \varphi, t_j) > 0 \implies (\zeta, t_j) \models_S \varphi \implies r(\zeta, \varphi, t_j) \geq 0 \tag{5}$$
$$r(\zeta, \varphi, t_j) > 0 \implies (\zeta, t_j) \models_W \varphi \implies r(\zeta, \varphi, t_j) \geq 0 \tag{6}$$

Theorem 3. *Given a labeled set of interval trajectories $\mathcal{D}_{unc} = \{([\underline{\zeta}, \overline{\zeta}]^i, l_i)\}_{i=1}^{N_D}$ and an STL formula φ, if $F(\mathcal{D}_{unc}, \varphi) > 0$, then φ perfectly classifies $\mathcal{D}_{unc}$; and if φ perfectly classifies $\mathcal{D}_{unc}$, then $F(\mathcal{D}_{unc}, \varphi) \geq 0$.*

6 Uncertainty-Aware STL Inference

In this section, we propose and explain two uncertainty-aware algorithms for STL inference. The first uncertainty-aware algorithm is denoted as *TLI-UA*.

The second algorithm relies on the first one and uses decision trees to infer STL formulas which is denoted as *TLI-UA-DT*.

Satisfiabilty Modulo Theories (SMT) and OptSMT Solvers: One of the common concepts involved in the process of inferring STL formulas is *satisfiabilty*. Satisfiability addresses the following problem statement: *How can we assess whether a logical formula is satisfiable?* Based on the type of problem we deal with, we can exploit different solvers. For example, if the satisfiability problem is in the Boolean domain, we can use *Boolean satisfiability* (SAT) solvers; or if the satisfiability problem is in the continuous domain, we can use *satisfiability modulo theories* (SMT) solvers. In this paper, we consider trajectories in the real domain, as well as time-bounds of temporal operators as integers, thus we use SMT instead of SAT. SMT solvers, based on some theories including *arithmetic theories* or *bit-vectors theory*, determine whether an STL formula is satisfiable or not [16].

Another important concept involved is the incorporation of *optimization* procedures in a SMT problem. Optimization modulo theories (OMT) is an extension of SMT that allows finding models that optimizes a given objective function [38]. There exists several variants of OMT [39], in particular OptSMT, where an explicit objective function is given, and MaxSMT, where soft constraints with different costs are assigned. Our proposed methods rely on OptSMT.

OptSMT-Based Learning Algorithm: In the proposed algorithms, the input to the algorithms is in the form of interval trajectories. This input contains the data whose behaviors we wish to infer STL formulas for, and consists of two possibly non-separable labeled sets P_{unc}, N_{unc}. We categorize P_{unc} as the set containing interval trajectories with desired property (or behavior) and N_{unc} as the set containing interval trajectories with the undesired property (or behavior).

We represent the input as a set $\mathcal{D}_{unc} = P_{unc} \cup N_{unc}$. We present an STL formula by a syntax DAG. The syntax DAG encodes the STL formula by propositional variables. The propositional variables are [18]: 1) $x_{i,\lambda}$ where $i \in \{1, ..., n\}$ and $\lambda \in \Pi \cup C$; 2)$l_{i,k}$ where $i \in \{2, .., n\}$ and $k \in \{1, .., i-1\}$; 3)$r_{i,k}$ where $i \in \{2, .., n\}$ and $k \in \{1, .., i-1\}$.

To facilitate the encoding, a *unique identifier* is assigned to each node of the DAG, which is denoted by $i \in \{1, 2, .., n\}$. Two mandatory properties of this identifier are: 1) The identifier of the root is n, and 2) the identifiers of the children of Node i are less than i. It should be noted that the node with identifier 1 is always labeled with an atomic predicate ($\pi \in \Pi$). In the listed variables, $x_{i,\lambda}$ is in charge of encoding a labeling system for the syntax DAG such that if a variable $x_{i,\lambda}$ becomes *True*, then Node i is labeled with λ. The variables $l_{i,k}$ and $r_{i,k}$ encode the left and right children of the inner nodes. If the variable $l_{i,k}$ is set to *True*, then k is the identifier of the left child of Node i. If the variable $r_{i,k}$ is set to *True*, then k is the identifier of the right child of Node i. Moreover, if Node i is labeled with an unary operator, the variables $r_{i,k}$ are ignored and, both of the variables $l_{i,k}$ and $r_{i,k}$ are ignored in the case that Node i is labeled with an atomic predicate. Moreover, the reason that identifier i ranges from 2 to n for variables $l_{i,k}$ and $r_{i,k}$ is that Node 1 is always labeled with an atomic predicate and cannot have children. Lastly, k ranging from 1 to $i - 1$ reflects the point of children of a node having identifiers smaller than their root node. It is crucial to guarantee that each node has exactly one right and one left child. This matter is enforced by Eqs. (7), (8) and (9). In addition, Eq. (10) ensures that Node 1 is labeled with an atomic predicate.

$$\left[\bigwedge_{1 \leq i \leq n} \bigvee_{\lambda \in \Pi \cup C} x_{i,\lambda} \right] \wedge \left[\bigwedge_{1 \leq i \leq n} \bigwedge_{\lambda \neq \lambda' \in \Pi \cup C} \neg x_{i,\lambda} \vee \neg x_{i,\lambda'} \right] \tag{7}$$

$$\left[\bigwedge_{2 \leq i \leq n} \bigvee_{1 \leq k < i} l_{i,k} \right] \wedge \left[\bigwedge_{2 \leq i \leq n} \bigwedge_{1 \leq k < k' < i} \neg l_{i,k} \vee \neg l_{i,k'} \right] \tag{8}$$

$$\left[\bigwedge_{2 \leq i \leq n} \bigvee_{1 \leq k < i} r_{i,k} \right] \wedge \left[\bigwedge_{2 \leq i \leq n} \bigwedge_{1 \leq k < k' < i} \neg r_{i,k} \vee \neg r_{i,k'} \right] \tag{9}$$

$$\bigvee_{\pi \in \Pi} x_{1,\pi} \tag{10}$$

We introduce two sets of integer variables to the syntax DAG to add the time bounds on the temporal operators. These variables are denoted by a_i and b_i (where subscript i is the node identifier). These two variables are used to store the range of time-step indices $[j + a_i, j + b_i)$ within which the STL formula φ_i (valuation of formula φ at Node i) holds *True* when evaluated at time-step t_j. In the proposed algorithms, only the temporal operators $\mathbf{F}$, $\mathbf{G}$, and $\mathbf{U}$ use these a_i and b_i. We add the following constraint to these variables in Eq. (11).

$$\bigwedge_{1 \leq i \leq n} 0 \leq a_i < b_i \leq |\zeta| \tag{11}$$

Let the propositional formula Φ_n^{DAG} be the conjunction of Eqs. (7) to (11). Φ_n^{DAG} encodes the syntax DAG structural constraints for a yet unknown formula of size n. We can reconstruct a syntax DAG from a model v, i.e., a valuation of the propositional variables in Φ_n^{DAG}, as follows. 1) Label Node i with unique label λ such that $v(x_{i,\lambda}) = 1$ (if label is $\mathbf{F}$, $\mathbf{G}$, or $\mathbf{U}$, assign time interval $I = [v(a_i), v(b_i))$ to the operator), 2) set the node n as the root and finally, 3) arrange the nodes of the DAG according to $v(l_{i,k})$ and $v(r_{i,k})$. From this syntax DAG, we can derive an STL formula denoted by φ_v.

To implement the framework which is introduced in Sect. 5 in the proposed algorithms, we define two real-valued variables: $\underline{y}_{i,j}^\zeta$ and $\overline{y}_{i,j}^\zeta$. These two variables are equivalent to the robustness margin at the worst-case and the best-case, respectively.

$$\underline{y}_{i,j}^\zeta = \min_{\zeta \in [\underline{\zeta}, \overline{\zeta}]} r(\zeta, \varphi_i, t_j) \tag{12}$$

$$\overline{y}_{i,j}^\zeta = \max_{\zeta \in [\underline{\zeta}, \overline{\zeta}]} r(\zeta, \varphi_i, t_j) \tag{13}$$

In this section, the time length of an interval trajectory T is represented by $|\zeta|$, and for the better explanation of the algorithm, we denote the index of the time-step as a position in an interval trajectory; hence, in $\underline{y}^{\zeta}_{i,j}$ Eq. (12) and $\overline{y}^{\zeta}_{i,j}$ Eq. (13), $i \in \{0, ..., n\}$ represents a node in the syntax DAG and $j \in \{0, .., |\zeta| - 1\}$ is a position in the finite interval trajectory $[\underline{\zeta}, \overline{\zeta}]$.

Specifically, $\overline{y}^{\zeta}_{i,j}$ is used for implementing the robust semantics of negation of an STL formula Eq. (14).

$$r([\underline{\zeta}, \overline{\zeta}], \neg\varphi, t_j) = \min_{\zeta \in [\underline{\zeta}, \overline{\zeta}]} (-r(\zeta, \varphi, t_j)) = - \max_{\zeta \in [\underline{\zeta}, \overline{\zeta}]} r(\zeta, \varphi, t_j) \qquad (14)$$

To implement the semantics of the temporal operators and Boolean connectives, we apply the constraints shown in formulas Eqs. (15) to (18). These constraints are inspired by bounded model checking [40]. It should be noted that these constraints are defined similarly for both $\underline{y}^{\zeta}_{i,j}$, $\overline{y}^{\zeta}_{i,j}$. Equation (15) implements the semantics of the atomic predicates. Equation (16) implements the semantics of negation. In that formula, if Node i is labeled with $\neg$ and node k is its left child, then $\underline{y}^{\zeta}_{i,j}$ is the negation of $\overline{y}^{\zeta}_{k,j}$ and its value is $-\overline{y}^{\zeta}_{k,j}$. Similarly, Eq. (17) implements the semantics of disjunction. In this case, if Node i is labeled with $\vee$, and node k is its left child and node k' is its right child, then $\underline{y}^{\zeta}_{i,j}$ is equal to the maximum value between $\underline{y}^{\zeta}_{k,j}$ and $\underline{y}^{\zeta}_{k',j}$. Equation (18) implements the semantics of $\mathbf{U}_{[a,b)}$ operator. In formula (18), $a, b \in \{0, 1, \ldots, |\zeta|\}$ denote the starting position and the ending position in which a given STL formula φ holds *True* in interval trajectory $[\underline{\zeta}, \overline{\zeta}]$. Similarly, we can define the semantics of other operations: $\mathbf{F}_{[a,b)}, \mathbf{G}_{[a,b)}, \rightarrow, \wedge, \top$.

$$\bigwedge_{1 \leq i \leq n} \bigwedge_{\pi \in \Pi} x_{i,\pi} \rightarrow \left[\bigwedge_{0 \leq j < |\zeta|} \left\{ \underline{y}^{\zeta}_{i,j} = r([\underline{\zeta}, \overline{\zeta}], \pi, t_j) \right\} \right] \qquad (15)$$

$$\bigwedge_{\substack{1 < i \leq n \\ 1 \leq k < i}} (x_{i,\neg} \wedge l_{i,k}) \rightarrow \bigwedge_{0 \leq j < |\zeta|} \left[\underline{y}^{\zeta}_{i,j} = -\overline{y}^{\zeta}_{k,j} \right] \qquad (16)$$

$$\bigwedge_{\substack{1 < i \leq n \\ 1 \leq k, k' < i}} (x_{i,\vee} \wedge l_{i,k} \wedge r_{i,k'}) \rightarrow \bigwedge_{0 \leq j < |\zeta|} \left[\underline{y}^{\zeta}_{i,j} = \max (\underline{y}^{\zeta}_{k,j}, \underline{y}^{\zeta}_{k',j}) \right] \qquad (17)$$

$$\bigwedge_{\substack{1 < i \leq n \\ 1 \leq k, k' < i}} (x_{i,\mathbf{U}_{[a,b)}} \wedge l_{i,k} \wedge r_{i,k'}) \rightarrow$$

$$\left[\bigwedge_{0 \leq j < |\zeta|} \underline{y}^{\zeta}_{i,j} = \max_{j+a \leq j' < j+b} \left(\min \left(\underline{y}^{\zeta}_{k',j''}, \min_{j+a \leq j'' < j'} \underline{y}^{\zeta}_{k,j''} \right) \right) \right] \qquad (18)$$

We construct the actual objective function $Y_n^{\mathcal{D}_{unc}}$ equivalent to $F(\mathcal{D}_{unc}, \varphi_v)$ in Eq. (19). We use the negated best-case robustness margin for trajectories labeled as -1 to take into account the $\neg$ in Eq. (4).

$$Y_n^{\mathcal{D}_{unc}} := \min_{i=1,..,N_{\mathcal{D}}} \begin{cases} +\underline{y}_{n,0}^{\zeta^i}, & \text{if } l_i = +1. \\ -\overline{y}_{n,0}^{\zeta^i}, & \text{if } l_i = -1. \end{cases} \tag{19}$$

Remark 1. Given $N_{\mathcal{D}}$ interval trajectories of time length $|\zeta|$ and a set of atomic predicates Π, inferring an STL formula of size n is an OptSMT problem of size $|\Phi_n^{DAG}| + |Y_n^{\mathcal{D}_{unc}}| = \mathcal{O}(N_{\mathcal{D}} \cdot |\zeta| \cdot |\Pi| \cdot n + N_{\mathcal{D}} \cdot |\zeta|^3 \cdot n^3)$; solving OptSMT belongs to the complexity class NP.

Algorithm 1: *TLI-UA*

Input: Sample $\mathcal{D}_{unc} = \{([\underline{\zeta}, \overline{\zeta}]^i, l_i)\}_{i=1}^{N_{\mathcal{D}}}$
    Maximum iteration $N \in \mathbb{N}^+$
    Minimum robustness margin $R \in \mathbb{R}$

1 $n \leftarrow 0$
2 **repeat**
3 | $n \leftarrow n + 1$
4 | Construct formula Φ_n^{DAG}
5 | Assign objective function $Y_n^{\mathcal{D}_{unc}}$ to be maximized
6 | Find model v using OptSMT solver
7 | Construct φ_v and evaluate $r \leftarrow F(\mathcal{D}_{unc}, \varphi_v)$
8 **until** $r \geq R$ *or* $n > N$
9 **return** φ_v

Uncertainty-Aware Temporal Logic Inference Algorithm (*TLI-UA*): Algorithm 1 shows the procedure of *TLI-UA*. We increase the size of the searched formula n (starting from 1) until either of the stopping criterion (described later) is triggered. In each iteration, we first construct at line 4 the formula of the structural constraints of the DAG (denoted by Φ_n^{DAG}). On top of it, we assign at line 5 the objective function $Y_n^{\mathcal{D}_{unc}}$, defined in Eq. (19). We then use OptSMT to get a model v of Φ_n^{DAG} that maximizes $Y_n^{\mathcal{D}_{unc}}$ (line 6), reconstruct the inferred formula and evaluate the attained objective function value (line 7).

The first stopping criterion is triggered when the maximum iteration $N \in \mathbb{N}^+$ (given as a parameter) is reached, which produces a formula of maximum size N. The second stopping criterion is triggered when the robustness margin threshold $R \in \mathbb{R}$ (given as a parameter) is reached.

To solve Problem 3, one can set N to the predetermined positive integer described in this problem, and $R = +\infty$ in order to ignore the second stopping criterion. With only the N as the stopping criterion, the loop of the algorithm could be ignored and we could directly start at $n = N$. In that case, Algorithm 1 returns one of the formula of size N that maximizes $F(\mathcal{D}_{unc}, \varphi)$ (such formula is not unique). When a finite R is specified, Algorithm 1 returns an STL formula with size possibly less than N but with $F(\mathcal{D}_{unc}, \varphi_v) \geq R$. This is particularly useful when the expected size of the STL formula is unknown and $N = +\infty$.

Using Algorithm 1 on sufficiently long separable labeled interval trajectories $\mathcal{D}_{unc}$ always terminates when $R \leq 0$. Indeed, a formula that perfectly classifies $\mathcal{D}_{unc}$ exists (Theorem 1) and has a robustness greater than or equal to zero (Theorem 3), and Algorithm 1 is able to infer it when N is large enough. Moreover, Algorithm 1 with $R > 0$ and $N = +\infty$ returns only STL formulas that perfectly classify $\mathcal{D}_{unc}$ (Theorem 3), if such formulas exist.

Decision Trees over STL Formulas: A decision tree over STL formulas is a tree-like structure where all nodes of the tree are labeled by STL formulas.

While the leaf nodes of a decision tree are labeled by either *True* or *False*, the non-leaf nodes are labeled by (non-trivial) STL formulas which represent decisions for predicting the class of a trajectory. Each inner node leads to two subtrees connected by edges, where the left edge is represented with a solid edge and the right edge with a dashed one. Figure 3 depicts a decision tree over STL formulas.

A decision tree τ over STL formula corresponds to an STL formula $\varphi_\tau :=$ $\bigvee_{\rho \in \mathfrak{R}} \bigwedge_{\varphi \in \rho} \varphi'$, where $\mathfrak{R}$ is the set of paths that originate in the root node and end in a leaf node labeled with *True*, $\varphi' = \varphi$ if it appears before a solid edge in $\rho \in \mathfrak{R}$, and $\varphi' = \neg\varphi$ if it appears before a dashed edge in $\rho \in \mathfrak{R}$ (see Fig. 3).

Algorithm 2: *TLI-UA-DT*

Input: Sample $\mathcal{D}_{unc} = \{([\underline{\zeta}, \overline{\zeta}]^i, l_i)\}_{i=1}^{N_{\mathcal{D}}}$
   Maximum iteration $N \in \mathbb{N}^+$
   Minimum robustness margin $R \in \mathbb{R}$

1 $\varphi \leftarrow$ Algorithm 1 $(\mathcal{D}_{unc}, R, N)$
2 Split $\mathcal{D}_{unc}$ into $\mathcal{D}_{unc}^+$, $\mathcal{D}_{unc}^-$ using φ
3 **if** $stop(\mathcal{D}_{unc}^+, \mathcal{D}_{unc}^-)$ **then**
4 | **return** $leaf(\mathcal{D}_{unc})$
5 **else**
6 | $\tau_1 \leftarrow$ Algorithm 2 $(\mathcal{D}_{unc}^+, R, N)$
7 | $\tau_2 \leftarrow$ Algorithm 2 $(\mathcal{D}_{unc}^-, R, N)$
8 | **return** *decision tree with root node φ and subtrees*
   | τ_1, τ_2

Decision Tree Variant of *TLI-UA* (*TLI-UA-DT*):
We propose this second method for uncertainty aware STL inference based on decision trees, outlined by Algorithm 2. First, we infer an STL formula using *TLI-UA* (line 1). Given the inferred formula φ, we need a way to split $\mathcal{D}_{unc}$ into two labeled sets $\mathcal{D}_{unc}^+$ and $\mathcal{D}_{unc}^-$. Note that the set of $[\underline{\zeta}, \overline{\zeta}]^i$ with label $l_i = +1$ that strongly satisfies φ and the set of $[\underline{\zeta}, \overline{\zeta}]^i$ with the label $l_i = -1$ that strongly violates φ do not necessarily partition the $\mathcal{D}_{unc}$. As an alternative, we choose to split $\mathcal{D}_{unc}$ with respect to an averaged robustness margin as in Eqs. (20) and (21), in order to have a partition (line 2):

Fig. 3. A decision tree over STL formulas

$$\mathcal{D}_{unc}^{+} = \left\{ ([\underline{\zeta}, \overline{\zeta}], l) \in \mathcal{D}_{unc} \,\middle|\, \frac{\underline{r}([\underline{\zeta}, \overline{\zeta}], \varphi, t_0) + \overline{r}([\underline{\zeta}, \overline{\zeta}], \varphi, t_0)}{2} > 0 \right\} \qquad (20)$$

$$\mathcal{D}_{unc}^{-} = \mathcal{D}_{unc} \setminus \mathcal{D}_{unc}^{+} \qquad (21)$$

Based on $\mathcal{D}_{unc}^{+}$ and $\mathcal{D}_{unc}^{-}$, Algorithm 2 is applied recursively (lines 6 and 7), if Algorithm 2 does not terminate at lines 3 and 4. We define the stopping criteria, $stop(\mathcal{D}_{unc}^{+}, \mathcal{D}_{unc}^{-})$, for Algorithm 2 as the following: if $\mathcal{D}_{unc}^{+} = \emptyset$ or $\mathcal{D}_{unc}^{-} = \emptyset$, then $stop(\mathcal{D}_{unc}^{+}, \mathcal{D}_{unc}^{-}) = True$; otherwise, $stop(\mathcal{D}_{unc}^{+}, \mathcal{D}_{unc}^{-}) = False$. This stopping criterion guarantees the termination of this method, as the sample size decreases at each split until no split is possible anymore.

7   Experimental Evaluation

In this section, we evaluate the performance of the proposed uncertainty-aware algorithms. In the following, we compare *TLI-UA* with *TLI-RS*, and compare *TLI-UA-DT* with *TLI-RS-DT*. We implement all following four algorithms in a C++ toolbox[1] using Microsoft Z3 [15]:

– *TLI-RS*:
  MaxSMT-based algorithm on finitely many randomly sampled trajectories within the interval trajectories (first baseline);
– *TLI-RS-DT*: Decision tree variant of *TLI-RS* (second baseline);
– *TLI-UA*: Uncertainty-aware OptSMT-based algorithm on interval trajectories (first proposed algorithm);
– *TLI-UA-DT*: Decision tree variant of *TLI-UA* (second proposed algorithm).

Execution Time: For STL inference using *TLI-RS* and *TLI-RS-DT*, we randomly sample a certain number of trajectories from each interval trajectory in the dataset $\mathcal{D}_{unc}$. For STL inference using *TLI-UA* and *TLI-UA-DT*, we directly encode the interval trajectories to the OptSMT solver. First, we generate 10 datasets to evaluate the performance of the proposed uncertainty-aware algorithms. Among these datasets, five datasets are non-separable, and five datasets are separable. In each dataset, both of the sets P_{unc} and N_{unc} contain up to three interval trajectories with the time length up to 10. For comparing the the results obtained from the *TLI-UA* and *TLI-UA-DT* with the baseline algorithms *TLI-RS* and *TLI-RS-DT*, we randomly sample first 50 and then 200 trajectories from each interval trajectory in each dataset. We denote the former sampled datasets by $\mathcal{D}_{50}$ and the latter datasets by $\mathcal{D}_{200}$. We choose 1000 s for the criterion of timeout for each execution of the algorithms (TO). For both *TLI-UA* and *TLI-RS*, we use the same values of parameter N. similarly, we use same values of parameter N for both *TLI-UA* and *TLI-UA-DT*.

The comparison of the execution time of *TLI-RS* and *TLI-UA* for $\mathcal{D}_{50}$ can be seen in Fig. 4a, and the comparison time of *TLI-RS* and *TLI-UA* for $\mathcal{D}_{200}$ can

---

[1] https://github.com/cryhot/uaflie

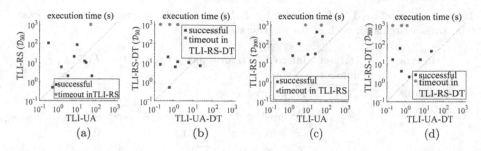

Fig. 4. The comparison of the execution time between *TLI-UA* and *TLI-RS*: a) the execution time of *TLI-UA* is 1/7 of the execution time of *TLI-RS* for $\mathcal{D}_{50}$ on average; b) *TLI-UA-DT* outperforms *TLI-RS-DT*, for $\mathcal{D}_{50}$, by having the execution time of 1/88 of the execution time of *TLI-RS-DT* on average; c) for $\mathcal{D}_{200}$, the execution time of *TLI-UA* is 1/17 of the execution time of *TLI-RS* on average; d) *TLI-UA-DT* outperforms *TLI-RS-DT*, for $\mathcal{D}_{200}$, by having the execution time of 1/95 of the execution time of *TLI-RS-DT* on average.

be seen in Fig. 4c. In the comparison between *TLI-UA* and *TLI-RS*, for $\mathcal{D}_{50}$, the execution time of *TLI-UA* is 1/7 of the execution time of *TLI-RS* on average. In the comparison between *TLI-UA* and *TLI-RS* for $\mathcal{D}_{200}$, the results show that the execution time of *TLI-UA* is 1/17 of the execution time of *TLI-RS* on average.

Figure 4b presents the comparison between the execution time of *TLI-UA-DT* and *TLI-RS-DT* for $\mathcal{D}_{50}$. *TLI-UA-DT* outperforms *TLI-RS-DT* by having the execution time of 1/88 of the execution time of *TLI-RS-DT* on average. Figure 4d shows the similar comparison for $\mathcal{D}_{200}$. Similarly, *TLI-UA-DT* outperforms *TLI-RS-DT* by having the execution time of 1/95 of the execution time of *TLI-RS-DT* on average.

In the next step, we asses the effectiveness of exploiting decision trees in *TLI-UA* and *TLI-RS*. We start with evaluating the effectiveness of using decision tress in the baseline algorithm *TLI-RS*. The comparison of the execution time between *TLI-RS* and *TLI-RS-DT* for $\mathcal{D}_{50}$ can be seen in Fig. 5a. Results show that the execution time of *TLI-RS-DT* is 1/3 of the execution time of *TLI-RS* on average. Figure 5b presents the comparison between the execution time of *TLI-RS* and *TLI-RS-DT* for $\mathcal{D}_{200}$. The results show that the execution time of *TLI-RS-DT* is 1/2 of the the execution time of *TLI-RS* on average. Finally, Fig. 5c shows the comparison between the execution time of *TLI-UA* and *TLI-UA-DT*. *TLI-UA-DT* outperforms *TLI-UA* by inferring STL formulas faster. The execution time of *TLI-UA-DT* is 1/6 of the execution time of *TLI-UA* on average.

Table 1. The inferred STL formulas by *TLI-UA*, and the corresponding worst-case robustness margins for each of the 10 generated datasets.

Data type	Dataset number	Inferred STL formulas φ by *TLI-UA*	$F(\mathcal{D}_{unc}, \varphi)$
Separable datasets	1	$\mathbf{F}_{[6,10)}(x^1 + x^2 < 20)$	0
	2	$\mathbf{F}_{[3,10)}(x^1 - x^2 < 0) \to (x^1 - x^2 < 0)$	0
	3	$(x^1 > 10) \vee (x^2 < -12)$	0
	4	$\mathbf{F}_{[3,4)}(x^1 + x^2 > 15.5)$	2.5
	5	$\mathbf{G}(x^1 > 2.5)$	1.6
Non-separable datasets	6	$(x^2 > -0.8)\mathbf{U}_{[5,10)}(x^2 > -0.8)$	-5.2
	7	$(x^1 < 10) \wedge (x^1 - x^2 > 8.9)$	-10
	8	$\mathbf{G}_{[9,10)}(x^1 - x^2 > -1.5)$	-2
	9	$\mathbf{F}_{[0,2)}(x^1 + x^2 > 8) \to (x^1 + x^2 > 8)$	-4
	10	$\mathbf{F}_{[1,10)}(\neg(x^2 < 4.5))$	-0.5

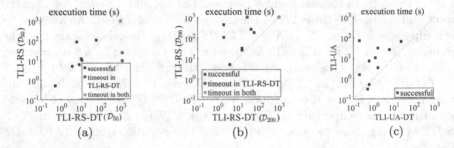

(a)   (b)   (c)

Fig. 5. The effectiveness of adding decision trees to *TLI-RS* and *TLI-UA*: a) the execution time of *TLI-RS-DT*, for $\mathcal{D}_{50}$, is 1/3 of the execution time of *TLI-RS* on average; b) the execution time of *TLI-RS-DT*, for $\mathcal{D}_{200}$, is 1/2 of the execution time of *TLI-RS* on average; c) the execution time of *TLI-UA-DT* is 1/6 of the execution time of *TLI-UA* on average.

Robustness Margin: The inferred STL formulas by *TLI-UA* are listed in Table 1 with the corresponding optimal worst-case robustness margins for 10 datasets. A comparison between the optimal worst-case robustness margins of Table 1 and the obtained optimal worst-case robustness margins for $\mathcal{D}_{50}$ and $\mathcal{D}_{200}$ reveals that using *TLI-UA* improves the worst-case robustness margins by 330% on average for $\mathcal{D}_{200}$ and 98% on average for $\mathcal{D}_{50}$[2].

---

[2] The numerical results of the robustness margins for $\mathcal{D}_{50}$ and $\mathcal{D}_{200}$, and the inferred formulas by *TLI-RS* are not illustrated due to space limitations. The complete numerical results and proofs can be found in [41].

8   Conclusion

In this paper, we proposed two uncertainty-aware STL inference algorithms. Our results showed that uncertainty-aware STL inference expedites the inference process in the presence of uncertainties along with enhancing the worst-case robustness margin. Exploiting uncertainty-aware STL inference to enhance RL is one future research direction (in a similar manner as in [42]). Moreover, we aim to develop the proposed learning algorithms to uncertainty-aware *graph temporal logic* (GTL) inference, where we can infer spatial-temporal properties from data with uncertainties [43].

Acknowledgment. The authors thank Dr. Rebecca Russell and the entire ALPACA team for their collaboration. This material is based upon work supported by the Defense Advanced Research Projects Agency (DARPA) under Contract No. HR001120C0032.

Appendix 1   Supplementary Mathematical Materials

1.1   Proof of Theorem 1

Proof. For two given disjoint intervals, $[\underline{a}, \overline{a}]$ and $[\underline{b}, \overline{b}]$, we know that $\underline{a} \leq \overline{a}$ and $\underline{b} \leq \overline{b}$. If $\overline{a} < \underline{b}$, then we define $[\underline{a}, \overline{a}] < [\underline{b}, \overline{b}]$; or if $\overline{b} < \underline{a}$, then $[\underline{a}, \overline{a}] > [\underline{b}, \overline{b}]$.

For two interval trajectories, $[\underline{\zeta}, \overline{\zeta}]^i$ with label $l_i = +1$ and $[\underline{\zeta}, \overline{\zeta}]^{\tilde{i}}$ with label $l_{\tilde{i}} = -1$, if there exists one time-step t_j and one dimension k such that $[\underline{\zeta}_j^k, \overline{\zeta}_j^k]^i \cap [\underline{\zeta}_j^k, \overline{\zeta}_j^k]^{\tilde{i}} = \emptyset$; then, either $[\underline{\zeta}_j^k, \overline{\zeta}_j^k]^i > [\underline{\zeta}_j^k, \overline{\zeta}_j^k]^{\tilde{i}}$ or $[\underline{\zeta}_j^k, \overline{\zeta}_j^k]^i < [\underline{\zeta}_j^k, \overline{\zeta}_j^k]^{\tilde{i}}$. Without loss of generality, we take $[\underline{\zeta}_j^k, \overline{\zeta}_j^k]^i > [\underline{\zeta}_j^k, \overline{\zeta}_j^k]^{\tilde{i}}$. Moreover, we know that $\overline{\zeta}_j^k \in [\underline{\zeta}_j^k, \overline{\zeta}_j^k]^{\tilde{i}}$ and $\underline{\zeta}_j^k \in [\underline{\zeta}_j^k, \overline{\zeta}_j^k]^i$ are real numbers. If we represent $\overline{\zeta}_j^k \in [\underline{\zeta}_j^k, \overline{\zeta}_j^k]^{\tilde{i}}$ by $\tilde{d}$, and represent $\underline{\zeta}_j^k \in [\underline{\zeta}_j^k, \overline{\zeta}_j^k]^i$ by d, we know for any two real numbers $\{d, \tilde{d} \mid d > \tilde{d}\}$, there is a real value $\delta = \frac{\tilde{d}+d}{2}$ such that $d > \frac{\tilde{d}+d}{2} > \tilde{d}$. Then, we can conclude that $[\underline{\zeta}_j^k, \overline{\zeta}_j^k]^i > \delta$. Therefore, there exists at least one STL formula in the form of $\mathbf{F}_{[t_j, t_{j+1})}(x^k > \delta)$ that perfectly classifies the two interval trajectories. $\square$

1.2   Proof of Theorem 2

Proof. Given a labeled set of interval trajectories $\mathcal{D}_{unc} = \{([\underline{\zeta}, \overline{\zeta}]^i, l_i)\}_{i=1}^{N_D}$, we represent interval trajectories with label $l_i = +1$ by $[\underline{\zeta}, \overline{\zeta}]^i$ and represent interval trajectories with label $l_{i'} = -1$ by $[\underline{\zeta}, \overline{\zeta}]^{i'}$.

By relying on Theorem 1, if all the pairs of interval trajectories $[\underline{\zeta}, \overline{\zeta}]^i$ and $[\underline{\zeta}, \overline{\zeta}]^{i'}$ are separable, then a formula $\varphi_{ii'}$ can be found that is strongly satisfied by interval trajectories $[\underline{\zeta}, \overline{\zeta}]^i$ with the label $l_i = +1$ and is strongly violated by interval trajectories $[\underline{\zeta}, \overline{\zeta}]^{i'}$. This formula can be in the form of $\varphi := \bigvee_{([\underline{\zeta}, \overline{\zeta}]^i, +1) \in \mathcal{D}_{unc}} \bigwedge_{([\underline{\zeta}, \overline{\zeta}]^{i'}, -1) \in \mathcal{D}_{unc}} \varphi_{ii'}$. This formula can strongly classify the two sets of interval trajectories since φ is strongly satisfied by all $[\underline{\zeta}, \overline{\zeta}]^i$ and strongly violated by all $[\underline{\zeta}, \overline{\zeta}]^{i'}$. $\square$

1.3   Proof of Lemma 1

Proof. This statement can be proven by induction over robustness semantics and Definitions 1 and 2. Equations (5) and (6) are true on the formulas of size one (the predicates π) when $t_j \leq T$, i.e., when the trajectory is sufficiently long enough. We now prove that Eqs. (5) and (6) hold on longer STL formulas, i.e., assuming they hold for a formula of size n, that they hold for a formula of size $n + 1$. For example, we present the induction for the "not" operator and the weak view (similar induction can be done for the strong view, and for the other operators): we assume that Eq. (5) holds for formula φ (Eq. (22)), and we deduce that Eq. (6) holds for formula $\neg\varphi$ (Eq. (24)). We use the semantic rules to transform Eq. (22) into Eq. (23), and Eq. (24) is the contrapositive of Eq. (23).

$$r(\zeta, \varphi, t_j) > 0 \implies (\zeta, t_j) \models_S \varphi \implies r(\zeta, \varphi, t_j) \geq 0 \tag{22}$$
$$r(\zeta, \neg\varphi, t_j) < 0 \implies (\zeta, t_j) \not\models_W \neg\varphi \implies r(\zeta, \neg\varphi, t_j) \leq 0 \tag{23}$$
$$r(\zeta, \neg\varphi, t_j) \geq 0 \impliedby (\zeta, t_j) \models_W \neg\varphi \impliedby r(\zeta, \neg\varphi, t_j) > 0 \tag{24}$$

$\square$

1.4   Proof of Theorem 3

Proof. We consider here only the interval trajectories $[\underline{\zeta}, \overline{\zeta}]^i$ such that $l_i = +1$. If $F(\mathcal{D}_{unc}, \varphi) > 0$ holds, then by definition (Eqs. (4) and (3)) we have $\underline{r}([\underline{\zeta}, \overline{\zeta}]^i, \varphi, t_0) > 0$; using Eq. (1), we deduce $\forall \zeta \in [\underline{\zeta}, \overline{\zeta}]^i, r(\zeta, \varphi, t_0) > 0$; using Lemma 1, we finally deduce $\forall \zeta \in [\underline{\zeta}, \overline{\zeta}]^i, (\zeta, t_0) \models_S \varphi$. We can prove the same way that for every $[\underline{\zeta}, \overline{\zeta}]^i$ such that $l_i = -1$, if $F(\mathcal{D}_{unc}, \varphi) > 0$ holds, then $\forall \zeta \in [\underline{\zeta}, \overline{\zeta}]^i, (\zeta, t_0) \models_S \neg\varphi$. This means that if $F(\mathcal{D}_{unc}, \varphi) > 0$ holds, then φ perfectly classifies $\mathcal{D}_{unc}$. We can prove in a similar way that if φ perfectly classifies $\mathcal{D}_{unc}$, then $F(\mathcal{D}_{unc}, \varphi) \geq 0$. $\square$

Appendix 2   Baseline Algorithms

Random Sampling over Interval Trajectories: We present two other algorithms, *TLI-RS* and *TLI-RS-DT*, that we use as baseline algorithms. For both of the baseline algorithms, we first randomly sample finitely many trajectories within each labeled interval trajectory from $\mathcal{D}_{unc}$ and these labeled sampled trajectories $\mathcal{D}$ are input to the baseline algorithms. Algorithm 3 and Algorithm 4 present the detailed procedures for the two baseline algorithms *TLI-RS* and *TLI-RS-DT*, respectively.

Algorithm 3: TLI

Input: Sample $\mathcal{D} = \{(\zeta^i, l_i)\}_{i=1}^{N_{\mathcal{D}}}$
Minimum classification rate $\kappa \in [0,1]$
Maximum iteration $N \in \mathbb{N}^+$

1 $n \leftarrow 0$
2 **repeat**
3 $\quad$ $n \leftarrow n + 1$
4 $\quad$ Construct formula $\Phi_n^{DAG} \wedge \Phi_n^{\mathcal{D}}$
5 $\quad$ Assign weights to soft constraints
6 $\quad$ Find model v using MaxSMT solver (or SMT
$\quad\quad$ solver if $\kappa = 1$)
7 $\quad$ Construct φ_v and evaluate $s \leftarrow \dfrac{\{(\zeta^i, l_i) \in \mathcal{D} \mid \zeta^i \models \varphi_v\}}{|\mathcal{D}|}$
8 **until** $s \geq \kappa$ *or* $n > N$
9 **return** φ_v

Baseline Temporal Logic Inference Algorithm (*TLI-RS*): Algorithm 3 shows the procedure of *TLI-RS* after the random sampling of $\mathcal{D}_{unc}$ into $\mathcal{D}$. This algorithm is inspired by [44] and presents similarities with Algorithm 1 in its structure. We cover the key differences of Algorithm 3 here.

We define propositional formulas Φ_ζ^n for each trajectory ζ that tracks the valuation of the STL formula encoded by Φ_n^{DAG} on ζ. These formulas are built using variables $y_{i,j}^\zeta$, where $i \in \{1, \ldots, n\}$ and $j \in \{1, \ldots, |\zeta|-1\}$, that corresponds to the value of $(\zeta, t_j) \models_S \varphi_i$ (φ_i is the STL formula rooted at Node i).

We now define the constraint that ensure consistency with the sample $\Phi_n^{\mathcal{D}}$:

$$\Phi_n^{\mathcal{D}} = \bigwedge_{(\zeta,l) \in Z} \Phi_\zeta^n \wedge \bigwedge_{(\zeta,+1) \in \mathcal{D}} y_{n,0}^\zeta \wedge \bigwedge_{(\zeta,-1) \in \mathcal{D}} \neg y_{n,0}^\zeta$$

Each of the $y_{n,0}^\zeta$ and $\neg y_{n,0}^\zeta$ are soft constraints (for sake of simplicity, each one is attributed a weight of 1); all the other constraints are hard constraints.

The previously defined soft constraints aim at correctly classifying a maximum number of trajectories in $\mathcal{D}$. We introduce a new stopping criterion that is triggered when the percentage of correctly classified trajectories exceeds a given threshold $\kappa \in [0,1]$. With $\kappa = 1$ and $N = +\infty$, and assuming that $\mathcal{D}$ is separable, Algorithm 3 terminates and return a formula φ that perfectly classifies $\mathcal{D}$. However, due to the nature of random sampling, it is not ensured that φ perfectly classifies $\mathcal{D}_{unc}$.

Algorithm 4: TLI-DT

Input: Sample $\mathcal{D} = \{(\zeta^i, l_i)\}_{i=1}^{N_{\mathcal{D}}}$
   Minimum classification rate $\kappa \in [0, 1]$
   Maximum iteration $N \in \mathbb{N}^+$

1 $\varphi \leftarrow$ Algorithm 3 $(\mathcal{D}, \kappa, N)$
2 Split $\mathcal{D}$ into $\mathcal{D}^+$, $\mathcal{D}^-$ using φ
3 **if** $stop(\mathcal{D}^+, \mathcal{D}^-)$ **then**
4 | **return** $leaf(\mathcal{D})$
5 **else**
6 | $\tau_1 \leftarrow$ Algorithm 4 $(\mathcal{D}^+, \kappa, N)$
7 | $\tau_2 \leftarrow$ Algorithm 4 $(\mathcal{D}^-, \kappa, N)$
8 | **return** *decision tree with root node* φ *and subtrees*
   | τ_1, τ_2

Decision Tree Variant of *TLI-RS* (*TLI-RS-DT*): Algorithm 4 shows the procedure of *TLI-RS-DT* after the random sampling of $\mathcal{D}_{unc}$ into $\mathcal{D}$. This algorithm is inspired by [44] and presents similarities with Algorithm 2 in its structure. Note that we split at line 2 $\mathcal{D}$ into strong satisfied and weakly violated samples as in Eqs. (25) and (26):

$$\mathcal{D}^+ = \{(\zeta, l) \in \mathcal{D} | (\zeta, t_0) \models_S \varphi\} \tag{25}$$

$$\mathcal{D}^- = \{(\zeta, l) \in \mathcal{D} | (\zeta, t_0) \not\models_S \varphi\} \tag{26}$$

Appendix 3   Supplementary Numerical Evaluation Results

3.1   Numerical Results of Sampling-Based Baseline Algorithm *TLI-RS*

In Tables 2 and 3, the inferred formulas by *TLI-RS* with corresponding worst-case robustness margins can be seen for $\mathcal{D}_{50}$ and $\mathcal{D}_{200}$, respectively.

Table 2. The inferred STL formulas by *TLI-RS* for $\mathcal{D}_{50}$, and the corresponding worst-case robustness margins for each of the 10 generated datasets.

Dataset number	Inferred STL formulas φ by *TLI-UA*	$F(\mathcal{D}_{unc}, \varphi)$
1	$(x^1 + x^2 < 2.7)$	−9.3
2	$\mathbf{G}_{[4,5)}(x^1 - x^2 < 0)$ $\rightarrow (x^1 - x^2 < 0)$	0
3	$\mathbf{G}_{[8,9)}(x^1 > 3)$	−0.2
4	$\mathbf{G}_{[0,5)}(x^1 + x^2 > 12.5)$	−25.5
5	$\mathbf{F}_{[1,4)}(x^1 > 4)$	0.1
6	TO	N/A
7	$\neg(x^1 < 1.5)$	−12.5
8	$(x^1 - x^2 > -2.5)\mathbf{U}_{[1,5)}(\neg(x^1 - x^2 > -2.5))$	−5
9	$(x^1 + x^2 > 1.5)\mathbf{U}(\neg(x^1 + x^2 > 1.5))$	−9
10	$\mathbf{F}_{[1,3)}(x^1 < 4)$	−3

We used the same N values for each dataset in the scenarios of Tables 1, 2 and 3 (including *TLI-UA* for interval trajectories, *TLI-RS* for $\mathcal{D}_{50}$, and *TLI-RS* for $\mathcal{D}_{200}$). By comparing the derived worst-case robustness margins for the 10 randomly generated datasets, it can be concluded that *TLI-UA* infer STL formulas with higher worst-case robustness margins. This trend is consistent in both the separable datasets (datasets 1 to 5) and the non-separable datasets (datasets 6 to 10). Finally, a comparison between Tables 1, 2, and 3 reveals that using *TLI-UA* improves the worst-case robustness margins by 330% on average in comparison with the worst-case robustness margins in Table 2 ($\mathcal{D}_{50}$), and by 98% on average in comparison with the worst-case robustness margins in Table 3 ($\mathcal{D}_{200}$).

Table 3. The inferred STL formulas by *TLI-RS* for $\mathcal{D}_{200}$, and the corresponding worst-case robustness margins for each of the 10 generated datasets.

Dataset number	Inferred STL formulas φ by *TLI-UA*	$F(\mathcal{D}_{unc}, \varphi)$
1	$(x^1 + x^2 < 2.5)$	−9.5
2	$\mathbf{F}_{[3,10)}(x^1 - x^2 < 0)$ $\rightarrow (x^1 - x^2 < 0)$	0
3	$(\neg(x^2 < 3))\mathbf{U}_{[4,10)}(x^2 > 3)$	−1
4	$\mathbf{F}(x^1 + x^2 > 20)$	−2
5	$(x^1 > 4)\mathbf{U}_{[1,10)}(x^1 > 4)$	0
6	TO	N/A
7	$\neg(x^1 < 1.6)$	−12.6
8	$\mathbf{G}_{[4,7)}(x^1 - x^2 > -3.3)$	−3.3
9	$(x^1 + x^2 > 1.6)\mathbf{U}(\neg(x^1 + x^2 > 1.6))$	−8.8
10	TO	N/A

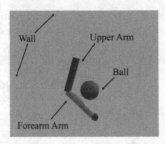

Fig. 6. The illustration of the Pusher-robot in the simulation environment with the two components denoted as the forearm and the upper arm, where the goal of the Pusher-robot is to interact with a ball and a wall with four different strategies.

3.2 Strategy Inference of Pusher-Robot Scenario

In this case study, we infer uncertainty-aware STL formulas to describe the behavior of the interval trajectories of a Pusher-robot with the goal of interacting with a ball and a wall. The interval trajectories are generated by policies learned from reinforcement learning (RL) using *model-based reinforcement learning* (MBRL) algorithm [45]. The intervals represent the uncertainties associated with the policies and the environment. This Pusher-robot consists of two components denoted as the "forearm" and the "upper arm" (Figure 6). In this paper, we investigate four different strategies of this Pusher-robot: 1) Tap the ball toward the wall. 2) Tap the ball, rotate around, and stop the ball. 3) Tap the ball, stop the ball with the upper arm. 4) Bounce the ball off the wall. We infer an STL formula for each strategy versus the other three strategies based on the change of the speed (m/s) of the ball during performing the current strategy which is denoted by x^1. For the dataset, P_{unc} includes the interval trajectories of the current strategy, and N_{unc} includes the interval trajectories of the other three strategies. The inferred STL formulas are presented in Table 4. If $x^1 < 0$, the contact (the contact between the robot and the wall or contact between the ball and the ball) absorbs the momentum of the ball, and if $x^1 > 0$, then the contact adds momentum to the ball.

Table 4. The inferred STL formulas by *TLI-UA*, in the Pusher-robot scenario, for strategies 1 to 4, and the corresponding worst-case robustness margins for the change in the speed of the ball when performing the current strategy.

Strategy	Inferred STL formula φ by *TLI-UA*	$F(\mathcal{D}_{unc}, \varphi)$
Strategy 1	$(x^1 > -0.232)$	-0.848
	$\mathbf{U}_{[2,4)}(x^1 > -0.232)$	
Strategy 2	$(x^1 > 0.21)$	-0.4
	$\mathbf{U}_{[0,3)}(\mathbf{G}_{[1,3)}(x^1 > 0.21))$	
Strategy 3	$\mathbf{G}_{[1,4)}(x^1 > 0.266)$	-0.35
Strategy 4	$(x^1 > 0.231)$	-0.385
	$\mathbf{U}_{[4,5)}(x^1 > 0.231)$	

The interpretations of the inferred STL formulas for the strategies, respectively from 1 to 4, are: 1) The change in the speed of the ball is greater than −0.232 m/s, until some time from time-step 2 to time-step 4, the change in the speed of the ball is greater than −0.232 m/s (transition from losing momentum to gaining momentum). 2) The change in the speed of the ball is greater than 0.21 m/s , until some time from time-step 0 to time-step 3, the change of the speed of the ball is always greater than 0.21 m/s (gaining momentum from time-step 0 to time-step 3). 3) Some time from time-step 1 to time-step 4, the change of the speed of the ball is always greater than 0.266 m/s and gaining momentum. 4) The change in the speed of the ball is greater than 0.231 m/s, until some time from time-step 4 to time-step 5, the change in the speed of the ball is greater than 0.231 m/s (gaining momentum).

References

1. Essien, A., Petrounias, I., Sampaio, P., Sampaio, S.: Improving urban traffic speed prediction using data source fusion and deep learning. In: 2019 IEEE International Conference on Big Data and Smart Computing, BigComp 2019 - Proceedings (March 2019)
2. Essien, A., Petrounias, I., Sampaio, P., Sandra, S.: A deep-learning model for urban traffic flow prediction with traffic events mined from twitter. World Wide Web (2020)
3. Boukerche, A., Wang, J.: Machine learning-based traffic prediction models for intelligent transportation systems. Comput. Netw. **181**(August), 107530 (2020). https://doi.org/10.1016/j.comnet.2020.107530
4. Fujiyoshi, H., Hirakawa, T., Yamashita, T.: Deep learning-based image recognition for autonomous driving. IATSS Res. **43**(4), 244–252 (2019). http://www.sciencedirect.com/science/article/pii/S0386111219301566
5. Sarker, I.H.: Machine learning: algorithms, real-world applications and research directions. SN Comput. Sci. **2**(3) (2021). https://doi.org/10.1007/s42979-021-00592-x
6. Anzai, Y.: Pattern Recognition and Machine Learning, no. 1992. Elsevier, Amsterdam (2012)
7. Sintov, A., Kimmel, A., Bekris, K.E., Boularias, A.: Motion planning with competency-aware transition models for underactuated adaptive hands. In: Proceedings–IEEE International Conference on Robotics and Automation, pp. 7761–7767 (2020)
8. Shvo, M., Li, A.C., Icarte, R.T., McIlraith, S.A.: Interpretable sequence classification via discrete optimization. arXiv, vol. 1 (2020)
9. Basudhar, A., Missoum, S., Sanchez, A.H.: Limit state function identification using support vector machines for discontinuous responses and disjoint failure domains. Probab. Eng. Mech. **23**(1), 1–11 (2008)
10. Raman, V., Donzé, A., Sadigh, D., Murray, R.M., Seshia, S.A.: Reactive synthesis from signal temporal logic specifications. In: Proceedings of the 18th International Conference on Hybrid Systems: Computation and Control, HSCC 2015, pp. 239–248 (2015)
11. Bae, K., Lee, J.: Bounded model checking of signal temporal logic properties using syntactic separation. Proc. ACM Program. Lang. **3**, 1–30 (2019)

12. Asarin, E., Donzé, A., Maler, O., Nickovic, D.: Parametric identification of temporal properties. In: Khurshid, S., Sen, K. (eds.) RV 2011. LNCS, vol. 7186, pp. 147–160. Springer, Heidelberg (2012). https://doi.org/10.1007/978-3-642-29860-8_12

13. Maler, O., Nickovic, D.: Monitoring temporal properties of continuous signals. In: Lakhnech, Y., Yovine, S. (eds.) FORMATS/FTRTFT -2004. LNCS, vol. 3253, pp. 152–166. Springer, Heidelberg (2004). https://doi.org/10.1007/978-3-540-30206-3_12

14. Budde, C.E., D'Argenio, P.R., Hartmanns, A., Sedwards, S.: Qualitative and Quantitative Trace Analysis with Extended Signal Temporal Logic, vol. 1, pp. 340–358 (2018). http://dx.doi.org/10.1007/978-3-319-89963-3_20

15. De Moura, L., Bjørner, N.: Z3: an efficient SMT solver. In: Ramakrishnan, C.R., Rehof, J. (eds.) TACAS 2008. LNCS, vol. 4963, pp. 337–340. Springer, Heidelberg (2008). https://doi.org/10.1007/978-3-540-78800-3_24

16. De Moura, L., Bjørner, N.: Satisfiability modulo theories: an appetizer. In: Oliveira, M.V.M., Woodcock, J. (eds.) SBMF 2009. LNCS, vol. 5902, pp. 23–36. Springer, Heidelberg (2009). https://doi.org/10.1007/978-3-642-10452-7_3

17. Clarke, E.M., Henzinger, T.A., Veith, H., Bloem, R.: Handbook of model checking (2018)

18. Neider, D., Gavran, I.: Learning linear temporal properties. In: Proceedings of the 18th Conference on Formal Methods in Computer-Aided Design, FMCAD 2018, pp. 148–157 (2019)

19. Bombara, G., Vasile, C.I., Penedo, F., Yasuoka, H., Belta, C.: A decision tree approach to data classification using signal temporal logic. In: HSCC 2016–Proceedings of the 19th International Conference on Hybrid Systems: Computation and Control, pp. 1–10 (2016)

20. Xu, Z., Birtwistle, M., Belta, C., Julius, A.: A temporal logic inference approach for model discrimination. IEEE Life Sci. Lett. **2**(3), 19–22 (2016)

21. Xu, Z., Belta, C., Julius, A.: Temporal logic inference with prior information: an application to robot arm movements. IFAC-PapersOnLine **48**(27), 141–146 (2015). http://dx.doi.org/10.1016/j.ifacol.2015.11.166

22. Moosavi, A., Rao, V., Sandu, A.: Machine learning based algorithms for uncertainty quantification in numerical weather prediction models. J. Comput. Sci. **50**(September 2020), 101295 (2021). https://doi.org/10.1016/j.jocs.2020.101295

23. Malinin, A., Gales, M.J.F.: Uncertainty estimation in deep learning with application to spoken language assessment, no. August (2019). https://www.repository.cam.ac.uk/handle/1810/298857

24. Hubschneider, C., Hutmacher, R., Zollner, J.M.: Calibrating uncertainty models for steering angle estimation. 2019 IEEE Intelligent Transportation Systems Conference, ITSC 2019, pp. 1511–1518 (2019)

25. Abdar, M., et al.: A review of uncertainty quantification in deep learning: Techniques, applications and challenges, arXiv (2020)

26. Jin, X., Donzé, A., Deshmukh, J.V., Seshia, S.A.: Mining requirements from closed-loop control models. IEEE Trans. Comput. Aided Des. Integr. Circuits Syst. **34**(11), 1704–1717 (2015)

27. Jha, S., Tiwari, A., Seshia, S.A., Sahai, T., Shankar, N.: TeLEx: passive STL learning using only positive examples. In: Lahiri, S., Reger, G. (eds.) RV 2017. LNCS, vol. 10548, pp. 208–224. Springer, Cham (2017). https://doi.org/10.1007/978-3-319-67531-2_13

28. Vazquez-Chanlatte, M., Jha, S., Tiwari, A., Ho, M.K., Seshia, S.A.: Learning task specifications from demonstrations, arXiv, no. NeurIPS, pp. 1–11 (2017)

29. Kong, Z., Jones, A., Medina Ayala, A., Aydin Gol, E., Belta, C.: Temporal logic inference for classification and prediction from data. In: HSCC 2014 - Proceedings of the 17th International Conference on Hybrid Systems: Computation and Control (Part of CPS Week), no. August, pp. 273–282 (2014)
30. Bombara, G., Belta, C.: Online learning of temporal logic formulae for signal classification. In: 2018 European Control Conference, ECC 2018, pp. 2057–2062 (2018)
31. Nguyen, L.V., Deshmukh, J.V., Kapinski, J., Butts, K., Jin, X., Johnson, T.T.: Abnormal data classification using time-frequency temporal logic. In: HSCC 2017 - Proceedings of the 20th International Conference on Hybrid Systems: Computation and Control (part of CPS Week), pp. 237–242 (2017)
32. Akazaki, T., Hasuo, I.: Time robustness in MTL and expressivity in hybrid system falsification. In: Kroening, D., Păsăreanu, C.S. (eds.) CAV 2015. LNCS, vol. 9207, pp. 356–374. Springer, Cham (2015). https://doi.org/10.1007/978-3-319-21668-3_21
33. Xu, Z., Duan, X.: Robust Pandemic Control Synthesis with Formal Specifications: A Case Study on COVID-19 Pandemic (2021). http://arxiv.org/abs/2103.14262
34. Xu, Z., Saha, S., Hu, B., Mishra, S., Julius, A.A.: Advisory temporal logic inference and controller design for semiautonomous robots. IEEE Trans. Autom. Sci. Eng. 16(1), 459–477 (2019)
35. Schneider, K.: Temporal logics. Verif. React. Syst. 8(October), 279–403 (2004)
36. Fainekos, G.E., Pappas, G.J.: Robustness of temporal logic specifications for continuous-time signals. Theor. Comput. Sci. 410(42), 4262–4291 (2009). http://dx.doi.org/10.1016/j.tcs.2009.06.021
37. Jiang, P., Missoum, S., Chen, Z.: Optimal SVM parameter selection for non-separable and unbalanced datasets. Struct. Multidiscip. Optim. 50(4), 523–535 (2014)
38. Sebastiani, R., Trentin, P.: On optimization modulo theories, MaxSMT and sorting networks, CoRR, vol. abs/1702.02385 (2017). http://arxiv.org/abs/1702.02385
39. Bjørner, N., Phan, A.-D., Fleckenstein, L.: νz - an optimizing SMT solver. In: Baier, C., Tinelli, C. (eds.) TACAS 2015. LNCS, vol. 9035, pp. 194–199. Springer, Heidelberg (2015). https://doi.org/10.1007/978-3-662-46681-0_14
40. Biere, A., Cimatti, A., Clarke, E.M., Strichman, O., Zhu, Y.: Bounded model checking. Adv. Comput. 58(C), 117–148 (2003)
41. Baharisangari, N., Gaglione, J.R., Neider, D., Topcu, U., Xu, Z.: Uncertainty-aware signal temporal logic inference (2021)
42. Xu, Z., et al.: Joint inference of reward machines and policies for reinforcement learning. In: Proceedings of the 30th International Conference on Automated Planning and Scheduling (ICAPS). AAAI Press, 2020, pp. 590–598 (2020)
43. Xu, Z., Nettekoven, A.J., Julius, A.A., Topcu, U.: Graph temporal logic inference for classification and identification. In: Proceedings of the IEEE Conference on Decision and Control, vol. 2019-December, pp. 4761–4768 (2019)
44. Gaglione, J.-R., Neider, D., Roy, R., Topcu, U., Xu, Z.: Learning linear temporal properties from noisy data: a MaxSAT-based approach. In: Hou, Z., Ganesh, V. (eds.) ATVA 2021. LNCS, vol. 12971, pp. 74–90. Springer, Cham (2021). https://doi.org/10.1007/978-3-030-88885-5_6
45. Nagabandi, A., Konolige, K., Levine, S., Kumar, V.: Deep dynamics models for learning dexterous manipulation, pp. 1–12 (2019)

Designing and Proving Properties
of the Abaco Autoscaler Using TLA+

Smruti Padhy$^{(\boxtimes)}$ and Joe Stubbs

Texas Advanced Computing Center, Austin, TX, USA
{spadhy,jstubbs}@tacc.utexas.edu

Abstract. The Abaco (Actor Based Containers) platform is an open-source software system funded by the National Science Foundation and hosted at the Texas Advanced Computing Center, providing national-scale functions-as-a-service to the research computing community. Abaco utilizes the Actor Model of concurrent computation, where computational primitives, referred to as actors, execute in response to messages sent to the actor's inbox. In this paper, we use formal methods to analyze Abaco and create an improved design which corrects a race condition in one of its critical subsystems. More precisely, we present a specification of an updated version of the autoscaler subsystem of Abaco, responsible for automatically scaling the number of worker processes associated with an actor based on the actor's inbox size, using TLA+, a formal specification language for modeling concurrent systems. We analyze the new design using both the TLC model checker and the TLAPS proof system. We include results of our use of TLC for manually checking safety and liveness properties for some small state spaces, and we provide proofs in TLAPS of all safety properties. To the best of our knowledge, our work is the first analysis of a large, real-world production software system with open-source code, openly available TLA+ specification and complete TLAPS proofs of all key safety properties.

Keywords: TLA+ · TLAPS · TLC · Functions-as-a-Service · Abaco · Autoscaler · Cloud computing · Distributed systems

1 Introduction

The Abaco (Actor Based Containers) platform [4,15,16] is an NSF-funded project providing functions-as-a-service to the research computing community. Hosted at the Texas Advanced Computing Center at the University of Texas at Austin, Abaco enables research projects to execute workloads on demand without having to manage any servers. The Abaco system is used in a critical way

This material is based upon work supported by the National Science Foundation Office of Advanced CyberInfrastructure, Collaborative Proposal: Frameworks: Project Tapis: Next Generation Software for Distributed Research (Award #1931439), and SI2-SSE: Abaco - Flexible, Scalable, and Usable Functions-As-A-Service via the Actor Model (Award #1740288).

R. Bloem et al. (Eds.): NSV 2021/VSTTE 2021, LNCS 13124, pp. 86–103, 2022.
https://doi.org/10.1007/978-3-030-95561-8_6

by several projects including major efforts funded by DARPA, NASA, NIH and NSF. To date, more than 50,000 functions have been registered with Abaco and over one million executions performed.

Abaco is designed around the Actor Model of concurrent computation where functions are referred to as *actors* which execute in response to *messages*. Internally, Abaco queues each message it receives in a queue dedicated to the actor, and a separate subsystem, referred to as the *autoscaler*, asynchronously starts and stops processes, referred to as *workers*, that supervise actor executions for messages in the order they were received. Additionally, Abaco must handle concurrent updates to actor definitions. Abaco's API contract states that, at the time an actor is updated, any currently running executions will finish using the version of the actor they were started with, but all subsequent executions will be started with the new version of the actor. We refer to this feature as "zero downtime updates" because updating the actor definition does not incur an interruption in message processing.

The autoscaler must ensure that actor executions are processed with low latency while simultaneously making efficient use of the underlying computing resources. Key properties of the autoscaler include ensuring that:

1. After an initialization step, each actor with pending messages has a minimum number of workers.
2. The total number of Abaco workers does not exceed the maximum number of allowable workers configured for the system.
3. Whenever a worker dequeues a message as part of starting an actor execution, the worker uses the current version of the actor.

Note that, in particular, it is not acceptable for Abaco to use the version of the actor defined when Abaco received a message to process the message. If an actor's code contains a defect, and an actor has many pending messages, users want to update the actor definition and use the new version to process as many pending messages as possible.

A previous version of Abaco contained a race condition which caused property 3 to be violated under certain conditions. To better understand this issue and develop an improved design to correct it, we analyzed the Abaco autoscaler subsystem by defining a specification for it in the TLA+ language. We present this specification as well as safety and liveness properties of the Abaco autoscaler, including properties that ensure it is well behaved with respect to the three key properties listed above. We use TLC, the TLA+ model checker, to explore the entire state space and check that the specification adheres to the safety and liveness properties in some small cases. We then use TLAPS, the TLA+ proof system, to prove that the safety properties hold for the specification in all cases.

This work is related to a number of other works presenting specifications for cloud-based, distributed systems. For example, in [19], a basic specification is given for implementing zero downtime updates across servers in a load balancer while [12] describes how Amazon Web Services has used TLA+ on 10 large, complex projects; in niether case are complete source code, TLA+ specifications and TLAPS proofs all available. Also, the challenge of autoscaling with zero downtime updates comes up in numerous settings in industry, such as with autoscaling EC2 instances with "Instance Refresh", as described in [14].

To the best of our knowledge, our work provides the first analysis in TLA+ of a large, real-world production software system with open-source code, an openly available TLA+ specification, and complete TLAPS proofs of all key safety properties. This paper can serve as a blueprint for modeling similar cloud-based distributed software systems, reducing the barrier to adopting these formal methods tools by a large and growing software developer community.

In summary, the main contributions of this paper are as follows:

- A TLA+ specification of the Abaco autoscaler, including key safety and liveness properties.
- Model checking of the specification using TLC with numerical data showing the state space explosion and corresponding time to validation.
- Proofs of the safety properties using TLAPS and associated metrics.

The rest of the paper is organized as follows: in Sect. 2 we provide the background material needed to read the rest of the paper; in Sect. 3 we give an overview of the TLA+ specification; Sect. 4 contains the main results, including the results of model checking with TLC and our proofs utilizing TALPS; in Sect. 5 we discuss techniques and benefits to using TLA+; in Sect. 6 we present related work and we conclude in Sect. 7.

2   Background

In this section we provide background on concepts that will be used throughout the rest of the paper.

2.1   Functions-as-a-Service

Functions-as-a-service (Faas) platforms provide application developers with programming interfaces to deploy small, standalone units of software, referred to as *functions*, on top of cloud computing resources. These platforms are sometimes called *serverless* because the application developer does not need to be concerned with deployment and maintenance of the functions – these concerns are abstracted away by the Faas APIs. For example, the Faas platform will typically manage starting and stopping functions in response to events or other actions. In particular, many Faas provide an autoscaling capability (e.g. [5]) to automatically start and stop instances of functions based on different rules. With autoscaling, the high-level objective is to make efficient use of the underlying cloud resources while still providing good overall application performance.

2.2   The Abaco API

The Abaco project provides functions-as-a-service through a novel combination of Linux container technology and the Actor Model for concurrent computation.

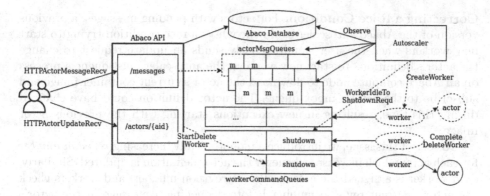

Fig. 1. Abaco architecture

In the Actor Model, fundamental computational primitives, called *actors*, are assigned an *inbox* where they can receive messages. In response to a message, an actor can perform local computation, create additional actors, and send messages to existing actors. In Abaco, actors are defined with a reference to a Docker image available on the public Docker Hub, and thus, actors in Abaco can be thought of as functions packaged in Docker container images. Abaco exposes its functionality as a set HTTP APIs utilizing a RESTful architecture, with endpoints available for all possible actions that can be taken, including creating, updating and deleting actors, and sending an actor a message. When an actor is registered with Abaco, the system generates a unique URL for the actor's inbox, and a message can be sent to the actor by making an HTTP POST request to the URL.

When Abaco receives a message for an actor, it stores it in an internal queue assigned to the actor. Asynchronously, Abaco starts and stops additional processes, referred to as *workers*, which are responsible for facilitating actor executions. After downloading the current Docker image associated with the actor, each worker repeats the following steps:

1. Retrieve a message from the actor's message queue.
2. Start a container from the Docker image and inject the message (as an environment variable in the case of text, and over a unix socket in the case of binary).
3. Monitor the container execution to completion while streaming container logs and resource utilization data to Abaco's internal database.
4. Finalize the execution details and clean up the actor container.

The Abaco autoscaler subsystem starts and stops workers associated with different actors based on a simple rule: if the actor has pending messages in its queue, the autoscaler will start an additional worker for the actor so long as the actor does not already have the maximum number of workers allowed. Similarly, if the actor has zero pending messages, the autoscaler will shut down its workers. Figure 1 presents a high-level overview of the autoscaler architecture.

Correcting a Race Condition: For actors with pending messages, a previous version of the Abaco autoscaler could encounter a race condition trying to start new workers when the user simultaneously sends an update request to change the actor's definition. To start new workers, the autoscaler must queue a process on an Abaco compute node to download the actor's current container image and subscribe to the actor's inbox queue. The actor definition could have changed during this time, resulting in new executions starting with the previous actor image.

To correct this issue, we introduce a monotonically increasing *revision number* for each actor which increases whenever the actor definition is updated. Similarly, each worker is assigned the actor's current revision number, and workers check the actor's current revision number before dequeuing a message; if the actor's revision number is greater than the worker's revision number, the message is requeued. Analysis with TLA+ led us to this improved design.

2.3   TLA+

TLA+ [8] is a formal language based on set theory and the temporal logic of actions (TLA) for specifying software systems. In TLA+, a specification for a system is defined in terms of variables, their initial values, and the allowable set of transitions (actions) that can take place during the lifetime of the system. Variables are assigned values in a *state*, and transitions describe how the values of variables change from one state to the next. A *behavior* is defined to be a single sequence of states that can be reached via the specification, and the *state-space* of a specification is the set of all possible behaviors.

2.4   TLC and TLAPS

TLC [8] is the state space model checker for TLA+. TLC computes the behaviors associated with a *model*, a TLA+ specification optionally supplemented with additional definitions to provide values for constants, configurations for the checker, and so on. While computing the behaviors, a TLC model can be configured to check *safety properties*, or expressions that should be true at every state in all behaviours, as well as *liveness properties*, or expressions that should eventually by true in all behaviors (i.e., true at some state and remain true for all subsequent states in the behaviour). TLC reports failures as counterexamples with a complete trace of all states in the behavior leading to the failure.

TLAPS [11] is the proof system for TLA+ which can be used to write and validate proofs concerning statements written in TLA+. In TLAPS, authors compose proofs as a series of steps, and TLAPS translates each step into a set of formal proof obligations. It then leverages one or more backend provers to verify each proof obligation. If all obligations for a step can be verified, the step is proved true; otherwise, the author must try to decompose the step further. TLAPS currently supports a number of backend provers, including SMT, Zenon and Isabelle.

Our interest in TLAPS is in using it to prove safety properties for all behaviors of a given specification. Note that TLC and TLAPS are designed to be used within the TLA+ Tooblbox IDE [6].

3 Overview of Abaco Specification

In this section we provide an overview of our Abaco specification in TLA+.

3.1 Constants

Our Abaco specification includes a set of five constants which serve two purposes. First and foremost, constants allow us to control the size of the state-space when using the TLC model checker. For example, the *MaxHTTPRequests* constant controls the total number of HTTP requests that can be sent through the specification. Of course, in the real system there is no such upper bound, but limiting the total number of requests is critical for controlling the size of the state-space (see Sect. 4.4).

In addition to controlling the state-space, constants represent configurable aspects of the Abaco platform itself. For example, the constant *MinimumWorkers − AlwaysUpPerActor* represents a configuration in the Abaco config file that puts a lower bound on the number of workers each actor should have at any given time.

3.2 Variables

For the most part, variables in the specification represent runtime state stored in the Abaco persistence layers, including its internal database and message broker (queues). For example, *actorStatus*, *workerStatus*, and *actorWorkers* represent state about the existing actors and workers stored in the Abaco database, while *actorMsgQueues*, *commandQueues* and *workerCommandQueues* represent queue data structures stored in the internal Abaco message broker.

The *clock* variable is an exception, as it represents a global clock used in all actions throughout the specification. A key point is that the *clock* variable is used for verification purposes only, when establishing the safety property *RevisionNumberInv* ensuring that each execution is started with the current version of the actor (see Subsect. 4.1).

3.3 Assumptions

The Abaco specification includes a *SpecAssumptions* which makes assertions regarding the constants; for example, that various constants are non-zero, non-negative natural numbers, that *MinimumWorkersAlwaysUpPerActor <= MaxWorkers*, etc. We require these assumptions because TLA+ is not a typed language and because specific values for the constants are not provided in the specification itself (different values are provided in individual models as part of model checking). In addition to helping "document" the nature of these constants in the context of the Abaco system, these assumptions are required for the proofs in TLAPS.

3.4 Entry Point Actions

Broadly, we categorize the actions defined in the Abaco specification as either "entry point" actions or "auxiliary" actions. By "entry point" actions, we mean actions that represent the initial agents of change in the system. For example, there are a set of actions corresponding to receiving each possible HTTP request, such as *HTTPActorMessageRecv* for receiving an HTTP POST request to an actor's inbox and *HTTPActorUpdateRecv* for receiving an HTTP PUT request to update the definition of an actor. Additional entry point actions include actions initiated by the autoscaler such as *CreateWorker* for creating a new worker and *StartDeleteWorker* for deleting an existing worker.

3.5 Auxiliary Actions

Auxiliary actions represent asynchronous processing that is typically triggered by some entry point action. For example, when the autoscaler determines a worker should be shutdown, it first sends a message to the worker. The *StartDeleteWorker* entry point action represents this first step. Then, eventually the worker receives this message and shuts down after completing the current execution. The auxiliary action *CompleteDeleteWorker* represents the worker processing this message and shutting itself down. Additional examples of auxiliary actions include actions representing subsequent states a worker moves through while supervising an execution, such as *WorkerIdleToBusy* and *WorkerBusyToIdle*.

4   Verification of Abaco Specification

We first define safety and liveness properties for the Abaco autoscaler subsystem. These properties ensure the correct behavior of the specification. We use TLC to verify these properties. However, this was only possible for a small state-space due to the inherent problem of state-space explosion in model checking. We then proved the safety properties using TLAPS.

4.1 Safety Properties

Type Invariants. *TypeInvariant* asserts the specification state variables' types. These assertions ensure all variables maintain proper types and values in every state of a behavior.

$TypeInvariant \triangleq$
$\quad \land actorStatus \in [Actors \rightarrow ActorState]$
$\quad \land Workers \in \{1 .. MaxWorkers\}$
$\quad \land workerStatus \in [Workers \rightarrow [status : workerState, actor : AllActors]]$
$\quad \land actorMsgQueues \in [Actors \rightarrow Seq(ActorMessage)]$
$\quad \land ...$
$\quad \land actorWorkers \in [Actors \rightarrow \text{SUBSET } Workers]$
$\quad \land idleWorkers \in \text{SUBSET } Workers$
$\quad \land \forall s1 \in idleWorkers : workerStatus[s1].status = \text{"IDLE"}$
$\quad \land busyWorkers \in \text{SUBSET } Workers$
$\quad \land \forall s2 \in busyWorkers : workerStatus[s2].status = \text{"BUSY"}$
$\quad \land idleWorkers \cap busyWorkers = \{\}$
$\quad \land actorRev \in [Actors \rightarrow [rnum : Nat, ts : Nat]]$
$\quad \land workerRev \in [Workers \rightarrow [rnum : Nat, ts : Nat]]$
$\quad \land clock \in Nat$

Note $actorRev$ is a function that maps $Actors$ to the set of records $[rnum : Nat, ts : Nat]$, where $rnum$ denotes the actor's current image revision number and ts denotes the timestamp at which the actor's image was updated. Similarly, $workerRev$ is a function that maps $Workers$ to the set of records $[rnum : Nat, ts : Nat]$, where $rnum$ denotes the worker's current image revision number and ts denotes the timestamp at which the worker updated that image. The variables $actorStatus$, $actorMsqQueues$, $commandQueues$, $workerStatus$, $workerCommandQueues$ represent the state/status of the actor, worker, and queues in the specification. The variables $idleWorkers$ and $busyWorkers$ represent the set of idle and busy workers, while $actorWorkers$ is the set of workers assigned to an actor. We have omitted a few trivial conjunctions here. The complete $TypeInvariant$ can be found in our specification available online [13].

Invariant About the Minimum Number of Workers per Actor. The $MinimalWorkerProperty$ asserts that each actor in $READY$ state has a minimum number of workers assigned to it, as stated in key property 1 in Sect. 1. This requirement is made explicit in the last conjunction. The first conjunctions also make basic assertions on the cardinality of the sets involved and the key property 2 as stated in Sect. 1. The complete $MinimalWorkersProperty$ can be found in our specification available online [13].

$MinimalWorkerProperty \triangleq$
$\quad \land Cardinality(idleWorkers) \in 0 .. MaxWorkers$
$\quad \land Cardinality(busyWorkers) \in 0 .. MaxWorkers$
$\quad \land IsFiniteSet(idleWorkers)$
$\quad \land IsFiniteSet(busyWorkers)$
$\quad \land Cardinality(idleWorkers) + Cardinality(busyWorkers) \leq MaxWorkers$
$\quad \land ...$
$\quad \land \forall a \in Actors : IsFiniteSet(actorWorkers[a])$
$\quad \land \forall a \in Actors : actorStatus[a] = \text{"READY"}$
$\qquad \Rightarrow (Cardinality(actorWorkers[a]) \geq MinimumWorkersAlwaysUpPerActor)$

Clock Invariant. We use a clock abstraction in our specification to keep track of the timestamp when the image associated with an actor gets updated and the timestamp when a worker is created with the actor's Docker image. The *clock* variable gets incremented in every action of the specification. *ClockInv* simply asserts that all saved timestamps should not exceed the current *clock* value.

$$ClockInv \triangleq \; \land \, \forall \, a \in Actors : actorRev[a].ts \leq clock$$
$$\land \, \forall \, w \in Workers : workerRev[w].ts \leq clock$$

Invariant About the Revision Number of Actor's Image. The key property 3 in Sect. 1 states that each execution is started with the current version of the actor's Docker's image. The *RevisionNumberInv* property asserts that for all workers for an actor, if the revision number of the Docker image used by a worker is less than the revision number of the Docker image registered for the corresponding actor, then the timestamp associated with the actor's revision number is greater than the timestamp associated with the worker's revision number; i.e., the worker started the execution before the update to the actor was made. Later in the Sect. 4.5, we proved that *RevisionNumberInv* is an invariant of the *Spec*.

$$RevisionNumberInv \triangleq \forall \, w \in Workers : \; workerStatus[w].actor \neq \text{``-''} \Rightarrow$$
$$(workerRev[w].rnum < actorRev[workerStatus[w].actor].rnum$$
$$\Rightarrow actorRev[workerStatus[w].actor].ts \geq workerRev[w].ts)$$

A

Time Stamp	t0	t1	t2	t3	t4	t5	t6	t7	t8
Action	Init	CW	WITB	HAUR	WBTI	SDW	CDW	CW	PUA
Actor Rev	(r1,t0)	(r1,t0)	(r1,t0)	(r2,t3)	(r2,t3)	(r2,t3)	(r2,t3)	(r2,t3)	(r2,t3)
Status	READY	READY	READY	UPDATING_IMAGE	UPDATING_IMAGE	UPDATING_IMAGE	UPDATING_IMAGE	UPDATING_IMAGE	READY
Worker Rev(w1)	(r0,t0)	(r1,t1)	(r1,t1)	(r1,t1)	(r1,t1)	(r1,t1)	(r0,t0)	(r1,t7) Incorrect (r2,t7) Correct	(r2,t7)
Status	-	IDLE	BUSY	BUSY	IDLE	SHUTDOWN_REQUESTED	-	IDLE	IDLE

B

Time Stamp	t0	t1	t2 ... t6	t7	t8	t9	t10	t11	t12
Action	Init	CW	WITB ... CDW	PUA	HAUR	CW	PUA	WITB	WBTI
Actor Rev	(r1,t0)	(r1,t0)	(r1,t0) ... (r2,t3)	(r2,t3)	(r3,t8)	(r3,t8)	(r3,t8)	(r3,t8)	(r3,t8)
Status	READY	READY	READY ... UPDATING_IMAGE	READY	UPDATING_IMAGE	UPDATING_IMAGE	READY	READY	READY
Worker Rev(w1)	(r0,t0)	(r1,t1)	(r1,t1)... (r0,t0)	(r0,t0)	(r0,t0)	(r1,t9) Incorrect (r2,t9) Incorrect (r3,t9) Correct	(r3,t9)	(r3,t9)	(r3,t9)
Status	-	IDLE	BUSY ... -	-	-	IDLE	IDLE	BUSY	IDLE

Fig. 2. Snapshots of sequence of states in two example behaviors for the scenario with actor update and worker creation. The following are the *Actions* Abbreviation used in the tables - Init: Initial state, CW: *CreateWorker*, WITB: *WorkerIdletoBusy*, HAUR: *HTTPActorUpdateRecv*, WBTI: *WorkerBusyToIdle*, SDW: *StartDeleteWorker*, CDW: *CompleteDeleteWorker*, PUA: *ProcessUpdateActor*

4.2 Example Behaviors-Safe vs Unsafe

RevisionNumberInv is a critical property for the operation of Abaco. Abaco serves the scientific research community by being part of their scientific workflow and addressing their infrastructural and computational needs. Reliability and reproducibility of such scientific findings depend on using the correct version of the software.

Figure 2 shows snapshots of a sequence of states of two example behaviors for the Abaco system with relevant state variables values. In both Tables A & B, we assumed only one actor and one worker in the system for demonstration purposes. In the tables, *Timestamp* denotes *clock* value and *Action* denotes the *Next* action in the Specification. *ActorRev* & *Status* denote the actor's Docker image revision number with timestamp and actor's status, respectively. *WorkerRev* & *Status* denote the revision number of the Docker image used during the worker's creation and worker's status, respectively. Table A shows the following sequence of states of an example behavior, say, behavior A:

- Initial state at $t0$
- Creation of a worker at $t1$ with actor's current image revision number $r1$
- Worker starts an execution for a message and changes worker's status from *IDLE* to *BUSY* at $t2$
- Abaco receives an HTTP actor update request and changes the actor's revision number from $r1$ to $r2$, and status from *READY* to *UPDATING_IMAGE* at $t3$
- Worker finishes the current execution and changes worker's status from *BUSY* to *IDLE* at $t4$
- Autoscaler decides to delete the worker as the revision number of the image used by the worker is not the same as that of the actor's current image revision number. The worker's status is changed to *SHUTDOWN_REQUESTED*, and a command message "SHUTDOWN" is sent to the worker's command queue at $t5$.
- Deletion of worker completes at $t6$. The status of the worker is reset to '$-$', the revision number is reset to $r0$ and timestamp to $t0$
- Creation of worker at $t7$. If the actor's current image revision number is used for worker creation, i.e., $r2$, it satisfies the *RevisionNumberInv*. However, if the actor's old image revision number is used for worker creation, i.e., $r1$, it violates the safety property, *RevisionNumberInv*. This is highlighted in the table.
- Once the worker is created with correct image revision number, the actor's status is changed from *UPDATING_IMAGE* to *READY* at $t8$.

Similarly, Table B shows the sequence of states of another example behavior, say behavior B. The sequence of states beginning at timestamp $t0$ remains the same until $t6$ of behavior A (explained above). At $t6$, the worker's status is reset to its initial status. Then, the actor's status changes from *UPDATING_IMAGE* to *READY* at $t7$. Before the creation of the worker, there is again an HTTP actor update request. The actor's revision number gets updated from $r2$ to $r3$ at time stamp $t8$. So, when a worker is created after that, it should use the actor's current image revision number $r3$. If it uses $r1$ or $r2$, it violates the *RevisionNumberInv*. Note that there is no worker ever created with image revision number $r2$ as before creation of worker, the actor's image got updated twice.

4.3 Temporal Property

We define one liveness property of the specification, *AllMessagesProcessed*, which asserts that all the messages in the actor message queue will get eventually be processed.

$$AllMessagesProcessed \triangleq \Diamond \Box (\forall\, a \in Actors : Len(actorMsgQueues[a]) = 0)$$

4.4 Model Checking with TLC

We used TLC to perform model checking of the Abaco specification. We created separate models with different values for the CONSTANTS of the specification as shown in Table 1. Note that we have set *ScaleUpThreshold* to one for all values of CONSTANTS. We conducted the experiments in a 3.5 GHz Dual-Core Intel Core i7 with 16 GB memory. We set the TLC options to 69% system memory, four workers threads, and profiling off for a performance speedup. In our model verification, we checked the invariants of the specification - *TypeInvariant*, *MinimalWorkerProperty*, *ClockInv*, and *RevisionNumberInv*. Table 2 shows the summary of the evaluation of our specifications using TLC for models specified in Table 1.

Table 1. Models and parameters for the experiments

Model name	#MaxHTTP-Requests	#Actors	#Max-Workers	#Minimum Workers Per Actor
Model_1	1	1	1	1
Model_2	1	1	2	1
Model_3	1	2	2	1
Model_4	2	2	2	1
Model_5	3	2	2	1
Model_6	3	2	3	1
Model_7	4	2	3	1
Model_8	4	2	4	2

The last row shows that checking took three hours and 30 min and led to a state space with 242,275,245 distinct states by then. It was incomplete as we had to stop the model checking when TLC reported 29 GB indicating that it exceeded the available memory and started using disk.

Table 2. Results of model checking Abaco Spec with TLC

Model name	States found	Distinct states	Diameter	Time
Model_1	11	11	8	3 s
Model_2	21	20	8	3 s
Model_3	673	543	10	3 s
Model_4	14,695	9835	15	4 s
Model_5	232,829	127,883	20	37 s
Model_6	1,568,647	718,719	20	1 m 48 s
Model_7	35,589,337	13,736,751	25	19 m 11 s
Model_8	598,496,471	242,275,245 (Incomplete*)	20	3 h 30 m

4.5 Proving Safety Properties Using TLAPS

In Sect. 4.4, we performed model checking of the specification for only small models. We could not verify large models with TLC because of the large number of reachable states involved, and therefore model checking did not provide much confidence that the specification was correct. To verify the safety properties of the system for any size model, we write formal and machine-checked proofs in TLA+ which TLAPS, the TLA+ proof system, then checks. The main theorem that we need to prove is:

$$\text{THEOREM } RevisionNumberTheorem \triangleq Spec \Rightarrow \Box RevisionNumberInv$$
$$where, \qquad\qquad Spec \triangleq Init \land \Box[Next]_{vars}$$

This theorem states that $Spec$ satisfies the safety property $RevisionNumberInv$. In the previous Subsect. 4.1, we defined the property $RevisionNumberInv$ We will prove this invariance property, i.e., the property is true for all states in every behavior of the $Spec$. This theorem is the mathematical expression for it. A TLA+ proof is hierarchically structured and uses proof by induction. To prove the theorem by induction, we are required to prove 1) the invariant is true for the initial state of any behavior of $Spec$, and 2) if the invariant is true in any state of the behavior of $Spec$, it is true in the next state of the behavior. An invariant satisfying an induction hypotheses like this is called an inductive invariant of $Spec$. Thus, we need to first find an inductive invariant satisfying the $RevisionNumberTheorem$, thereby proving $RevisionNumberInv$ is an invariant of $Spec$. The complete TLA+ proof for the $Spec$ is available online [13].

Proof Strategy: We first define a candidate inductive invariant for $Spec$ as shown below:

$$InductiveInvariant \triangleq \land TypeInvariant$$
$$\land MinimalWorkerProperty$$
$$\land ClockInv$$
$$\land RevisionNumberInv$$

Since the type correctness for all variables should be true for all states of the $Spec$'s behaviors, an inductive invariant needs to assert $TypeInvariant$ for the *Spec*. The second conjunction, *MinimalWorkerProperty*, also needs to be asserted for the type correctness and the minimal number of workers per actor to remain always available for safe operation. The third conjunction, *ClockInv*, asserts that the timestamp values never exceed the clock value at every state for all behaviors. It provides required conditions about the reachable states of the behaviors. The conjunction *RevisionNumberInv* needs to be asserted for a safe actor and worker update.

We used the approach provided in [10] where we prove one invariant and use it to prove the next invariant. We prove two theorems, first *TypeCorrect* and then *MinimalWorkerTheorem* as shown below:

THEOREM $TypeCorrect \triangleq Spec \Rightarrow \Box TypeInvariant$
THEOREM $MinimalWorkerTheorem \triangleq Spec \Rightarrow \Box MinimalWorkerProperty$

To prove *TypeCorrect* using induction, we first prove the induction basis, $Init \Rightarrow \Box TypeInvariant$. The proof was trivial, and TLAPS proved it automatically by just expanding the definition of *Init*, *TypeInvariant*, *SpecAssumption*, *workerState*, *ActorState*, *AllActors*, *ActorMessage*. Then we prove *TypeInvariant* $\wedge [Next]_{vars} \Rightarrow TypeInvariant'$. We use TLAPS to decompose the proof to prove all the conjunctions of the formula *TypeInvariant'*. $[Next]_{vars}$ is defined as a disjunction of *Next* and *UNCHANGED vars* of *Spec*. Thus, the proof is decomposed to 11 individual proof steps or cases corresponding to 11 *Next* sub-actions and one case for *UNCHANGED vars*. Out of 11 cases, the proofs of eight cases were trivial and handled automatically by TLAPS. For the remaining three cases corresponding to the actions *WorkerIBusyToIdle*, *WorkerIdleToShutdownReqd*, and *StartDeleteWorke*, we had to expand a few conjunctions in *TypeInvaraint'* that TLAPS failed to prove. TLAPS was then able to prove those stated assertions. TLAPS processes 84 obligations for the proof.

We used a similar approach to prove *MinimalWorkerTheorem*. First, we prove $Init \Rightarrow \Box MinimalWorkerTheorem$. This is not trivial as the smaller conjunctions in *MinimalWorkerProperty* involve a complex formula for sets and cardinality of *idleWorkers*, *busyWorkers* and *actorWorkers*. The proofs use *FiniteSets* and *FiniteSetTheorems* [18] to prove *idleWorkers'*, *busyWorkers'* and *actorWorkers'* are finite sets and to reason about how their cardinalities change in each action.

⟨2⟩4. ASSUME NEW $s \in Workers$, NEW $a \in Actors$, $WorkerIdleToBusy(s, a)$
       PROVE *MinimalWorkerProperty'*

⟨3⟩1. *IsFiniteSet(idleWorkers')*
         BY ⟨2⟩4, *FS_EmptySet*, *FS_Subset* DEF *WorkerIdleToBusy*

⟨3⟩2. *IsFiniteSet(busyWorkers')*
         BY ⟨2⟩4, *FS_EmptySet*, *FS_AddElement*, *FS_Subset* DEF *WorkerIdleToBusy*

⟨3⟩3. $Cardinality(busyWorkers') = Cardinality(busyWorkers) + 1$
         BY ⟨2⟩4, *FS_EmptySet*, *FS_AddElement*, *FS_Subset* DEF *WorkerIdleToBusy*

⟨3⟩4. $Cardinality(idleWorkers') = Cardinality(idleWorkers) - 1$
         BY ⟨2⟩4, *FS_EmptySet*, *FS_RemoveElement*, *FS_Subset* DEF *WorkerIdleToBusy*

⟨3⟩5. QED BY ⟨2⟩4, ⟨3⟩1, ⟨3⟩2, ⟨3⟩3, ⟨3⟩4, *FS_EmptySet*,
         FS_AddElement, *FS_RemoveElement*, *FS_Subset* DEF *WorkerIdleToBusy*

Next, we prove *RevisionNumberTheorem*. To prove the theorem, we prove the *InductiveInvariant* (IInv) as defined earlier. We use *TypeCorrect* and *Minimal-WorkerTheorem* to prove the IInv. The high-level proof structure of the theorem is shown below:

THEOREM *Spec* ⇒ □*RevisionNumberInv*
⟨1⟩1. *Init* ⇒ *RevisionNumberInv* ∧ *ClockInv*
⟨1⟩2. *TypeInvariant* ∧ *MinimalWorkerProperty* ∧ *ClockInv*
     ∧ *RevisionNumberInv* ∧ [*Next*]$_{vars}$ ⇒ *RevisionNumberInv'* ∧ *ClockInv'*
⟨1⟩3.QED BY ⟨1⟩1, ⟨1⟩2, *TypeCorrect*, *MinimalWorkerTheorem*, *PTL* DEF *Spec*

We first prove Step ⟨1⟩1. The proof was trivial and TLAPS automatically proves the assertion by expanding the definitions of *TypeInvariant*, *Init*, *workerState*, *ActorState*, *AllActors*, *ActorMessage*, *MinimalWorkerProperty*, *RevisionNumberInv*, *ClockInv* and *SpecAssumption*. Then we prove Step ⟨1⟩2. In all 11 *Next* cases, the proof can further be decomposed to *RevisionNumberInv'* and *ClockInv'*. *ClockInv'* is trivial to prove in all 11 cases. To prove *RevisionNumberInv'*, the *InitializeMinimalWorkers*, *CreateWorker*, and *HTTPActorUpdateRecv* cases require explicitly stating the formula *RevisionNumberInv'* with correct prime(′) placement in the complex formula. TLAPS is able to handle the rest of the cases automatically. A total of 108 obligations are processed for this theorem proof.

TLAPS Metrics: Table 3 shows a summary of TLAPS proof statistics. The proofs are checked using TLAPS in a 3.5 GHz Dual-Core Intel Core i7 with 16 GB memory.

Table 3. Summary of TLAPS proofs

Metrics	Values
Size of Spec (Lines)	435
Size of Proof (Lines)	527
Num of Obligations in TLAPS	876
Time taken by TLAPS to check	9 mins

5 Discussions

5.1 Experiences Using TLC

The TLC model checker is part of TLA+ Toolbox. It provides several features for efficient model checking. It allows model checking of the *Spec* for different models. It helped us uncover some of the errors in the *Spec* by providing counter-examples and where the safety property violation happens. An easy way to create different models in TLC is to clone an existing model and modify the specific constant value for the new model with all other configurations remaining the same.

TLC provides Additional Spec Options in which one can provide TLC with alternate definitions for individual operators. This is used when TLC cannot evaluate or enumerate the definition in *Spec*. An alternate definition overrides the existing one. For example, since TLC cannot enumerate a variable of type *Nat*, we override *Nat* with $0..N$ where N is a small natural number.

TLC also provides an option to specify State Constraints. This feature is very helpful for limiting the set of reachable states during model checking. For example, in our *Spec*, one can specify state constraint on *MaxHTTPRequests* and *clock* to restrict the number of messages in the queue and global clock value, which otherwise could lead to an infinite set of reachable states.

Understanding the model checking results took some time, mostly because it involves understanding how TLC computes its states and explores the state space ([8] and [20]).

5.2   Experiences Using TLAPS

The most crucial part of a TLA+ proof is finding an inductive invariant for the *Spec*. There could be several candidates for inductive invariants for the *Spec*. We used the approach stated in [10] and [9]. We first decided on a candidate inductive invariant, then checked the candidate with TLC for small models. If the invariant is satisfied, we then proceeded to prove it using TLAPS. We have experienced that even such candidate cannot be proved using TLAPS as they were not correct. Hints from TLC model checking and TLAPS failed obligation, helped us to modify and arrive at the correct candidate invariant. [11] provides a tutorial, hints and a list of supported and unsupported features in TLAPS. To use TLAPS for the proof, we heavily used the decompose proof command, which mechanically expands the proof, until we reached a fundamental fact or a leaf proof which could be proved easily. For Set related proofs, usually one has to use FiniteSetTheorems modules, and for Sequences, the SequenceOpTheorems module [18]. If the candidate invariant is still difficult to prove, we simplify it to a smaller problem and prove it.

5.3   Benefits to Abaco Project

The Abaco project benefited directly from the analysis with TLA+ in two primary ways. First, writing the specification uncovered a race condition with how Abaco implemented the actor update process. This race condition in turn could lead to situations where Abaco would break its contract. As a result of this effort, a fix to the race condition was implemented. In fact, earlier versions of Abaco and the TLA+ specification did not implement a monotonically increasing revision number for each actor. We were led to the idea by thinking in terms of the TLA+ specification, and it is now implemented in Abaco itself.

Second, the Abaco specification allows architects and senior engineers with no prior knowledge or exposure to Abaco to understand its design at a detailed level and with a precision that would be very difficult to otherwise achieve. At a little over 400 lines, including white space and comments, the specification is relatively easy to digest for anyone familiar with TLA+. On the other hand, the Abaco code base is over 10,000 lines of code across several packages and utilizes numerous third-party systems and libraries. Additionally, our experience suggests that the use of TLA+ for design specification is far more compact and precise than what could be produced using diagrams and written text.

6   Related Work

The Abaco specification in this paper is written in TLA+, model-checked with TLC, and proved using TLAPS. The description of TLA+ language and writing specification in TLA+ can be found in [8]. The TLC model checker and how it computes its states and explores the state space, and its usage are described in [8] and [20]. [1] provides details of TLAPS design and the features it supported at its first public release. Several examples of TLA+ specifications, proofs and usage of TLAPS are listed in [2,11,17]. We used TLA+ Toolbox, the Integrated Development Environment (IDE), for writing TLA+ specification, TLC, and TLAPS. Some of the latest features can be found in [6].

As mentioned in Sect. 1, there are several works that present TLA+ specifications and proofs for cloud-based distributed systems. [19] provides a basic specification for zero-downtime deployments of updates to servers in a load balancers in PlusCal. It used TLC to model checking for some invariant, and no proof was given. Recently, AWS launched "Instance Refresh" feature for EC2 Autoscaling to tackle zero-downtime deployment with instance updates [14]. Though it addresses similar problems mentioned in this paper, we did not find any specification for this feature. [7] lists some of the industrial works using TLA+. For example, at Microsoft, TLA+ has been used to write the specification and verify the correctness of the algorithm of Cosmos DB core algorithm and five consistency models, Xbox 360 protocol, management of Paxos rings, Azure Networking, and IoT services, while Amazon used TLA+ in verifying the replication and fault-tolerance mechanisms in DynamoDB. To the best of our knowledge, none of these examples addressed the problem of zero-downtime updates in a cloud-based autoscaler system.

7   Conclusion

This paper presented the results of analyzing the Abaco platform, a production Functions-as-a-service system funded by the NSF and utilized at scale by large research projects, using TLA+, including modeling checking with TLC and proofs of safety properties via TLAPS. We also discussed techniques we found to be useful when using TLC and TLAPS and presented some of the benefits to the Abaco project, including finding and fixing a race condition and allowing senior engineers with no prior knowledge of Abaco reason about its architecture. As a future work, we aim to explore different techniques [3] to ensure implementation conforms to the specification.

Acknowledgment. The authors would like to thank Dr. Stephen Merz, Markus Kuppe, and members of TLA+ Google group for their feedback and help with the understanding of the examples TLA+ proof and TLAPS.

References

1. Chaudhuri, K., Doligez, D., Lamport, L., Merz, S.: Verifying safety properties with the TLA$^+$ proof system. In: Giesl, J., Hähnle, R. (eds.) IJCAR 2010. LNCS (LNAI), vol. 6173, pp. 142–148. Springer, Heidelberg (2010). https://doi.org/10.1007/978-3-642-14203-1_12
2. Cousineau, D., Doligez, D., Lamport, L., Merz, S., Ricketts, D., Vanzetto, H.: TLA+ proofs. CoRR abs/1208.5933 (2012). http://arxiv.org/abs/1208.5933
3. Davis, A.J.J., Hirschhorn, M., Schvimer, J.: Extreme modelling in practice. Proc. VLDB Endow. **13**(9), 1346–1358 (2020). https://doi.org/10.14778/3397230.3397233
4. Garcia, C., Stubbs, J., Looney, J., Jamthe, A., Packard, M., Nguyen, K.: The abaco platform: a performance and scalability study on the jetstream cloud. In: The 16th International Conference on Grid, Cloud, and Cluster Computing (GCC 2020), World Congress in Computer Science, Computer Engineering, and Applied Computing (CSCE) (July 2020)
5. Kubeless: Autoscaling function deployment in kubeless. https://kubeless.io/docs/autoscaling/. Accessed 20 May 2021
6. Kuppe, M.A., Lamport, L., Ricketts, D.: The TLA+ toolbox. Electron. Proc. Theor. Comput. Sci. **310**, 50–62 (2019)
7. Lamport, L.: Industrial use of TLA+. https://lamport.azurewebsites.net/tla/industrial-use.html. Accessed 20 May 2021
8. Lamport, L.: Specifying Systems: The TLA+ Language and Tools for Hardware and Software Engineers. Addison-Wesley Longman Publishing Co., Inc., USA (2002)
9. Lamport, L.: Using tlc to check inductive invariance (2018). https://lamport.azurewebsites.net/tla/inductive-invariant.pdf. Accessed 20 May 2021
10. Lamport, L.: Proving safety properties (2019). https://lamport.azurewebsites.net/tla/proving-safety.pdf. Accessed 20 May 2021
11. Microsoft-Inria: TLA+ proof system. https://tla.msr-inria.inria.fr/tlaps/content/Home.html. Accessed 20 May 2021
12. Newcombe, C., Rath, T., Zhang, F., Munteanu, B., Brooker, M., Deardeuff, M.: How Amazon web services uses formal methods. Commun. ACM **58**(4), 66–73 (2015)
13. Padhy, S., Stubbs, J.: Abaco specification (2020). https://github.com/tapis-project/specifications/blob/master/generic-patterns/fmcad_abaco_proof.tla. Accessed 20 May 2021
14. Peven, B.: Introducing instance refresh for ec2 auto scaling (2020). https://aws.amazon.com/blogs/compute/introducing-instance-refresh-for-ec2-auto-scaling/. Accessed 20 May 2021
15. Stubbs, J., et al.: Enabling science with functions-as-a-service: new features and usage of the Abaco platform. Science Gateways Community Institute, Gateways (2020). osf.io/vd8am

16. Stubbs, J., Vaughn, M., Looney, J.: Rapid development of scalable, distributed computation with Abaco. In: Proceedings of the 10th International Workshop on Science Gateways, Edinburgh, Scotland, UK, 13–15 June 2018. CEUR Workshop Proceedings, vol. 2357. CEUR-WS.org (2018). http://ceur-ws.org/Vol-2357/paper3.pdf
17. TLA+-Community: TLA+ examples. https://github.com/tlaplus/Examples. Accessed 20 May 2021
18. TLAPS: Tlapm library. https://github.com/tlaplus/tlapm/tree/master/library. Accessed 20 May 2021
19. Wayne, H.: Modeling zero-downtime deployments with TLA+ (May 2017). https://www.hillelwayne.com/modeling-deployments/
20. Yu, Y., Manolios, P., Lamport, L.: Model checking TLA+ specifications. In: Pierre, L., Kropf, T. (eds.) CHARME 1999. LNCS, vol. 1703, pp. 54–66. Springer, Heidelberg (1999). https://doi.org/10.1007/3-540-48153-2_6

Case Study: Analysis of Autonomous Center Line Tracking Neural Networks

Ismet Burak Kadron[1]($\boxtimes$), Divya Gopinath[2], Corina S. Păsăreanu[3], and Huafeng Yu[4]

[1] University of California Santa Barbara, Santa Barbara, USA
`kadron@cs.ucsb.edu`
[2] KBR Inc., Nasa Ames, Mountain View, USA
`divya.gopinath@nasa.gov`
[3] KBR Inc., CMU, Nasa Ames, Mountain View, USA
`corina.s.pasareanu@nasa.gov`
[4] Boeing Research and Technology, Santa Clara, CA, USA
`huafeng.yu@boeing.com`

Abstract. Deep neural networks have gained widespread usage in a number of applications. However, limitations such as lack of explainability and robustness inhibit building trust in their behavior, which is crucial in safety critical applications such as autonomous driving. Therefore, techniques which aid in understanding and providing guarantees for neural network behavior are the need of the hour. In this paper, we present a case study applying a recently proposed technique, Prophecy, to analyze the behavior of a neural network model, provided by our industry partner and used for autonomous guiding of airplanes on taxi runways. This regression model takes as input an image of the runway and produces two outputs, cross-track error and heading error, which represent the position of the plane relative to the center line. We use the Prophecy tool to extract neuron activation patterns for the correctness and safety properties of the model. We show the use of these patterns to identify features of the input that explain correct and incorrect behavior. We also use the patterns to provide guarantees of consistent behavior. We explore a novel idea of using sequences of images (instead of single images) to obtain good explanations and identify regions of consistent behavior.

1 Introduction

Deep neural networks (DNNs) are increasingly impacting every aspect of our lives, by being used in many applications, some of them with safety-critical requirements, such as autonomous driving and flight. However, it is not well understood why a network gives a particular output which is essential for building trust in its behavior. Further, it is also crucial to obtain guarantees of consistent behavior of the network, specifically for safety-critical applications. There is thus a critical need for tools and techniques that can help analyze and understand neural network models. In this paper we report on our experience with

© Springer Nature Switzerland AG 2022
R. Bloem et al. (Eds.): NSV 2021/VSTTE 2021, LNCS 13124, pp. 104–121, 2022.
https://doi.org/10.1007/978-3-030-95561-8_7

applying a recent advancement in property inference for neural networks, i.e. Prophecy [1], to the analysis and understanding of neural networks used for autonomous guiding of airplanes on taxi runways.

The Autonomous Center line Tracking (ACT) neural network [2,3] is designed to take a single picture of the runway as input and return the plane's position with respect to the middle of the runway. It returns two numerical outputs; cross track error (y_0), which is the distance of the plane from the center line and heading error (y_1), which is the angle of the plane with respect to the center line. These outputs are typically fed to a controller which in turn manoeuvres the plane such that it remains close to the center of the runway. This forms a closed loop system wherein the ACT module continuously receives images in a sequence as the plane moves on the runway. ACT neural network models are typically trained and tested using the X-Plane simulator [4] that generates images at regular time intervals.

In this study, our goal is to understand (explain) the behavior of the ACT neural network model and provide guarantees for consistent behavior with respect to two types of output properties, indicated by the industrial partner. i) **Correctness properties** specify the conditions for correct behavior of the model using error bounds, by comparing the model outputs to ideal values; they have the following form: $|y_0 - y_{0ideal}| \leq 1.0\,\mathrm{m}, |y_1 - y_{1ideal}| \leq 5°$. ii) **Safety properties** specify conditions for safe operation by using runway dimensions; they have the following form: $|y_0| \leq 10.0\,\mathrm{m}, |y_1| \leq 90°$. To address these goals, we use Prophecy, which infers precondition properties from a deep neural network model with respect to its output behavior in terms of neuron activation patterns. Our previous work [1] shows the application of Prophecy to classification networks, for explaining perception models, proving behavioral properties and also using it at runtime to reduce inference time for classification. This work presents the first application of the tool on regression models for explaining correct and incorrect behaviors and for providing guarantees of consistent behavior with respect to output properties.

Most of the existing techniques for attribution, such as DeepLift [5], LIME [6], and SHAP [7], identify important pixels in an individual image impacting the output of a model and focus on classification tasks. In this work, we show how to leverage activation patterns to identify input features that impact network behavior with respect to output constraints for a regression model. Furthermore, we investigate the idea of leveraging sequences of images satisfying the same pattern to visualize features that impact network behavior across multiple similar images, thus providing more useful information for the developers.

Most existing neural network verification techniques have focused on checking local adversarial robustness for perception networks (e.g., Marabou [8]) and proving input-output properties for controller networks with low dimensional inputs [9]. In our work, we leverage activation patterns to identify regions of images that lead to consistent output behavior, which are potentially bigger than local neighborhoods. We identify image sequences satisfying the same pattern and leverage off-the-shelf solvers to prove that the network behaves consistently in the input region containing the sequence.

The activation patterns group together input sequences over which the output property acts as a *temporal invariant* for the network. Furthermore, counterexamples obtained from failed proofs highlight problematic scenarios, such as the plane going out of the runway. These scenarios can be used to debug and improve the network.

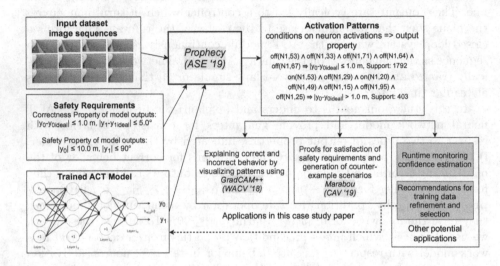

Fig. 1. Overview of our analysis framework.

2   Analysis of Autonomous Center Line Tracking: An Overview

In this section, we provide an overview of the steps performed in this case study for analyzing neural networks built for Autonomous Center Line Tracking. Centerline tracking on runway or taxiway is one of the most important ground operations in an airport. An airplane is required to follow the center lines of taxiway and runway during taxiing. Center lines have standardized shapes and colors on the pavement of airport runways and taxiways, but may be less visible for a number of reasons, including skid marks, poor lighting conditions and bad weather.

Figure 1 presents our analysis framework. Given a trained model for autonomous center line tracking, input sequences comprising of runway images and safety requirements in terms of constraints on the model outputs, the Prophecy tool is invoked to extract activation patterns. Figure 1 shows examples of safety requirements; correctness and safety properties in terms of outputs y_0 and y_1, and example patterns extracted by Prophecy; pre-conditions in terms of neuron activations that imply the output property. More explanation about the

activation patterns are provided in Sects. 3 and 4.2. For a given correctness or
safety property, patterns with high support on the input data are selected for
both the satisfaction and violation of the respective properties. Analysis of these
patterns has the potential to aid in a number of applications. In this case study,
we use the patterns to explain the correct and incorrect behavior of the model.
To enable this we employ the GradCAM++ tool (refer to Sect. 3.3) to visualize
the patterns and identify the input features on the runway images that impact
network behavior. We also explore the use of patterns to provide guarantees of
consistent behavior of the network by obtaining proofs for the satisfaction of the
requirements. We employ the Marabou tool (refer to Sect. 3) for this purpose. We
also generate counter-example scenarios or sequences of images that violate the
safety requirements. We envisage the use of the patterns in other applications
such as runtime monitoring, confidence estimation and training data refinement
(refer to Sect. 7 for more details on these potential applications).

3   Background

3.1   Deep Neural Networks

A deep neural network (DNN) (Fig. 2) is a machine learning model which when
given an input such as an image produces a prediction of the respective outputs.
A neural network is typically made up of multiple layers, each of which performs
an input transformation. Each layer is made up of neurons, and each neuron
takes in a weighted sum of the outputs from the previous layer and applies an
activation function on it. The Rectified Linear Unit (ReLU) is a popular function
that returns the value of the weighted sum as is if it is positive and returns 0
otherwise. The respective neuron is said to be OFF when its output is 0 and
ON otherwise. Exponential Linear Units (ELU) are activation functions which
display the same behavior as ReLU for positive inputs but display non-linear
exponential behavior on negative inputs. Dense layers or fully connected layers
are the most commonly used in networks, where each neuron in a layer receives
input from every neuron in the previous layer. Convolutional layers are popularly
used in image processing to blur and sharpen images, detect and enhance edges
so on. They make use of filters or kernels, to detect what features are present
throughout an image.

3.2   Prophecy

Prophecy [1] is a recently proposed technique that aims to analyze a complex
DNN model to extract a set of compact properties. Each property is a rule of
the form Pre $\Rightarrow$ Post, where Pre is a constraint in terms of (on/off) neuron
activation patterns and Post is a constraint on the output of the network. An
example of such a property is shown in Fig. 2, which states that for any input
to the network, if the activation of the first neuron in layer 1 ($N_{1,0}$) is off and
the activation of the second neuron ($N_{1,1}$) is on, then the output y_1 is greater

than the output y_0. Prophecy extracts these properties by applying decision tree learning over the activation patterns recorded for a given set of labeled data for the DNN model. The properties are proven using an off-the-shelf verification tool such as Marabou [8]. Each such property is associated with a support, which indicates the number of data instances that satisfy the rule. This information can be used to assess the extracted rules, in cases they can not be proved formally.

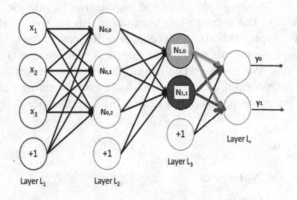

ReLU(x) = x (on) if x > 0; 0 (off) otherwise

Fig. 2. Example DNN with ReLU activation and example layer property that can be extracted by the Prophecy; $\text{off}(N_{1,0}) \wedge \text{on}(N_{1,1}) \Rightarrow y_1 > y_0$

3.3 GradCAM++

GradCAM++ [10] is a recently proposed approach for explaining the decisions of convolutional neural network models used for image classification. It aims to generate class activation maps that highlight pixels of the image the model used to make the classification decision. It builds on the basic idea proposed in [11] of using the gradients of any target concept flowing into the final convolutional layer to produce a coarse localization map highlighting the important regions in the image for predicting the concept. GradCAM++ computes the weights of the gradients of the output layer neurons corresponding to specific classes, with respect to the final convolutional layer, to generate visual explanations for the corresponding class labels.

4   Details of the Case Study

In this section, we provide details of the network used in our case study and explain the steps of our analysis on this network.

4.1   Autonomous Center Line Tracking Networks

Our industry partner developed a research prototype of machine learning component based on neural networks to identify center lines on runways/taxiways and predict the CTE (distance between the nose wheel and centerline) during taxi. The network was demonstrated and evaluated using the X-Plane simulator. We analyzed a model for Autonomous Center line Tracking supplied by our industry partner, which we denote as ACT. The model is a sequential convolutional neural network model (CNN) with 24 layers including an input layer that takes in images of dimensions $360 \times 200 \times 3$, 5 convolution layers, and four dense layers at the end. The first dense layer has 100 neurons, the second has 50 neurons, the third has 10 neurons; the output layer has 2 neurons. Each neuron has an ELU (Exponential Linear Unit) activation function. As ACT could not be analyzed with formal verification tools due to its complex structure, we also analyzed a second network, TinyNet, as described in the next section.

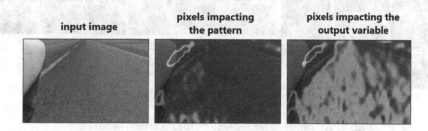

Fig. 3. GradCAM++ based attribution

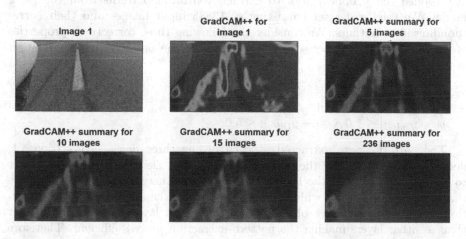

Fig. 4. Attribution over single image and summary over sequences of varying length.

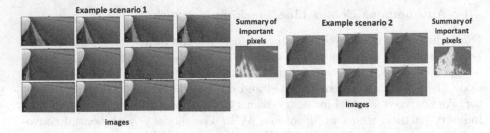

Fig. 5. Attribution for sequences for correct behavior.

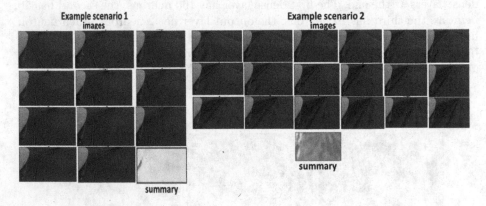

Fig. 6. Attribution for sequences for incorrect behavior.

4.2   Study of the ACT Network Provided by Our Industry Partner

We applied the Prophecy tool to extract activation patterns from the ACT model. We used a dataset consisting of 13885 input images and their corresponding ideal outputs. We consider the following three correctness properties of the outputs and extract separate patterns for the satisfaction and violation of each of them:

- $|y_0 - y_{0ideal}| \leq 1.0$,
- $|y_1 - y_{1ideal}| \leq 5.0$, and
- $|y_0 - y_{0ideal}| \leq 1.0 \wedge |y_1 - y_{1ideal}| \leq 5.0$.

The patterns were extracted at each of the three dense layers (dense_1, dense_2, dense_3) and all the dense layers together. Dense layers appear closer to the output and hold the logic that impacts the network's predictions more than convolutional layers which focus on processing the input for feature extraction. Further, the number of neurons at the dense layers is typically smaller than at other layers making the pattern-extraction process efficient. Therefore we focused on the three dense layers of the ACT model.

Each pattern is a rule in terms of the activations of the neurons in the respective layers. A neuron with the ELU activation function is considered to be off if its value is ≤ 0 and on otherwise. Patterns were generated for the satisfaction of the output property (denoted here as class 1) and their violation (denoted here as class 0). We obtained a total of 396 patterns for class 1 and 418 for class 0, with a minimum support of 10 instances satisfying a pattern.

Note that the model is coded to ensure that the outputs y_0 and y_1 do not have values beyond the runway dimensions for safety (10 m and 90 °C, respectively), therefore we could not extract patterns that discriminate between satisfaction and violation of the safety property on this model.

Using Patterns for Explaining Behavior. Each layer in a neural network typically extracts and processes features of the input image. Each layer pattern thus potentially represents the logic of the network in terms of the input features which in turn impact the network's behavior with respect to the specific output property. Therefore, visualization of the features represented by layer patterns has the potential to identify the portion of the input that impacts correct or incorrect network behavior.

Here is an example pattern for the correct behavior extracted from the first dense layer of the ACT network model:

$$\text{off}(N_{1,53}) \land \text{off}(N_{1,33}) \land \text{off}(N_{1,71}) \land \text{off}(N_{1,64}) \land \text{off}(N_{1,67}) \Rightarrow |y_0 - y_{0ideal}| \leq 1.0.$$

The pattern states that for input images satisfying the neuron activations as prescribed in the pattern, the cross-track error output of the network would be close to the ideal. There were 1792 images (from the initial dataset used to extract the patterns) that satisfy the respective activations and also satisfy the output correctness property. We refer to this as the support of the pattern; note that the higher the value of the support, the higher is the confidence that the pattern would hold true for all possible inputs.

In order to use the pattern to explain the network behavior, we aim to visualize the features represented by the pattern. This can be done by identifying the pixels in the input that impact the neurons that appear in the rule representing the pattern. Attribution approaches such as the GradCAM++ (refer to Sect. 3.3) technique identify pixels in the input that impact the output neuron corresponding to a given label. We use this technique to identify pixels in the input (image satisfying the pattern) impacting the neurons in the pattern by making the following modifications. Instead of using GradCAM++ to target output neurons and generate class explanations, we use GradCAM++ to target neurons in the pattern. GradCAM++ computes the partial derivatives of the last convolutional layer with respect to the neurons in the pattern and generates a visual explanation for the pattern.

The first picture in Fig. 3 shows an image satisfying the example pattern for correct behavior. The picture in the center shows the pixels identified with the help of the pattern, which highlight the portion of the image between the nose of the plane and the center-line of the runway. This represents the relevant input features which the network appears to use to determine the cross-track error output, and corresponds to the expected behaviour according to the domain experts.

We note that existing attribution approaches for image classification networks, including GradCAM++, typically aim to identify pixels of an input image that directly impact the respective output variable of interest. This works for classification models, since the output nodes represent the labels and the pixels that increase the magnitude of the output node could be considered responsible for the decision. However, such an approach does not make too much sense for regression models. We did try to use GradCAM++ to highlight input pixels that directly impact the output y_0 for the given input image. However, as seen in the last picture in Fig. 3, this seems to highlight most of the image and does not appear to help in localizing the features that impact the satisfaction of the correctness property. This example highlights the benefit of using patterns for explainability of regression models. The pattern enables the representation of the inequality constraint $|y_0 - y_{0ideal}| \leq 1.0$ as a binary classification condition, thereby aiding in the discrimination of the pixels that impact the satisfaction of the correctness property vs its violation. This enables localization of the input features impacting the correct behavior of the network better than identifying the pixels that directly impact the output variable (as is done with traditional attribution approaches).

Leveraging Image Sequences. Attribution with respect to a single image highlights important pixels that may be specific to the image but they may not capture the more general feature that the pattern represents. Summarizing the important pixels over multiple images satisfying the same pattern has the potential to extract this general feature. However, summarizing over a large number of images may be too noisy. Such a case is shown in Fig. 4, where the summary over 236 images (all satisfying the same activation pattern) highlights only a very small portion of the image. Note that the ACT network receives images sequentially, one after the other, representing the plane moving on the runway. Thus, the same feature may appear in different parts of the input images, corresponding to different times in the sequence. We therefore propose to consider images in *contiguous sequences* that satisfy the same pattern. Each such sequence represents similar images that were taken in succession while the airplane was moving on the taxiway. We then summarize the important pixels over all images in a sequence (by considering the average GradCAM++ value for each pixel) and use this to visualize the feature that the pattern represents for that sequence.

Explaining Correct Behavior over Image Sequences. We were able to identify a number of sequences of considerable lengths that satisfied the patterns for correct behavior. For instance, for the correctness property constraining y_0, there were 62 individual sequences, one of them being 236 images in length, that satisfied the pattern for correct behavior. For the correctness property constraining y_1, there were 50 sequences with the highest length being 795 that satisfied the pattern for correct behavior.

Figure 5 shows two sequences that satisfy our example pattern for correct behavior for y_0 and their respective attribution summaries. These represent two different input scenarios which are viewed similarly by the network since they satisfy the same pattern. Note that the important pixels highlighted are different in both cases, however, both of them represent the same feature in their respective scenarios; the distance between the nose of the plane and the center line. This feature being relevant to determining the cross-track error, it explains why the network produces the correct outputs for these scenarios.

Explaining Incorrect Behavior over Image Sequences. We used the patterns for the violation of the correctness properties and the respective sequences, to explain the incorrect behavior of the network. For the violation of the correctness property constraining y_0, the pattern with the maximum support (403) had 24 sequences with maximum length of 34 images. For the violation of the correctness property constraining y_1, the pattern with the maximum support (558) had 30 sequences with maximum length of 65 images.

Here is an example pattern for the violation of the correctness property for the cross-track error output, $on(N_{1,53}) \wedge off(N_{1,29}) \wedge on(N_{1,20}) \wedge off(N_{1,49}) \wedge off(N_{1,15}) \wedge off(N_{1,95}) \wedge off(N_{1,25}) \Rightarrow |y_0 - y_{0ideal}| > 1.0$.

Figure 6 shows two scenarios that satisfy this pattern and their respective summaries. In scenario 1, we can understand based on the pixels highlighted that the blue line probably acts as noise and interferes with the correct determination of the cross-track error output. In scenario 2, none of the pixels are highlighted indicating the absence of a distinct feature that the network could use to make a correct estimation of the cross-track error.

Patterns for Guaranteeing Consistent Behavior. All inputs satisfying a pattern potentially satisfy the output property as well. A formal proof is a guarantee of consistent behavior of the network on regions of inputs that are similar to each other with respect to the semantic features that the pattern represents.

Solvers such as Marabou [12] can be used to prove properties of neural networks. However, the ACT model from our industry partner is complex, involving convolutions, and ELU activations, which cannot be handled by existing solvers such as Marabou. We tried training a simpler feed-forward ReLU network on the provided data but could not obtain a network with good accuracy. We therefore resorted to validating each pattern statistically by calculating its precision, recall and F1-score on a separate test set of 2777 images. Figure 7 shows that the patterns for the satisfaction of correctness properties display very good precision on the test set. There were also patterns for the violation of each of the three properties that displayed fairly good precision, greater than 80%. These statistical results provide confidence that the patterns could be used to identify valid and invalid behaviors, although we could not formally prove them.

Layer	Precision (%)	Recall (%)	F1-Score
	y0 - y0ideal| ≤ 1.0		
2	100.00	6.90	12.91
ALL	99.42	6.55	12.29
ALL	100.00	6.13	11.55
2	98.76	6.06	11.42
3	98.76	5.99	11.29
1	100.00	4.69	8.96
ALL	100.00	2.94	5.71
ALL	100.00	2.62	5.11
ALL	100.00	2.51	4.90
ALL	98.28	2.15	4.21

Layer	Precision (%)	Recall (%)	F1-Score
	y1 - y1ideal| ≤ 5.0		
ALL	100.00	20.95	34.64
1	100.00	9.09	16.67
2	100.00	6.65	12.47
1	100.00	6.14	11.57
ALL	100.00	5.88	11.11
1	100.00	4.18	8.02
1	100.00	3.77	7.27
2	100.00	3.70	7.14
ALL	100.00	2.62	5.11
2	98.21	2.07	4.05

Layer	Precision (%)	Recall (%)	F1-Score
	y0 - y0ideal| ≤ 1.0 ∧	y1 - y1ideal| ≤ 5.0		
2	100.00	6.97	13.03
ALL	100.00	6.54	12.28
1	100.00	4.77	9.11
ALL	100.00	1.74	3.42
1	100.00	1.22	2.41
2	86.49	1.21	2.39
1	100.00	1.10	2.18
ALL	100.00	1.03	2.04
ALL	81.25	0.98	1.94
1	100.00	0.92	1.82

Layer	Precision (%)	Recall (%)	F1-Score
	y0 - y0ideal| > 1.0		
1	86.67	18.31	30.23
ALL	73.91	23.94	36.17
ALL	33.33	0.66	1.29
1	25.00	0.66	1.29
ALL	20.83	4.07	6.81
1	18.18	2.82	4.88
1	18.18	2.82	4.88
ALL	5.88	0.81	1.42
1	5.88	0.66	1.19
ALL	4.35	0.81	1.37

Layer	Precision (%)	Recall (%)	F1-Score
	y1 - y1ideal| > 5.0		
ALL	100.00	8.55	15.75
1	100.00	7.24	13.50
ALL	100.00	1.41	2.78
ALL	87.50	9.21	16.67
1	73.33	15.49	25.58
ALL	66.67	1.63	3.18
1	60.00	4.23	7.90
2	12.50	2.63	4.35
1	8.11	3.95	5.31

Layer	Precision (%)	Recall (%)	F1-Score
	y0 - y0ideal| > 1.0 ∨	y1 - y1ideal| > 5.0		
ALL	70.00	9.21	16.28
ALL	90.91	6.58	12.27
ALL	20.83	4.07	6.81
1	50.00	2.82	5.34
ALL	2.75	12.50	4.51
1	4.11	4.88	4.46
1	3.39	4.88	4.00
ALL	2.09	9.76	3.44
1	2.09	9.21	3.41
1	1.91	8.94	3.15

Fig. 7. Patterns for the violation and satisfaction of every correctness property which had a support greater than 10 were validated on a separate test set. The figure displays for each property, the layer and test-set metrics for the patterns with top 10 F1-scores.

5   Analysis of the TinyNet Network

As mentioned, we could not analyze ACT with Marabou, due to its complex structure (convolutions, ELU activations that can not be handled by the verification tool). We therefore analyzed another network for autonomous center-line tracking, TinyNet [13], which is a smaller network that is more amenable to formal verification. The TinyNet neural network takes a single picture of the runway of size $360 \times 200 \times 3$, crops a segment of the image of size 205×135 to remove the nose of the plane from the image, make it black and white, reduce the size of the image to 256×128 and downsample it to dimensions 16×8 by taking the average brightness of 16 pixels with most brightness in each 16×16 pixel block. TinyNet has one input layer of dimension 128, three fully connected layers of sizes 16, 8, 8 with ReLU activation function and an output layer of size 2 with no activation function. The output layer returns the two outputs, the cross track error (y_0) and heading error (y_1).

We performed a study of a smaller, fully connected network with ReLU activations (TinyNet, refer to Sect. 4) for the same purpose of centering the plane on the runway specifically to highlight the benefit of using patterns to obtain **formal proofs of consistent behavior**. We used a labeled dataset of 51462 images in the down-sampled input space of TinyNet and extracted patterns at each intermediate layer and all layers together.

Sequence of images satisfying a pattern for the correctness or safety property potentially represent an interval of time where the network displays consistent behavior. We selected sequences of images satisfying the same pattern and bounded the input region as an over-approximation box covering all images within the sequence ($[x_{\min}, x_{\max}]$, represents the minimum and maximum values for each pixel calculated based on all images in the sequence). We then used Marabou to perform the following check for the safety property; $\forall x \in [x_{\min}, x_{\max}] \land pattern_{class=1} \Rightarrow |y_0| \leq \theta$. $pattern_{class=1}$ represents a pattern for the satisfaction of the property and θ represents the threshold on the runway dimensions. If proved successfully, the output property could be considered as a temporal invariant over input sequences within the region, else the counterexample represents a scenario of a sequence of images resulting in violation.

It is a challenge to prove that the correctness property holds true for all the inputs satisfying a pattern. This is because the ground truth is not known for all the input images and can not be expressed in a checkable form. Thus we focused on the safety properties instead.

We experimented with different threshold values for encoding the safety properties, in order to get more insights into the network behavior. We were able to extract patterns for the following safety properties.

- $|y_0| \leq 10.0 \, \mathrm{m}$,
- $|y_0| \leq 8.0 \, \mathrm{m}$,
- $|y_0| \leq 5.0 \, \mathrm{m}$.

For instance, for $|y_0| \leq 5.0 \, \mathrm{m}$, the pattern satisfying the property with the maximum support (750) has 108 sequences with maximum length of 18 images.

The pattern violating the property (support of 259) has 76 sequences with maximum length of 11 images. For $|y_0| \leq 10.0\,\mathrm{m}$, we obtained proofs for 33 out of 111 sequences with at least 5 images, the longest sub-sequence where we can obtain proofs has 17 images. For $|y_0| \leq 8.0\,\mathrm{m}$ and $|y_0| \leq 5.0\,\mathrm{m}$, the longest sequence on which a proof was obtained was 9 images long. We performed similar experiments for the safety properties involving y_1.

We would like to point out that some of the proofs could be obtained even without the inclusion of the pattern in the constraint formulation; i.e., $\forall x \in [x_{\min}, x_{\max}] \Rightarrow |y_0| \leq \theta$ would suffice. Even in these cases, the pattern was used to identify sequence of images satisfying them and thereby obtain the minimum and maximum values for each pixel, i.e. the input region bounded by $[x_{\min}, x_{\max}]$. In order to further evaluate the benefit of using activation patterns, we attempted proofs on random sequences of images satisfying the output property (but not necessarily satisfying any pattern for correct behavior) and computing $[x_{\min}, x_{\max}]$ over them. However, we were unable to obtain any proofs. These observations highlight that the patterns help select sequences of images (thereby input regions) which are processed similarly by the network and hence have higher chances of consistent behavior.

Fig. 8. Counterexample for an image sequence of length 39 for $|y_0| \leq 10\,\mathrm{m}$ safety property.

Fig. 9. Counterexample for an image sequence of length 5 for $|y_0| \leq 10\,\mathrm{m}$ safety property.

5.1   Counterexamples

The generation of scenarios where the plane can run out of the runway is very useful for debugging and improving the network. However, it is a challenge to generate a scenario that is realistic or is plausible to occur in a close loop system, using just the neural network model. We describe in this section how we use the counterexamples reported by Marabou for the failed proofs of the patterns to generate such scenarios.

Recall that the pattern for correct behavior in the check $\forall x \in [x_{min}, x_{max}] \wedge$ $pattern_{class=1} \Rightarrow |y_0| \leq \theta$, represents the neuron activations that are satisfied by valid inputs within $[x_{min}, x_{max}]$, that also satisfy the output safety property. A counterexample to this proof represents an input that is similar to the other valid images in the sequence and hence has similar context. It also satisfies $pattern_{class=1}$, which is a temporal invariant of the system over the given sequence of valid images. This increases the chances of this image not being a random input, but an image that is possible to occur in the sequence.

We illustrate such a counterexample scenario showing the first and last image of a sequence and the generated counterexample image in the downsampled input space of TinyNet in Figs. 8 and 9. In order to better understand the counterexample, we mapped it back to the original input space, denoted as 'upsampled counterexample' in Figs. 8 and 9. The check was formulated as follows; $\forall x \in [x_{min}, x_{max}] \wedge pattern(x) \Rightarrow |y_0| \leq 10.0$ m. Here the pattern represents the activation pattern for the satisfaction of the safety property $|y_0| \leq 10.0$ m and all the images in the sequence satisfy this pattern.

Marabou solves the check to find a counterexample to the given constraint. To map the counterexample image back to the original input space, we leverage input sequences again and we find the closest downsampled image from the image sequence to use the regular version as the reference. We modify the segment of the image used in downsampling to match the brightness of the image to the counterexample we have. Some downsampling operations done by TinyNet are irreversible, for that reason our method creates an upsampled counterexample image that is very close to the original counterexample when downsampled.

We are able to generate counterexamples with Marabou in 19 out of 58 sequences of minimum length of 2 images for the constraint $\forall x \in [x_{min}, x_{max}] \wedge$ $pattern(x) \Rightarrow |y_0| \leq 10$ m in a labeled dataset of downsampled images of size 7385 and our upsampling satisfies the pattern in 17 out of 19 counterexamples.

6   Related Work

Existing formal verification techniques for neural networks have focused on verifying input-output properties of neural network models using approaches such as the simplex method, mixed integer linear programming, and symbolic interval analysis [14–18]. Recent work has attempted to prove properties of models used in safety-critical applications such aircraft collision avoidance policies [9]. However, when the input dimensionality is high such as in the case of perception networks, most existing work has only been able to provide local adversarial robustness guarantees.

The work presented in [19] considers the TinyNet model that we also consider here, for the purpose of centering the plane on the runway. It employs Marabou to provide local adversarial robustness guarantees; specifically it ensures that given an input X and its respective model output Y, for all inputs within a certain distance or in the neighborhood of X, the network produces output values that are within a certain distance of Y. The work reported in [13] presents a method that searches for sequences of image disturbances that to lead to failure in the aircraft taxiway application using TinyNet model in a closed-loop system. The method employs local robustness verification techniques along with adaptive stress testing and simulation to search for such sequences. In contrast, our approach only involves the analysis of the neural network to find problematic scenarios.

Most existing work on explaining neural network behavior focuses on explaining the behavior of classification models [6,11,20–23] and is based on class activations, perturbations or gradients. The recent work in [24] presents a database and an experimental setup to quantitatively evaluate techniques for explaining model behavior. It highlights that techniques used traditionally for classification networks do not work well for regression problems. They tend to produce noisy and inconsistent results. The paper proposes a new technique for explaining regression model outputs, which averages out results from different training runs of the model. The technique seems to produce better explanations than existing techniques, however, it is very expensive in practice. In our work, we show how we could use the activation patterns computed with respect to the output properties of regression models to represent the regression problem as a classification, thereby enabling the use of existing techniques for explainability.

7 Lessons Learned and Applications

We have found that while there is vast literature on attribution techniques for classification models there is much less work on providing explanations for regression models, and none that aims to generalize said explanations across multiple inputs. More research is needed for finding explanations in regression models. Another take-away from our experiments is that it may be better to build neural networks which are verifiable by design. We were able to obtain proofs on the smaller TinyNet network for the safety properties, however, we were unable to use existing solvers to obtain proofs for the more complex ACT model.

We envision several applications for the activation patterns that are mined with our approach. First, the activation patterns can be used for reducing redundancy in the training data set. For patterns that lead to correct behaviour and have very high support, this may be an indication that the images are redundant and can be removed from the trainset, leading to faster training time with similar accuracy. Similarly, patterns mined for incorrect behaviour can contribute to trainset augmentation by identifying input areas requiring more training. The counter-example scenarios could also be used to debug and improving the network by adversarial re-training.

Second, we envision using the patterns for correctness properties in a *predictive manner* at runtime, to determine how confident the network is in its prediction. In real-world decision making systems, neural networks must not only be accurate, but also should indicate when they are likely to be incorrect. While there are related works that attempt to provide a measure of *confidence* in the network outputs, we find that they are again limited to classification problems (see e.g. [25]). Our patterns can potentially provide a solution (albeit partial) to regression models.

Finally, another avenue for further research is to use more information from the simulator to obtain explanations of the network behavior in terms of the semantic features used by the image renderer, thereby enabling the generation of rules over these features that may help test, debug and improve the model (see the work based on SCENIC [26]).

8 Conclusion and Next Steps

In this paper, we presented an industrial case study applying a recently proposed technique, Prophecy, to analyze the behavior of neural network models used for autonomous guiding of airplanes on taxi runways. We showed the usefulness of the patterns extracted by Prophecy to identify features of the input that explain correct and incorrect behavior. We also used the patterns to obtain proofs for the satisfaction of safety requirements. We explored a novel idea of using sequences of images (instead of single images) to obtain good explanations and identify regions of consistent behavior.

This is our first effort to apply Prophecy on aviation applications. Other visual perception applications will also be considered in the future, such as autonomous takeoff or landing, detect and avoid, object detection and identification. We will further explore definitions of confidence and coverage for these analyses. Confidence and coverage, built on analyses with formal methods and/or statistical methods, will provide quantitative support to artificial intelligence (AI) trustworthiness and potential certification of AI-enabled systems. Our future research also includes using design time analysis results during operations via runtime monitors. Pre-recorded activation patterns can be used by the monitors to identify or predict potential safety violations for unseen images.

References

1. Gopinath, D., Converse, H., Pasareanu, C., Taly, A.: Property inference for deep neural networks. In: 34th International Conference on Automated Software Engineering (ASE), pp. 797–809. IEEE (2019)
2. Beland, S., et al.: Towards assurance evaluation of autonomous systems. In: ICCAD (2020)
3. Frew, E., et al.: Vision-based road-following using a small autonomous aircraft. In: 2004 IEEE Aerospace Conference Proceedings (IEEE Cat. No. 04TH8720), vol. 5, pp. 3006–3015 (2004)
4. X-plane flight simulator. https://www.x-plane.com/
5. Shrikumar, A., Greenside, P., Kundaje, A.: Learning important features through propagating activation differences. In: Proceedings of the 34th International Conference on Machine Learning, ICML 2017, Sydney, NSW, Australia, 6–11 August 2017, pp. 3145–3153 (2017)

6. Ribeiro, M.T., Singh, S., Guestrin, C.: Why should i trust you?: Explaining the predictions of any classifier. In: Proceedings of the 22nd ACM SIGKDD International Conference on Knowledge Discovery and Data Mining, San Francisco, CA, USA, 13–17 August, pp. 1135–1144 (2016)

7. Nohara, Y., Matsumoto, K., Soejima, H., Nakashima, N.: Explanation of machine learning models using improved Shapley additive explanation. In: Proceedings of the 10th ACM International Conference on Bioinformatics, Computational Biology and Health Informatics, BCB 2019, Niagara Falls, NY, USA, 7–10 September 2019, p. 546 (2019)

8. Katz, G., Barrett, C., Dill, D.L., Julian, K., Kochenderfer, M.J.: Towards proving the adversarial robustness of deep neural networks. In: Proceedings First Workshop on Formal Verification of Autonomous Vehicles, FVAV@iFM 2017, Turin, Italy, 19th September, 2017, pp. 19–26 (2017)

9. Julian, K.D., Kochenderfer, M.J.: Guaranteeing safety for neural network-based aircraft collision avoidance systems, CoRR, vol. abs/1912.07084 (2019)

10. Chattopadhay, A., Sarkar, A., Howlader, P., Balasubramanian, V.N.: Grad-cam++: generalized gradient-based visual explanations for deep convolutional networks. In: 2018 IEEE Winter Conference on Applications of Computer Vision (WACV), pp. 839–847. IEEE (2018)

11. Selvaraju, R.R., Cogswell, M., Das, A., Vedantam, R., Parikh, D., Batra, D.: Grad-CAM: visual explanations from deep networks via gradient-based localization. Int. J. Comput. Vis. **128**(2), 336–359 (2020)

12. Katz, G., et al.: The Marabou framework for verification and analysis of deep neural networks. In: Dillig, I., Tasiran, S. (eds.) CAV 2019. LNCS, vol. 11561, pp. 443–452. Springer, Cham (2019). https://doi.org/10.1007/978-3-030-25540-4_26

13. Julian, K.D., Lee, R., Kochenderfer, M.J.: Validation of image-based neural network controllers through adaptive stress testing. In: 23rd IEEE International Conference on Intelligent Transportation Systems, ITSC 2020, Rhodes, Greece, 20–23 September, pp. 1–7 (2020)

14. Akintunde, M., Lomuscio, A., Maganti, L., Pirovano, E.: Reachability analysis for neural agent-environment systems. In: Principles of Knowledge Representation and Reasoning: Proceedings of the Sixteenth International Conference, KR 2018, Tempe, Arizona, 30 October–2 November 2018, pp. 184–193 (2018)

15. Wang, S., Pei, K., Whitehouse, J., Yang, J., Jana, S.: Efficient formal safety analysis of neural networks. In: Advances in Neural Information Processing Systems 31: Annual Conference on Neural Information Processing Systems 2018, NeurIPS 2018, Montréal, Canada, 3–8 December 2018, pp. 6369–6379 (2018)

16. Liu, C., Arnon, T., Lazarus, C., Strong, C.A., Barrett, C.W., Kochenderfer, M.J.: Algorithms for verifying deep neural networks. Found. Trends Optim. **4**(3–4), 244–404 (2021)

17. Ivanov, R., Weimer, J., Alur, R., Pappas, G.J., Lee, I.: Verisig: verifying safety properties of hybrid systems with neural network controllers, CoRR, vol. abs/1811.01828 (2018)

18. Yang, X., Tran, H.D., Xiang, W., Johnson, T.: Reachability analysis for feed-forward neural networks using face lattices, CoRR, vol. abs/2003.01226 (2020)

19. Wu, H., et al.: Parallelization techniques for verifying neural networks. In: 2020 Formal Methods in Computer Aided Design, FMCAD 2020, Haifa, Israel, 21–24 September 2020, pp. 128–137 (2020)

20. Zhou, B., Khosla, A., Lapedriza, À., Oliva, A., Torralba, A.: Learning deep features for discriminative localization. In: 2016 IEEE Conference on Computer Vision and Pattern Recognition, CVPR 2016, Las Vegas, NV, USA, 27–30 June 2016, pp. 2921–2929 (2016)
21. Patro, B.N., Lunayach, M., Patel, S., Namboodiri, V.P.: U-CAM: visual explanation using uncertainty based class activation maps, CoRR, vol. abs/1908.06306 (2019)
22. Zeiler, M.D., Fergus, R.: Visualizing and understanding convolutional networks. In: Fleet, D., Pajdla, T., Schiele, B., Tuytelaars, T. (eds.) ECCV 2014. LNCS, vol. 8689, pp. 818–833. Springer, Cham (2014). https://doi.org/10.1007/978-3-319-10590-1_53
23. Simonyan, K., Vedaldi, A., Zisserman, A.: Deep inside convolutional networks: visualising image classification models and saliency maps. In: Bengio, Y., LeCun, Y. (eds.) 2nd International Conference on Learning Representations, ICLR 2014, Banff, AB, Canada, 14–16 April 2014, Workshop Track Proceedings (2014)
24. Millan, M., Achard, C.: Explaining regression based neural network model, CoRR, vol. abs/2004.06918 (2020)
25. Guo, C., Pleiss, G., Sun, Y., Weinberger, K.Q.: On calibration of modern neural networks, CoRR, vol. abs/1706.04599 (2017). http://arxiv.org/abs/1706.04599
26. Kim, E., Gopinath, D., Pasareanu, C., Seshia, S.A.: A programmatic and semantic approach to explaining and debugging neural network based object detectors. In: 2020 IEEE/CVF Conference on Computer Vision and Pattern Recognition, CVPR 2020, Seattle, WA, USA, 13–19 June 2020, pp. 11 125–11 134 (2020)

Abstract Interpretation of LLVM
with a Region-Based Memory Model

Arie Gurfinkel[1]([⊠]) and Jorge A. Navas[2]([⊠])

[1] University of Waterloo, Waterloo, Canada
arie.gurfinkel@uwaterloo.ca
[2] SRI International, Menlo Park, USA
jorge.navas@sri.com

Abstract. Static analysis of low-level programs (C or LLVM) requires
modeling memory. To strike a good balance between precision and performance, most static analyzers rely on the C memory model in which
a pointer is a numerical offset within a memory object. Finite partitioning of the address space is a common abstraction. For instance,
the *allocation-site* abstraction creates partitions by merging all objects
created at the same allocation site. *Recency* abstraction refines the
allocation-site abstraction by distinguishing the most recent allocated
memory object from the previous ones. Unfortunately, these abstractions
are not often precise enough to infer invariants that are expressed over
the contents of dynamically allocated data-structures such as linked lists.
In those cases, more expensive abstractions such as *shapes* that consider
connectivity patterns between memory locations are often needed.

Instead of resorting to expensive memory abstractions, we propose
a new memory model, called *region-based memory model* (*RBMM*).
RBMM is a refinement of the C memory model in which pointers have
an extra component called *regions*. Thus, a memory object can spawn
multiple regions which can greatly limit aliasing since regions are pairwise disjoint. Since RBMM requires that each memory instruction refers
explicitly to a region, we first present a new intermediate representation
(IR) based on regions which is the input of our abstract interpreter CRAB.
Second, we show how abstractions such as allocation-site and recency can
be easily adapted to RBMM. Third, we evaluate CRAB using our new
IR and a simple allocation-site abstraction on widely-used C projects.

1 Introduction

One of the most difficult problems in Abstract Interpretation of a low-level language, such as C or LLVM, is modeling memory. An abstract interpreter must
strike a balance between a model that is sufficiently abstract to allow for efficient
analysis, yet sufficiently precise to reduce false positives. Abstracting memory

Jorge A. Navas has been supported in part by NSF grant 1816936. We also acknowl-
edge the support of the Natural Sciences and Engineering Research Council of Canada
(NSERC).

R. Bloem et al. (Eds.): NSV 2021/VSTTE 2021, LNCS 13124, pp. 122–144, 2022.
https://doi.org/10.1007/978-3-030-95561-8_8

consists of partitioning the unbounded number of concrete memory objects at run-time into a finite set of abstract objects, sometimes, further sub-divided into fields. Popular memory abstractions vary from cheaply *smashing* all memory objects originated from the same *allocation site* into a summarized abstract object to more precise but expensive modeling of connectivity between objects allowing to reason about *shapes*. In between, abstractions that partition memory by the *recency* of the objects are also popular because they can allow to distinguish objects allocated in different loop iterations while still being efficient to compute.

In this paper, we focus on Abstract Interpretation of general-purpose, modern (portable) C programs. Our goal is to compute non-trivial invariants that involve both scalar variables and values stored in memory for programs that allocate memory dynamically. We propose a new memory model, called *region-based memory model* (RBMM), which can boost the precision of existing memory abstractions such as smashing[1] and recency while retaining their efficiency.

RBMM partitions memory into a finite set of *regions*. In its simplest form, a *region* is a set of memory objects. More generally, a region is a set of slices (i.e., contiguous sub-fields) of objects. A *reference*[2] is an offset within a memory object refined with a region. In RBMM, all regions are pairwise disjoint and, therefore, a write into one region cannot affect data stored in another region. In this paper, we show that an abstract interpreter based on RBMM can infer interesting properties on realistic programs that manipulate dynamically allocated data structures using very simple memory abstractions such as smashing.

Our approach consists of the following steps: (1) translate the C program into LLVM bitcode and apply a whole-program pointer analysis on the LLVM program so that memory is statically partitioned into regions. The analysis also identifies which parts of the program might not satisfy the assumptions of our memory model; (2) translate the LLVM program into a novel intermediate-representation (IR), called CRABIR, where all LLVM memory instructions are translated to instructions over regions and references; (3) run the CRAB abstract interpreter on the CRABIR program.

We argue that having a specialized IR (CRABIR) for our memory model poses several advantages. First, we separate the source language (LLVM in this case) from the language analyzed by the abstract interpreter. This makes the abstract interpreter reusable as long as the memory model is compatible. Second, the use of CRABIR simplifies the design of the abstract interpreter without jeopardising precision. In CRABIR, each memory instruction is explicitly defined over regions. This allows the abstract interpreter to reason about memory contents without necessarily a complex memory abstract domain. Nevertheless, the precision of the analysis in this case would depend on how precise is the pointer analysis from Step 1. In a pessimistic scenario, all the memory instructions can be mapped to

---

[1] In this paper, we use the terms *smashing* and *allocation-site* interchangeably.

[2] Usually, the term *reference* is used as an alias for an address that precludes pointer arithmetic. We do not place such a restriction. We use reference as an alternative to *pointer*, to stress that a reference belongs to a statically known region.

a single region. For those cases, more complex memory abstractions (e.g., [20]) can be used. Third, our multi-step approach allows us to benefit from the active area of pointer analysis of LLVM (e.g., SeaDsa [14,19], SVF [24]) saving us from dealing with all the intricacies of the LLVM pointer semantics.

Assumptions of RBMM. The soundness of RBMM relies on two key assumptions: (1) memory is *word-addressable*[3], and (2) programs do not exhibit *undefined behaviour* (UB) under C11 standard. The former highly simplifies the semantics of CRABIR and the abstract transfer functions. The latter allows to restrict aliasing by assuming that the strict aliasing rules are always satisfied (the effective type of a *lvalue* must be compatible[4] with the effective type of the object being accessed). Moreover, absence of UB allows our analysis to use abstractions such as smashing by assuming, for instance, that a memory read can only access to initialized data. Although it may seem counter-intuitive, this assumption does not limit our analysis from proving absence of UB. As shown by Conway et al. [8], conditionally sound analyses can prove absence of errors (e.g., memory violations) or otherwise, produce one counterexample although it cannot produce all possible counterexamples. Informally, this means that we can still use our analysis to find the first instruction that causes UB. If the analysis does not find such an instruction then the analysis proves soundly that UB is not possible. In Sect. 7, we show that these assumptions are reasonable and not too restrictive for the analysis of modern C programs.

Contributions. In summary, the contributions of this paper are: (1) A memory model based on regions that refines the C memory model (Sect. 3). (2) Describe the syntax and concrete semantics of a new intermediate representation called CRABIR, based on RBMM (Sect. 4 and Sect. 5). (3) Adapt abstractions such as smashing and recency to our RBMM (Sect. 6). (4) An implementation in the CRAB (https://github.com/seahorn/crab) abstract interpretation library and empirical evidence of the practicality of our approach on a set of widely-used C projects (Sect. 7).

2   Motivating Example

In this section, we motivate the benefits of our memory model using an example program shown in Fig. 1. Note that while our tool works at the level of LLVM intermediate representation, we present the example in C for readability.

Our analysis understands three special functions: `int_nd` returns an integer chosen non-deterministically; `assume(b)` blocks if the condition b is false, and,

---

[3] Memory is *word-addressable* if all reads and writes access to the same, fixed amount of bytes (the CPU word length). Note that any C program can be ported to word-addressable memory by adding extra instructions that fill a word with empty bytes before a memory write or extract some bytes from a word after a memory read.

[4] Informally, casting any pointer to a `char*` type is allowed but the opposite is not. Moreover, signedness and constness do not affect the strict aliasing rules.

```
1   typedef struct node{
2     int   *data;
3     size_t len; size_t cap;
4     struct node *n;
5   } *List;
6
7   int* init(size_t sz, int val) {
8     int* data =
9       (int*)malloc(sizeof(int)*sz);
10    assume(data > 0);
11    for (int i=0;i<sz;++i)
12      data[i] = val;
13    return data;
14  }
15  List mk_list(size_t list_sz,
              size_t data_sz, int val) {
16    List l = 0;
17    for(size_t i=0;i<list_sz;i++){
18      List tmp = (List)malloc(sizeof
                (struct node));
19      assume(tmp > 0);
20      tmp->data = init(data_sz,val);
21      int used = int_nd();
22      assume(used>=0);
23      assume(used<data_sz);
24      tmp->len = used;
25      tmp->cap = data_sz;
26      tmp->n = l ;
27      l = tmp;
28    }
29    return l;
30  }
```

```
31  void main() {
32    // Create a linked-list
33    size_t list_sz = int_nd();
34    size_t data_sz = int_nd();
35    int val = int_nd();
36    List node = mk_list(list_sz,
            data_sz, val);
37
38    // Check properties
39    for(;node;node=node->n) {
40      sassert(node->data > 0);
41      sassert(node->len < data_sz);
42      sassert(node->len <= node->cap);
43
44        sassert(node->data[i] == val);
45    }
46  }
```

Fig. 1. C program that creates a linked-list and checks some properties.

otherwise, restricts the execution by setting b to true; and, sassert(b) *statically* reports an error if b is false, or it behaves as assume(b) otherwise.

In the example, struct node defines the type of a node of a singly linked list with a pointer n pointing to the next node in the list. The node has also some data (data) defined as an array of integers. The field cap is the amount of space allocated (capacity) for data and the field len is the number of actual bytes held in the node which is not necessarily equal to cap. First, the program creates an unbounded, non-empty linked list of list_sz nodes and for each node it creates some data of capacity data_sz (lines 33–36). Both the contents of the data and its length are chosen non-deterministically. Lines 22–23 ensures that len is always less than cap. Second, the program iterates over the linked list (lines 39–45) and checks for the following four properties:

1. (Line 40) For every node n in the list, n→data is not null.
2. (Line 41) For every node n in the list, n→len is less than data_sz.
3. (Line 42) For every node n in the list, n→len is less or equal than n→cap.
4. (Line 44) For every node n in the list, $\forall i :: $ n→data[i] == val.

This program is challenging for automatic static analysis tools. In fact, mature abstract interpreters such as Infer [6] and IKOS [5] fail to prove more than one of the four properties. The reason is that the analyzer needs to reason

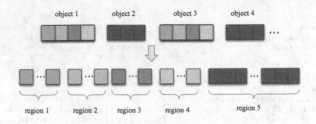

Fig. 2. The C versus the region-based memory model.

about two difficult but different aspects. First, it needs to quantify over all nodes of the linked list. Second, it requires inferring numerical relationships between the contents of the linked list. None of the above-mentioned tools can do both.

We argue that these properties should not be hard to prove automatically without resorting to complex memory abstractions. All properties rely on the fact that they uniformly hold on every node in the linked list (Property 1–3) or every array `data` element (Property 4). Smashing or recency do not work because each node of the linked list consists of two different groups of fields: the data (`cap`, `len`, and `data`) and the pointer to the next node (`n`). Smashing both groups make the analysis unable to infer anything about the linked list.

RBMM partitions memory in such a way that smashing alone[5] can prove the four properties. Using an inexpensive flow-insensitive pointer analysis, our memory model partitions memory into four regions: one for every field in the linked list node. This is what makes smashing to be successful in proving all the properties because, properties about the next pointer are not mixed with the other fields, and properties among `cap`, `len`, and `data` are also kept separate.

3   Standard C versus Region-Based Memory Model

A memory model defines the semantics of pointers together with the assumptions that are made about how memory is addressed. We start by defining the most popular memory model for C programs, which we call the standard C memory model, and then we define our new region-based memory model (RBMM).

In the standard C memory model, a pointer is of type $\mathrm{ptr} = \mathcal{O} \times \mathbb{Z}$. That is, a pointer is a pair of a memory object and a numerical offset of integer type. $\mathcal{O}$ is the countable infinite set of memory objects. A memory object is a sequence of bytes. Pointer arithmetic or pointer comparison involving pointers from different memory objects is undefined. For instance, consider Line 18 in Fig. 1. Let us assume that each field of `struct node` occupies 8 bytes. Consider the first loop iteration ($i = 0$). The `malloc` instruction allocates a memory object o_{l20}^0 of 32 bytes (the superscript indicates the loop iteration and the subscript the line number of the allocation site). Then, `tmp->data`, `tmp->len`, `tmp->cap` and `tmp->n` are the pointers $\langle o_{l20}^0, 0 \rangle$, $\langle o_{l20}^0, 8 \rangle$, $\langle o_{l20}^0, 16 \rangle$, and $\langle o_{l20}^0, 24 \rangle$, respectively.

---

[5] CRAB proves the four properties using smashing abstraction and unrolling the loop one iteration. Finite loop unrolling would not help Infer and IKOS.

In RBMM, a pointer has an extra component, called a *region*. In the rest, we use the term "reference" instead of "pointer" to make clear that we refer to a pointer in the RBMM. A *reference* is of type ref $= \mathcal{R} \times \mathcal{O} \times \mathbb{Z}$, where $\mathcal{R}$ is the finite set of regions. In its simplest form, a region is a set (possibly singleton) of memory objects. More generally, a memory object can span multiple regions. That is, different object fields (i.e., subsequence of bytes) can be in different regions. Therefore, in general, a region represents field values of a set of objects.

In RBMM, every memory operation must indicate explicitly which region it is accessing. Since each memory operation indicates a region, accessing memory with a reference from a different region is undefined. To make RBMM compatible with the C memory model, pointer arithmetic and pointer comparison is allowed between references from different regions but they must point to the same memory object. Moreover, RBMM requires that no memory access can span multiple regions. Thus, every memory access must be a word and the partitioning of memory into regions must be done at the word level so that each region contain a multiple number of words. Note that in practice, this is also often required by most hardware platforms, and any potentially unaligned memory access is compiled into multiple aligned accesses. A key property in RBMM is that two references cannot alias if they point to different regions.

Back to Fig. 1, let us assume that in RBMM there are 4 regions $\{r_1, r_2, r_3, r_4\}$. Assume also that each field of struct node belongs to one of these regions. The loop at lines 17–28 might allocate multiple memory objects o_{l20}^i, where $0 \leq i < n$ is the loop counter. Then, tmp->data, tmp->len, tmp->cap and tmp->n hold the references $\{\langle r_1, o_{l20}^0, 0\rangle, \ldots, \langle r_1, o_{l20}^{n-1}, 0\rangle\}$, $\{\langle r_2, o_{l20}^0, 8\rangle, \ldots, \langle r_2, o_{l20}^{n-1}, 8\rangle\}$, $\{\langle r_3, o_{l20}^0, 16\rangle, \ldots, \langle r_3, o_{l20}^{n-1}, 16\rangle\}$, and $\{\langle r_4, o_{l20}^0, 24\rangle, \ldots, \langle r_4, o_{l20}^{n-1}, 24\rangle\}$, respectively.

The main differences between the two memory models are illustrated in Fig. 2. At the top, we show how memory is represented by the C memory model. Memory can be seen as a collection of memory objects. Each memory object is a sequence of consecutive bytes. At the bottom, we show how memory is organized under RBMM. The same combination of colors represents that the memory object is originated at the same allocation site. In this example, we assume that there are only two allocation sites (as_1 and as_2). Objects 1 and 3 (2 and 4) are allocated at as_1 (as_2). The first key difference is that the number of regions is finite. To achieve this, many (possibly infinite) objects are grouped into a single region (e.g., objects 2, 4, and any other object originated from as_2 into region 5). The second difference is that fields of the same memory object (represented with different colors) can be grouped into different regions. For instance, the green and yellow slices from object 1 are mapped to regions 1 and 3.

In conclusion, RBMM can be seen as a refinement of the standard C model by clustering together an unbounded number of object fields into a finite number of regions. As a result, RBMM can greatly simplify the design of abstract domains since two references cannot alias if they belong to different regions. On the other hand, RBMM does not impede the use of more precise memory abstractions since RBMM is compatible with the C memory model.

$$
\begin{array}{ll}
P & ::= F^* \\
F & ::= \texttt{declare } fun(v^*)\ B^+ \\
B & ::= \texttt{label} : S^*\ \texttt{goto label}^+\ | \\
  & \quad\ \ \texttt{label} : S^*\ \texttt{return } v^* \\
S & ::= S_{int}\ |\ S_{bool}\ |\ S_{rgn} \\
  & \quad\ \ [\ v^+ :=]\ \texttt{call } fun(v^*)\ | \\
  & \quad\ \ v := \texttt{havoc}()\ | \\
  & \quad\ \ \texttt{assume}(v_b)\ |\ \texttt{sassert}(v_b) \\
S_{int} & ::= v_i := aexp \\
S_{bool} & ::= v_b := bexp \\
aexp & ::= n\ |\ v_i\ |\ a_1\ op_a\ a_n \\
bexp & ::= \texttt{true}\ |\ \texttt{false}\ |\ \neg\ b\ |\ b_1\ op_b\ b_2\ | \\
  & \quad\ \ a_1\ op_r\ a_2\ |\ b_{ref}
\end{array}
$$

$$
\begin{array}{ll}
S_{rgn} & ::= v_{rgn} := \texttt{initrgn}()\ | \\
  & \quad\ \ v_{ref} := \texttt{makeref}(v_{rgn}, v_i)\ | \\
  & \quad\ \ \texttt{freeref}(v_{rgn}, v_{ref})\ | \\
  & \quad\ \ (v_{rgn}, v_{ref}) := \texttt{gepref}(v_{rgn},\ v_{ref}, v_i)\ | \\
  & \quad\ \ v_s := \texttt{loadref}(v_{rgn},\ v_{ref})\ | \\
  & \quad\ \ \texttt{storeref}(v_{rgn},\ v_{ref},\ v_s)\ | \\
  & \quad\ \ v_i := \texttt{reftoint}(v_{rgn},\ v_{ref})\ | \\
  & \quad\ \ v_{ref} := \texttt{inttoref}(v_{rgn}, v_i) \\
b_{ref} & ::= v_{ref}\ op_r\ v_{ref}\ |\ \texttt{isnull}(v_{ref})
\end{array}
$$

Fig. 3. CRABIR: Region-based intermediate representation.

4   CRABIR: An Intermediate Representation for RBMM

In RBMM, every memory operation must explicitly indicate on which region the memory access is taking place. This motivates us to introduce a new intermediate representation called CRABIR. In this section, we describe the main aspects of CRABIR which is the input of the CRAB abstract interpreter. In Sect. 5, we present its concrete semantics.

The simplified syntax[6] of CRABIR is shown in Fig. 3. A program P consists of a set of functions. A function consists of a name, zero or more input arguments, and a non-empty sequence of basic blocks. A basic block is denoted by a unique identifier label, containing zero or more statements S in three-address form. Each block must be terminated by either a goto or a return statement. The former is accompanied by one or more labels for each successor while the latter by zero or more output parameters of the function. Statements can only be one of these kinds: integers S_{int}, Booleans S_{bool}, and regions S_{rgn}. All statements are strongly typed. Integer, Boolean, reference, and region variables are denoted with symbols v_i, v_b, v_{ref}, v_{rgn}, respectively. Variables of any type are denoted by v. Scalar (non-region) variables are denoted by v_s. Integer variables are sized (i.e., of different bit-width). Control flow is modeled by goto and assume statements. The statement $v := \texttt{havoc}()$ assigns non-deterministically any value allowed by v's type to v. Properties can only be defined by adding sassert statements. The syntax of S_{int} and S_{bool} is self explanatory. Integer and Boolean expressions are described by $aexp$ and $bexp$.

We describe now informally the non-standard region statements. Detailed concrete semantics is given in Sect. 5. A key feature in CRABIR is that the language enforces that each reference is always associated uniquely to a region variable. Region variables must be initialized before used by calling initrgn. Reference variables can be created and destroyed by calling makeref and freeref, respectively. loadref reads the content of the reference v_{ref} within the region denoted by v_{rgn}, and assigns it to the scalar variable v_s. storeref writes the

---

[6] For instance, integer casts and casts between Boolean and integers are omitted.

value of v_s in the memory address pointed by v_{ref} within the region v_{rgn}. **gepref** performs pointer arithmetic. This is similar to the LLVM **getelementptr** instruction but it has been adapted to RBMM. **gepref** generates a new reference from adding an offset v_i (third input parameter) to the base reference v_{ref} (second input parameter). The region associated to the base reference must be provided (first input parameter). **gepref** has two output parameters: the new reference and its region. The key aspect of **gepref** is that it allows "switching" from one region to another as long as the references point to the same memory object. References can be compared to each other and to the null constant (b_{ref}). Finally, CRABIR allows to convert between references and integers (**inttoref** and **reftoint**). We show the translation of our example from Sect. 2 in Appendix A.

5   A Concrete Semantics for CRABIR

The goal of this section is twofold. First, it gives a formal meaning of the region statements in CRABIR by presenting a concrete interpreter. Second, it constitutes the basis for the structural abstractions presented in Sect. 6. By structural, we mean that each sub-component of a concrete state is separately abstracted.

Recall our memory model is *word-addressable* which means that all data location has the same size and all memory addresses are divisible by the *word size*, which is a fixed parameter in our model. Figure 4 defines the semantic domain to express the concrete semantics of CRABIR. The symbols $\mathcal{V_B}$, $\mathcal{V_I}$, $\mathcal{V_{Ref}}$, and $\mathcal{V_{Rgn}}$ denote the set of Boolean, integer, reference, and region variables such that $\mathcal{V_B} \cap \mathcal{V_I} \cap \mathcal{V_{Ref}} \cap \mathcal{V_{Rgn}} = \emptyset$. Memory is partitioned into a finite, disjoint set of regions. Each region is accessible by a handle $v \in \mathcal{V_{Rgn}}$. An *address* is an integer. A *reference* is an address within a region. The data associated with a reference is called a cell. A cell can represent either another reference or an integer value. A *cell* is a pair of the form of $\langle b, o \rangle$. If a cell represents a reference then b is a base address and o is a numerical offset. A cell can be trivially converted to an address (cell2Addr in Appendix B, Fig. 13). The special null reference is encoded as $\langle 0, 0 \rangle$. If a cell represents an integer k then it is encoded as $\langle 0, k \rangle$[7]. Note that since memory is word-addressable, the size of a cell is always the word size, and thus, it is omitted from the concrete semantics. A *valid* program state $\sigma \in$ State is represented by the tuple: $\langle refEnv, rgnEnv, numEnv, nextAddr, rgnAddrs, alloc \rangle$

The environment *refEnv* maps reference variables to cells. The content of a region is modeled by a map *rgnEnv* from addresses to cells. *numEnv* maps Boolean or integer variables to their values. The program state maintains the next available address (*nextAddr*), and for each region, the program state keeps track of all addresses owned by a region (*rgnAddrs*). The state also keeps track of all *allocated* memory objects (*alloc*) by keeping a list of pairs of: the base address and the past-the-end address of the object. *alloc* is mostly used for error checking and for converting addresses to cells (addr2Cell in Appendix B, Fig. 13). We use the symbol σ_Ω to denote either a valid state $\sigma \in$ State or the error state Ω. The semantics for statements is given by the function $[\![.]\!]_\Omega(.) : S \mapsto \sigma_\Omega \mapsto \sigma_\Omega$:

---

[7] Note that the cell $\langle 0, 0 \rangle$ can either mean the null reference or the integer 0.

$$
\begin{array}{llll}
\{a, nextAddr\} & \subseteq \text{Address} & = & \mathbb{Z} \\
c & \in \text{Cell} & = & \text{Address} \times \mathbb{Z} \\
refEnv & \in \text{RefEnv} & = & \mathcal{V}_{Ref} \mapsto \text{Cell} \\
rgnEnv & \in \text{RgnEnv} & = & \mathcal{V}_{Rgn} \mapsto (\text{Cell} \mapsto \text{Cell}) \\
numEnv & \in \text{NumEnv} & = & (\mathcal{V}_B \cup \mathcal{V}_I) \mapsto \mathbb{Z} \\
rgnAddrs & \in \text{RgnToAddrs} & = & \mathcal{V}_{Rgn} \mapsto 2^{\text{Address}} \\
\{objList, alloc\} & \subseteq \text{MemObjList} & = & \text{List}(\text{Address} \times \text{Address}) \\
\sigma & \in \text{State} & = & \text{RefEnv} \times \text{RgnEnv} \times \text{NumEnv} \times \\
& & & \text{Address} \times \text{RgnToAddrs} \times \text{MemObjList}
\end{array}
$$

Fig. 4. Semantic domains.

$[\![rgn := \texttt{initrgn}()]\!](\sigma) \equiv$

$\texttt{match } \sigma \texttt{ with } (refEnv, rgnEnv, numEnv, nextAddr, rgnAddrs, alloc) \rightarrow$
    $\texttt{if } isInitRegion(\sigma, rgn) \texttt{ then } \sigma$
    $\texttt{else } (refEnv, rgnEnv, numEnv, nextAddr, rgnAddrs[rgn \mapsto \emptyset], alloc)$

$[\![ref := \texttt{makeref}(rgn, n)]\!](\sigma) \equiv$

$\texttt{match } \sigma \texttt{ with } (refEnv, rgnEnv, numEnv, nextAddr, rgnAddrs, alloc) \rightarrow$
    $\texttt{if } \neg\, isInitRegion(\sigma, rgn) \texttt{ or } [\![n]\!](\sigma) \leq 0 \texttt{ then } \Omega$
    $\texttt{else}$
        $\texttt{let } \langle base, sz \rangle := \langle nextAddr, [\![n]\!](\sigma) \rangle \texttt{ in}$
        $\texttt{let } refEnv' = refEnv[ref \mapsto \langle base, 0 \rangle] \texttt{ in}$
        $\texttt{let } nextAddr' = base + sz \texttt{ in}$
        $\texttt{let } rgnAddrs' = rgnAddrs[rgn \mapsto rgnAddrs(rgn) \cup \{base\}] \texttt{ in}$
        $\texttt{let } alloc' = \langle base, base + sz \rangle :: alloc \texttt{ in}$
        $(refEnv', rgnEnv, numEnv, nextAddr', rgnAddrs', alloc')$

$[\![\texttt{freeref}(rgn, ref)]\!](\sigma) \equiv$

$\texttt{match } \sigma \texttt{ with } (refEnv, rgnEnv, numEnv, nextAddr, rgnAddrs, alloc) \rightarrow$
    $\texttt{if } ref \notin dom(refEnv) \texttt{ or } \neg\, isInList(refEnv(ref), alloc) \texttt{ then } \Omega$
    $\texttt{else}$
        $\texttt{match } removeFromList(refEnv(ref), alloc) \texttt{ with}$
            $\Omega \rightarrow \Omega$
            $alloc' \rightarrow (refEnv, rgnEnv, numEnv, nextAddr, rgnAddrs, alloc')$

$[\![(rgn_2, ref_2) := \texttt{gepref}(rgn_1, ref_1, n)]\!](\sigma) \equiv$

$\texttt{match } \sigma \texttt{ with } (refEnv, rgnEnv, numEnv, nextAddr, rgnAddrs, alloc) \rightarrow$
    $\texttt{if } \neg\, isInitRegion(\sigma, rgn_1) \texttt{ or } \neg isInitRegion(\sigma, rgn_2) \texttt{ or } ref_1 \notin dom(refEnv) \texttt{ then } \Omega$
    $\texttt{else}$
        $\texttt{let } \langle b, o \rangle = refEnv(ref_1) \texttt{ in}$
        $\texttt{let } c' = \langle b, o + [\![n]\!](\sigma) \rangle \texttt{ in}$
        $\texttt{let } refEnv' = refEnv[ref_2 \mapsto c'] \texttt{ in}$
        $\texttt{let } rgnAddrs' = rgnAddrs[rgn_2 \mapsto rgnAddrs(rgn_2) \cup \{cell2Addr(c')\}] \texttt{ in}$
        $(refEnv', rgnEnv, numEnv, nextAddr, rgnAddrs', alloc)$

Fig. 5. Concrete semantics for region-based statements (I).

$$
[\![stmt]\!]_{\Omega}(\sigma) = \begin{cases} \Omega & \text{if } \sigma = \Omega \\ [\![stmt]\!](\sigma) & \text{otherwse} \end{cases}
$$

$[\![lhs := \mathtt{loadref}(rgn, ref)]\!](\sigma) \equiv$

$\mathtt{match}\ \sigma\ \mathtt{with}\ (refEnv, rgnEnv, numEnv, nextAddr, rgnAddrs, alloc)\ \rightarrow$
  $\mathtt{if}\ \neg\ \mathsf{isInitRegion}(\sigma, rgn)\ \mathtt{or}\ \ ref \notin \mathsf{dom}(refEnv)\ \mathtt{or}$
    $\neg\ \mathsf{isInList}(refEnv(ref), alloc)\ \mathtt{then}\ \Omega$
  $\mathtt{else}$
    $\mathtt{let}\ c = refEnv(ref)\ \mathtt{in}$
    $\mathtt{let}\ \mathcal{M} = rgnEnv(rgn)\ \mathtt{in}$
    $\mathtt{if}\ c \notin \mathsf{dom}(\mathcal{M})\ \mathtt{then}\ \Omega$
    $\mathtt{else}$
      $\mathtt{let}\ (numEnv', refEnv') =$
      $\begin{cases} (numEnv, refEnv[lhs \mapsto \mathcal{M}(c)]) & \text{if } type(lhs) = \mathbf{Ref} \\ (numEnv[lhs \mapsto \mathsf{cell2Addr}(\mathcal{M}(c))], refEnv) & \text{otherwise} \end{cases}$
      $\mathtt{in}$
      $(refEnv', rgnEnv, numEnv', nextAddr, rgnAddrs, alloc)$

$[\![\mathtt{storeref}(rgn, ref, val)]\!](\sigma) \equiv$

$\mathtt{match}\ \sigma\ \mathtt{with}\ (refEnv, rgnEnv, numEnv, nextAddr, rgnAddrs, alloc)\ \rightarrow$
  $\mathtt{if}\ \neg\ \mathsf{isInitRegion}(\sigma, rgn)\ \mathtt{or}\ \ ref \notin \mathsf{dom}(refEnv)\ \mathtt{or}$
    $\neg\ \mathsf{isInList}(refEnv(ref), alloc)\ \mathtt{or}$
    $(type(val) \neq \mathbf{Ref}\ \mathtt{or}\ val \notin \mathsf{dom}(refEnv))\ \mathtt{then}\ \Omega$
  $\mathtt{else}$
    $\mathtt{let}\ c' = \begin{cases} refEnv(val) & \text{if } type(val) = \mathbf{Ref} \\ \langle 0, [\![val]\!](\sigma) \rangle & \text{otherwise} \end{cases}$
    $\mathtt{in}$
    $\mathtt{let}\ \mathcal{M} = rgnEnv(rgn)\ \mathtt{in}$
    $\mathtt{let}\ rgnEnv' = rgnEnv[rgn \mapsto \mathcal{M}[refEnv(ref) \mapsto c']]\ \mathtt{in}$
    $(refEnv, rgnEnv', numEnv, nextAddr, rgnAddrs, alloc)$

Fig. 6. Concrete semantics for region-based statements (II).

The definition of $[\![.]\!](.)$[8] for region statements is described in Figs. 5, 6, and 15. Our semantics is similar to a standard word-level C with two differences: (1) it keeps separate the memory space of each region ($rgnEnv$ is indexed by a region), and (2) it keeps track of all addresses owned by each region ($rgnAddrs$). We omit the semantics of other constructs (e.g., $\mathtt{assume}$, $\mathtt{goto}$) but they are defined in the usual way. The initial concrete state[9] is $\langle \lambda ref.\bot, \lambda rgn.(\lambda a.\bot), \lambda n.\bot, 1, \lambda rgn.\bot, nil \rangle$.

Region Initialization. The statement $\mathtt{initrgn}()$ returns a new region variable. All regions must be initialized before they can be used. The program state is updated by setting the set of owned address by the region to empty. If a region is already initialized then input state is returned.

Allocation and Deallocation. $ref := \mathtt{makeref}(rgn, n)$ returns a reference ref pointing to the base address of a newly allocated memory object of size n. The concrete semantics creates a new cell associated to ref and models the fact a

---

[8] We abuse notation and use $[\![.]\!](.)$ to evaluate integer and Boolean expressions defined as usual: $[\![c]\!](\sigma) = c$ for constant c, $[\![v]\!](\langle \_, \_, numEnv, \_, \_, \_ \rangle) = numEnv(v)$ for variable v, $[\![e_1 + e_2]\!](\sigma) = [\![e_1]\!](\sigma) + [\![e_2]\!](\sigma)$ for expressions e_1 and e_2, etc.

[9] We use the notation $\lambda x.\bot$ to represent the undefined function.

memory object has been allocated by adding it to *alloc* and increasing *nextAddr* by n. Moreover, the program state $(rgnAddrs)$ records that ref is owned by the region rgn. $\texttt{freeref}(rgn, ref)$ identifies the memory object associated to the reference ref and deletes the object from *alloc*. If the memory object was not allocated or already freed then it returns the error state.

Pointer Arithmetic. The semantics of $(rgn_2, ref_2) := \texttt{gepref}(rgn_1, ref_1, n)$ models pointer arithmetic in CRABIR. Similar to C pointer arithmetic, $\texttt{gepref}$ does not access memory and returns a new reference ref_2 obtained by adding the offset n to the input reference ref_1. What differs from the standard C memory model is that both reference variables ref_1 and ref_2 are associated with their corresponding regions denoted by variables rgn_1 and rgn_2, respectively. Therefore, the program state $(rgnAddrs)$ must update the set of owned addresses by rgn_2 by adding the address of ref_2.

Accessing Memory. Both $\texttt{storeref}$ and $\texttt{loadref}$ (Fig. 6) check first that the reference variable ref points to a valid memory object. If not then the error state is returned. $lhs := \texttt{loadref}(rgn, ref)$ reads the data associated to the ref's cell and updates either $numEnv$ or $rgnEnv$ depending on the type of lhs. $\texttt{storeref}(rgn, ref, val)$ modifies $rgnEnv$ by updating the data associated to ref's cell with val. Note that in both cases, the semantics is greatly simplified thanks to its word-level addressing.

Conversion Between References and Integers. Since CRABIR is strongly typed, all type conversions must be done explicitly. The statements $\texttt{reftoint}$ and $\texttt{inttoref}$ allow to convert a reference to an integer, and vice-versa. The semantics of these statements is shown in Appendix C.

6   Region Abstract Domains

This section illustrates how our region-based semantics from Sect. 5 can be efficiently computed by applying well-known *address abstractions*. The goal is not to introduce new abstractions but instead, to demonstrate that existing abstractions can be easily adapted to RBMM while they can benefit from the aliasing restrictions provided by our memory model. In this section, we revisit two address abstractions: *smashing*, where all memory objects within a region are grouped into one summarized variable, and *recency* [1], where the abstraction distinguishes between the most recent object and the previous ones. These two abstractions are pictorially shown in Fig. 7.

6.1   Smashing Region Abstract Domain

This domain uses the basic abstract domains: $\mathsf{Bool} = \{\bot_{\mathsf{Bool}}, \mathsf{True}, \mathsf{False}, \mathsf{All}\}$ where $\bot_{\mathsf{Bool}} \sqsubseteq \mathsf{True}, \bot_{\mathsf{Bool}} \sqsubseteq \mathsf{False}, \mathsf{True} \sqsubseteq \mathsf{All}, \mathsf{False} \sqsubseteq \mathsf{All}$; $\mathsf{SmallRange} = \{\bot_{\mathsf{SmallRange}}, 0, 1, 0{-}1, 1^+, 0^+\}$ where $\bot_{\mathsf{SmallRange}} \sqsubseteq 0, \bot_{\mathsf{SmallRange}} \sqsubseteq 1, 0 \sqsubseteq 0{-}1, 1 \sqsubseteq 0{-}1, 1 \sqsubseteq 1^+, 0{-}1 \sqsubseteq 0^+, 1^+ \sqsubseteq 0^+$; and Base, a numerical domain. As usual, we

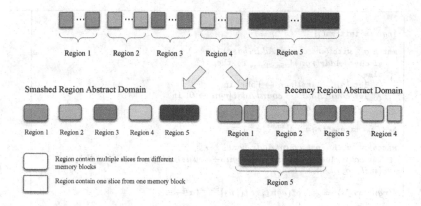

Fig. 7. Examples of simple region abstractions.

lift Bool and SmallRange to environment domains, BoolEnv, and SmallRangeEnv, respectively. These environments map variables to abstract values. If a variable is not found in the map then the corresponding top element (All or 0^+) is returned. An abstract state $\sigma^\# \in$ AState is defined as a triple where $init \in$ BoolEnv keeps track whether a region has been initialized, $countAddr \in$ SmallRangeEnv keeps track of the number of owned addresses by a region, and $base \in$ Base, is the base domain.

Abstract Operations. The binary abstract operators: inclusion, join, meet, widening, and narrowing are component-wise. Most relevant abstract transformers for the region-based statements are given in Fig. 8. For simplicity, the abstract transformers assume that the input abstract state is not $\bot$ (bottom). Also for simplicity, we omit the abstract transformer for `freeref`. Although conceptually simple, its transformer is a bit more elaborate because the abstract state needs to relate which regions may contain fields of the same memory object. This is because when a reference is being deallocating the whole memory object to which the reference points to must be freed. Our implementation models `freeref`. Most abstract transformers in Fig. 8 are self-explanatory. The idea is to count the number of possible references within each region. If more than one reference is possible then memory writes/reads are modeled as weak updates/reads, otherwise as strong updates/reads. For that, the abstract states uses *countAddr*. As usual, we assume that the base abstract domain supports the *expand* operation (e.g., [12]) such that $base' = \text{expand}(base, v_1, v_2)$ copies all the relationships between v_1 with other variables into a fresh, unconstrained v_2 without relate v_1 and v_2. This operation is used to perform "weak reads". Note that for the abstract domain to perform at least one strong update, it needs the counter of addresses per region to be set to the abstract value 0. This takes place in the abstract transformer of `initrgn`.

$[\![rgn := \mathtt{initrgn}()]\!]^{\mathsf{Smash}}(\sigma^{\#}) \equiv$

$\mathtt{match}\ \sigma^{\#}\ \mathtt{with}\ (init, countAddr, base)\ \rightarrow$
  $\mathtt{if}\ countAddr(rgn) \sqsubseteq_{\mathsf{SmallRange}} 1^{+}\ \mathtt{then}\ \sigma^{\#}$
  $\mathtt{else}$
    $\mathtt{let}\ init' = init[rgn \mapsto \mathsf{False}]\ \mathtt{in}$
    $\mathtt{let}\ countAddr' = countAddr[rgn \mapsto 0]\ \mathtt{in}$
    $(init', countAddr', base)$

$[\![ref := \mathtt{makeref}(rgn, n)]\!]^{\mathsf{Smash}}(\sigma^{\#}) \equiv$

$\mathtt{match}\ \sigma^{\#}\ \mathtt{with}\ (init, countAddr, base)\ \rightarrow$
  $\mathtt{let}\ countAddr' = countAddr[rgn \mapsto countAddr(rgn) +^{\mathsf{SmallRange}} 1]\ \mathtt{in}$
  $(init, countAddr', base)$

$[\![(rgn_2, ref_2) := \mathtt{gepref}(rgn_1, ref_1, n)]\!]^{\mathsf{Smash}}(\sigma^{\#}) \equiv$

$\mathtt{match}\ \sigma^{\#}\ \mathtt{with}\ (init, countAddr, base)\ \rightarrow$
  $\mathtt{if}\ rgn_1 \neq rgn_2\ \mathtt{or}\ [\![ref_2 \neq ref_1 + n]\!]^{\mathsf{Base}}(base) \neq \perp_{\mathsf{Base}}\ \mathtt{then}$
    $\mathtt{let}\ countAddr' = countAddr[rgn_2 \mapsto countAddr(rgn_2) +^{\mathsf{SmallRange}} 1]\ \mathtt{in}$
  $\mathtt{else}$
    $\mathtt{let}\ countAddr' = countAddr\ \mathtt{in}$
  $\mathtt{let}\ base' = [\![ref_2 := ref_1 + n]\!]^{\mathsf{Base}}(base)\ \mathtt{in}$
  $(init, countAddr', base')$

$[\![lhs := \mathtt{loadref}(rgn, ref)]\!]^{\mathsf{Smash}}(\sigma^{\#}) \equiv$

$\mathtt{match}\ \sigma^{\#}\ \mathtt{with}\ (init, countAddr, base)\ \rightarrow$
  $\mathtt{if}\ [\![ref \neq 0]\!]^{\mathsf{Base}}(base) = \perp_{\mathsf{Base}}\ \mathtt{or}\ init(rgn) = \mathsf{False}\ \mathtt{then}\ \perp$
  $\mathtt{else}$
    $\mathtt{if}\ countAddr(rgn) \sqsubseteq_{\mathsf{SmallRange}} 0\text{--}1\ \mathtt{then}$
      $\mathtt{let}\ base' = [\![lhs := rgn]\!]^{\mathsf{Base}}(base)\ \mathtt{in}$
    $\mathtt{else}$
      $\mathtt{let}\ base' = \mathtt{expand}(base, rgn, rgn_{fresh})\ \mathtt{in}$
      $(init, countAddr, [\![lhs := rgn_{fresh}]\!]^{\mathsf{Base}}(base'))$

$[\![\mathtt{storeref}(rgn, ref, val)]\!]^{\mathsf{Smash}}(\sigma^{\#}) \equiv$

$\mathtt{match}\ \sigma^{\#}\ \mathtt{with}\ (init, countAddr, base)\ \rightarrow$
  $\mathtt{if}\ [\![ref \neq 0]\!]^{\mathsf{Base}}(base) = \perp_{\mathsf{Base}}\ \mathtt{then}\ \perp$
  $\mathtt{else}$
    $\mathtt{if}\ init(rng) = \mathsf{False}\ \mathtt{or}\ countAddr(rgn) \sqsubseteq_{\mathsf{SmallRange}} 0\text{--}1\ \mathtt{then}$
      $\mathtt{let}\ base' = [\![rgn := val]\!]^{\mathsf{Base}}(base)\ \mathtt{in}$
    $\mathtt{else}$
      $\mathtt{let}\ base' = base \sqcup_{base} [\![rgn := val]\!]^{\mathsf{Base}}(base)\ \mathtt{in}$
    $(init[rgn \mapsto \mathsf{All}], countAddr, base')$

Fig. 8. Smashing abstraction for region-based statements.

6.2   Recency-Based Region Abstract Domain

We show now how recency abstraction [1] can be adapted to our region memory model. For each region variable $v \in \mathcal{V}_{\mathcal{R}gn}$, we introduce two *ghost variables* $v^r \in \mathcal{V}_{\mathcal{R}gn}$ and $v^o \in \mathcal{V}_{\mathcal{R}gn}$ where the former represents the field of the most recent allocated memory object within region v and the latter represents the same field but from the older memory objects allocated within same region. Moreover, we introduce a third ghost reference variable $v^l \in \mathcal{V}_{\mathcal{R}ef}$ that remembers the

$$[\![ref := \texttt{makeref}(rgn, n)]\!]^{\text{Recency}}(\sigma^{\#}) \equiv$$

```
match σ# with (init, countAddr, base)  →
    let init' = init[rgnᵒ ↦ init(rgnᵒ) ⊔_Bool init(rgnʳ)] in
    let countAddr' = countAddr[rgnᵒ ↦ countAddr(rgnᵒ) ⊔_SmallRange countAddr(rgnʳ)] in
    let ⟨init'', countAddr''⟩ = ⟨init'[rgnʳ ↦ False], countAddr'[rgnʳ ↦ 0–1]⟩ in
    let base' = forget(base ⊔_Base [rgnᵒ := rgnʳ]^Base(base), rgnʳ) in
    (init'', countAddr'', [rgnˡ := ref]^Base(base'))
```

$$[\![lhs := \texttt{loadref}(rgn, ref)]\!]^{\text{Recency}}(\sigma^{\#}) \equiv$$

```
match σ# with (_, _, base)  →
    if [ref < rgnˡ]^Base(base) = ⊥_Base then
        [lhs := loadref(rgnʳ, ref)]^Smash(σ#)
    else
        [lhs := loadref(rgnᵒ, ref)]^Smash(σ#)
```

$$[\![\texttt{storeref}(rgn, ref, val)]\!]^{\text{Recency}}(\sigma^{\#}) \equiv$$

```
match σ# with (_, _, base)  →
    if [ref < rgnˡ]^Base(base) = ⊥_Base then
        [storeref(rgnʳ, ref, val)]^Smash(σ#)
    else
        [storeref(rgnᵒ, ref, val)]^Smash(σ#)
```

Fig. 9. Recency abstraction for allocation and accessing memory statements.

address of the last allocated object. The abstract transformers for allocation and accessing memory statements are given in Fig. 9.

The most interesting case is `makeref`. When a new reference is allocated, the old region rgn^o must be joined with the most recent region rgn^r. Then, rgn^r is reset by making the region uninitialized and setting its counter of addresses to either 0 or 1 (0 if we assume that the allocation cannot fail). Moreover, the abstract state remembers the allocated reference in rgn^l. The rest of operations compare the corresponding references with rgn^l to determine whether the operation can be performed on the most recent region rgn^r or the old ones rgn^o.

7   Experimental Evaluation

To evaluate our RBMM, we aim to answer the following research questions:

RQ1: Are the assumptions of RBMM realistic for modern C projects?
RQ2: Can RBMM and the smashing domain analyze interesting properties?
RQ3: Is RBMM and the smashing domain efficient for realistic projects?

Implementation. We replaced the old IR in CRAB with CRABIR (Sect. 4), modified the interface of the abstract domains to support CRABIR, and implemented the smashing region domain (Sect. 6.1). These changes are now part of CRAB[10]. The implementation relaxes word-level addressability assumption as long as each memory read accesses the same number of bytes last written.

---

[10] Publicly available at https://github.com/seahorn/crab.

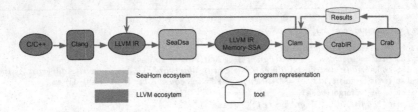

Fig. 10. Abstract Interpreter of LLVM programs.

Table 1. #I is the number of instructions in the LLVM program. Time(s) is the time in seconds of the translation to CRABIR, analysis, and checking phases. Trivial #A is the number of assertions proven by the CLAM preprocessor (without using CRAB). All Memory considers all dereferenced pointers while RBMM -compliant only checks a pointer if the analysis can ensure that RBMM assumptions hold. #P is the number of proved assertions by the analysis, #A is the number of checked assertions (excluding Trivial #A), and %P is $\lceil \frac{\#P}{\#A} \times 100 \rceil$.

Program	KLOC	# I	Time(s)	Trivial #A	All memory			RBMM-compl.		
					#P	#A	%P	#P	#A	%P
bftpd	4	11K	4	3 573	134	357	38	31	59	52
brotli	31	221K	101	9 470	7 741	14 945	52	535	1 221	43
brotli-mod	—	210K	860	8 328	3 937	7 843	51	1 339	2 128	63
curl	85	12K	152	840	820	1 601	52	92	125	77
thttpd	8	8K	52	1 480	661	1 326	50	149	258	58
vsftpd	16	16K	330	3 324	1 021	1 665	62	42	98	43

From LLVM to CRABIR. CRAB is a library for performing abstract interpretation of CRABIR programs, and thus, it does not support C or LLVM directly. The translation from LLVM to CRABIR is performed by CLAM, a LLVM frontend for CRAB. The main architecture of our C analyzer based on LLVM is shown in Fig. 10.[11]

CLAM[12] runs a whole-program pointer analysis, called SEADSA [14,19], on the LLVM bitcode and builds a *Memory SSA form* representation of the program [7]. In Memory SSA, each memory write is given a unique version of the heap and reads can only refer to one version. We use SEADSA to partition the heap into many disjoint sub-heaps. The translation from Memory SSA to CRABIR maps heap versions to different region variables.

---

[11] SEADSA, CLAM, and CRAB are also integrated into the SeaHorn verification framework [13].

[12] Publicly available at https://github.com/seahorn/clam.

Benchmarks and Setup. We selected popular C projects that focus on porta-bility and, therefore, do not rely on specific architectures. The projects are `bftpd`, `brotli`, `curl`, `thttpd`, and `vsftpd`. We implemented an LLVM instrumentation that adds assertions in CRABIR to check that each pointer is not null before being dereferenced. As the abstract domain, we use the smashing region domain from Sect. 6.1 with a simple reduced product of the sign and constant domain. We also tried the interval domain and differences were small. All artifacts to reproduce Table 1 are publicly available at http://doi.org/10.5281/zenodo.5129227.

Results. We evaluated our analysis on the selected benchmarks checking for null-dereferences. We present the results in Table 1 to answer each question.

RQ1: Are the assumptions of RBMM realistic for modern C projects?. To answer this question, we look at the columns #A in All Memory and RBMM-compliant, respectively. These numbers show that on average only nearly 10% of all checked pointers satisfy statically the assumptions of RBMM. For better understanding, we manually inspected our bigger program, brotli—a compression library.[13] By default, brotli is compiled to the host architecture, however, this can be disabled by a compile-time flag. The portable configuration of brotli complies with the assumptions of RBMM, and we use it for the rest of the experiments. Next, we saw that our pointer analysis, SEADSA, is not suffi-ciently precise. Luckily, brotli is designed to be very customizable. For example, it allows different memory managers in addition to the standard `malloc`, provides different layers of caches for small objects, and uses more than 10 different hash function implementations. We simplified the code (brotli-mod) by either special-ising some behaviour (e.g., allocating small objects on the heap, using default allocator, choosing fewer hash functions) and by abstracting away some hard-to-analyze functions (they can be analyzed by other less scalable but more precise approaches). With these simplifications, SEADSA was able to ensure that 30% of memory accesses are compliant with RBMM. Our takeaway is that modern C projects like brotli are designed to be portable and, thus, they are very likely to satisfy our RBMM assumptions. We also believe that it is possible to statically prove compliance with user help and/or using more precise pointer analyses.

RQ2: Can RBMM and the smashing domain analyze interesting prop-erties? The answer to this question is mixed. The results show that such a simple analysis can establish about 50-60% of all the non-trivial memory operations. Refactoring the code to be more analyzable, as we did in brotli, can have a significant positive impact. Unfortunately, there is no ground truth – we do not know how many memory accesses can be established safe automatically. We have tried number of existing tools, including IKOS and Infer, but none produce good quality results (either because of crashes or because of automatic hiding of warnings). In our opinion, the results show RBMM is a great building block to combine with more intricate abstract domain (i.e., not simple smashing). This is an avenue for future work.

---

[13] https://github.com/google/brotli

RQ3: Is RBMM and the smashing domain efficient for realistic projects? The results show that we can analyze a non-trivial project within 15 minutes, which is quite reasonable. Interestingly, the analysis time increases as precision increases (see the difference between `brotli` and `brotli-mod`. This is because more precision implies that the analysis does not generate "top" as often, thus, requiring more time to converge. It is interesting to see whether more aggressive widening strategy or less aggressive inlining can improve performance.

8 Related Work

Our approach can be seen as a form of abstract compilation (e.g., logic programs [27] and array-manipulating programs [9]) but it focuses on the pointer semantics of C. Our RBMM is inspired by similar memory models used by deductive verification tools such as Smack [22,23], Cascade [26], SeaHorn [13], FramaC/Jessie [10,21], Cadeceus [11] and [4]. Our work focuses on Abstract Interpretation and thus, it formalizes both its concrete and abstract semantics.

There is a variety of impressive C abstract interpreters such as Astrée [2], EVA [3], IKOS [5], Infer [6], MemCAD [15], Mopsa [17,18], and Verasco [16]. RBMM restricts further the memory models used by these tools with the goal of scaling on general-purpose C projects while proving interesting properties.

9 Conclusions

We have proposed a new region-based memory model (RBMM) suitable for static analysis based on abstract interpretation. We have formalized the semantics of the memory model and shown how to adapt existing memory abstractions. Our evaluation suggests that the assumptions of our memory model are realistic for modern C projects. However, more work needs to be done to fully prove absence of memory violations in those programs. One advantage of RBMM is its compatibility with standard C memory model and thus, more precise memory abstractions such as [20] and [25] can be used.

```
1   (ref,region(ref),region(int32),region(int32),region(ref),region(int32))
2   declare mk_list(n:int32,data_sz:int32,val:int32)
3   @entry:
4     initrgn(R1:region(ref));
5     initrgn(R2:region(int32));
6     initrgn(R3:region(int32));
7     initrgn(R4:region(ref));
8     initrgn(R5:region(int32));
9     havoc(l:ref)
10    assume(l == NULL_REF);
11    i = 0;
12    goto @bb_1;
13  @bb_1:
14    goto @bb_2,@bb_4;
15  @bb_2:
16    assume(i + 1 <= n);
17    goto @bb_3;
18  @bb_3:
19    n = 16;
20    tmp:ref = makeref(R1, n);
21    assume(tmp > NULL_REF);
22    (data:ref,R5) = call init(data_sz,val);
23    (R1,tmp#data:ref) = gepref(R1,tmp);
24    // update tmp->data
25    storeref(R1,tmp#data,data);
26    havoc(used:int32);
27    assume(used >= 0);
28    assume(used <= data_sz -1);
29    // update tmp->len
30    (R2,tmp#len:ref) = gepref(R1,tmp + 4);
31    storeref(R2,tmp#len,used);
32    // update tmp->cap
33    (R3,tmp#cap:ref) = gepref(R1,tmp + 8);
34    storeref(R3,tmp#cap,data_sz);
35    // update tmp->n
36    (R4,tmp#n:ref) = gepref(R1,tmp + 12);
37    storeref(R4,tmp#n,l);
38    // l = tmp
39    (R1,l) = gepref(R1,tmp);
40    i = i+1;
41    goto @bb_1;
42  @bb_4:
43    assume(n <= i);
44    goto @exit;
45  @exit:
46    return (l,R1,R2,R3,R4,R5);
```

Fig. 11. Simplified version of CRABIR code for mk_list function.

A Motivating Example from Sect. 2 in CRABIR

In this section, we show the translation of our motivating example from Sect. 2 to CRABIR. For readability purposes, variable names have been renamed to match those names used in the C program. We have also omitted types when they can be inferred from the context. We show two functions: mk_list in Fig. 11 and main in Fig. 12. The function init is translated in a very similar manner.

```
1    int32 declare main()
2    @entry:
3      havoc(list_sz:int32)
4      assume(list_sz >= 1);
5      havoc(data_sz:int32)
6      assume(data_sz >= 1);
7      havoc(val:int32)
8      (node:ref,R1:region(ref),R2:region(int32),
9       R3:region(int32),R4:region(ref),R5:region(int32)) =
10     call mk_list(list_sz:int32,data_sz:int32,val:int32);
11     goto @bb_1;
12   @bb_1:
13     goto @bb_2, @bb_9;
14   @bb_2:
15     assume(node > NULL_REF);
16     goto. @bb_3;
17   @bb_3:
18     (R1,node#data:ref)  = gepref(R1,node);
19     tmp1:ref  = loadref(R1,node#data);
20     sassert(tmp1 > NULL_REF);
21     (R2,node#len:ref)   = gepref(R1,node + 4);
22     tmp2:int32  = loadref(R2,node#len);
23     sassert(tmp2 <= data_sz-1);
24     (R3,node#cap:ref)   = gepref(R1,node + 8);
25     tmp3:int32  = loadref(R3,node#cap);
26     sassert(tmp2 <= tmp3);
27     i = 0;
28     goto @bb_4;
29   @bb_4:
30     goto @bb_5,@bb_7;
31   @bb_5:
32     assume(i <= data_sz-1);
33     goto @bb_6;
34   @bb_6:
35     tmp4:ref  = loadref(R1,node#data);
36     (R5,tmp5:ref)  = gepref(R5,tmp4 + 4*i);
37     tmp6:int32  = loadref(R5,tmp5);
38     sassert(tmp6 == val);
39     i = i+1;
40     goto @bb_4;
41   @bb_7:
42     assume(data_sz <= i);
43     goto @bb_8;
44   @bb_8:
45     (R4,node#n:ref)  = gepref(R1,node + 12);
46     tmp7:ref  = loadref(R4,node#n);
47     (R1,node)  = gepref(R1,tmp7);
48     goto @bb_1;
49   @bb_9:
50     assume(node == NULL_REF);
51     goto @exit;
52   @exit:
53     return 0;
```

Fig. 12. Simplified version of CRABIR code for main.

B Auxiliary Functions for Concrete Semantics

(See Fig. 14).

```
cell2Addr(c)
   match c with ⟨base, o⟩  →
      base + o


addr2Cell(a, objList)
   match objList with
      nil  →  ⟨0, 0⟩
      ⟨start, end⟩ :: tail  →
            if (start ≤ a and  a < end) then  ⟨start, a − start⟩
            else addr2Cell(a, tail)
```

Fig. 13. Conversion between addresses and cells.

```
isInitRegion(σ, rgn)
   match σ with (_, _, _, rgnAddrs, _)  →
      rgn ∈ dom(rgnAddrs)
```

```
isInList(⟨b, o⟩, objList)
   addr2Cell(cell2Addr(⟨b, o⟩), objList) ≠ ⟨0, 0⟩
```

```
removeFromList(c, objList)
   let a := cell2Addr(c) in
   match objList with
      nil  →  Ω
      ⟨start, end⟩ :: tail  →
         if (start ≤ a and  a < end) then
            tail
         else match removeFromList(c, tail) with
            Ω → Ω
            objList'  →  ⟨start, end⟩ :: objList'
```

Fig. 14. Helpers for concrete semantics.

C   Concrete Semantics of reftoint and inttoref

The concrete semantics of reftoint and inttoref is shown in Fig. 15. It is straightforward by delegating to the functions cell2Addr and addr2Cell. The most interesting part occurs in $ref := \texttt{inttoref}(rgn, x)$ where the program state ($rgnAddrs$) must add the new reference ref to the set of owned addresses by the region rgn.

$[\![x := \mathtt{reftoint}(rgn, ref)]\!](\sigma) \equiv$

$\mathtt{match}\ \sigma\ \mathtt{with}\ (refEnv, rgnEnv, numEnv, nextAddr, rgnAddrs, alloc) \rightarrow$
    $\mathtt{if}\ \neg\ \mathsf{isInitRegion}(\sigma, rgn)\ \mathtt{or}\ ref \notin \mathsf{dom}(refEnv))\ \mathtt{then}\ \Omega$
    $\mathtt{else}$
        $\mathtt{let}\ numEnv' = numEnv[x \mapsto \mathsf{cell2Addr}(refEnv(ref))]\ \mathtt{in}$
        $(refEnv, rgnEnv, numEnv', nextAddr, rgnAddrs, alloc)$

$[\![ref := \mathtt{inttoref}(rgn, x)]\!](\sigma) \equiv$

$\mathtt{match}\ \sigma\ \mathtt{with}\ (refEnv, rgnEnv, numEnv, nextAddr, rgnAddrs, alloc) \rightarrow$
    $\mathtt{if}\ \neg\ \mathsf{isInitRegion}(\sigma, rgn)\ \mathtt{then}\ \Omega$
    $\mathtt{else}$
        $\mathtt{let}\ c = \mathsf{addr2Cell}([\![x]\!](\sigma), alloc)\ \mathtt{in}$
        $\mathtt{if}\ c = \langle 0, 0 \rangle\ \mathtt{then}\ \Omega$
        $\mathtt{else}$
            $\mathtt{let}\ refEnv' = refEnv[ref \mapsto c]\ \mathtt{in}$
            $\mathtt{let}\ rgnAddrs' = rgnAddrs[rgn \mapsto rgnAddrs(rgn) \cup \{[\![x]\!](\sigma)\}]\ \mathtt{in}$
            $(refEnv', rgnEnv, numEnv, nextAddr, rgnAddrs', alloc)$

Fig. 15. Concrete Semantics for `reftoint` and `inttoref`.

References

1. Balakrishnan, G., Reps, T.: Recency-abstraction for heap-allocated storage. In: Yi, K. (ed.) SAS 2006. LNCS, vol. 4134, pp. 221–239. Springer, Heidelberg (2006). https://doi.org/10.1007/11823230_15
2. Blanchet, B., et al.: A static analyzer for large safety-critical software. In: PLDI, pp. 196–207 (2003)
3. Blazy, S., Bühler, D., Yakobowski, B.: Structuring abstract interpreters through state and value abstractions. In: Bouajjani, A., Monniaux, D. (eds.) VMCAI 2017. LNCS, vol. 10145, pp. 112–130. Springer, Cham (2017). https://doi.org/10.1007/978-3-319-52234-0_7
4. Bouillaguet, Q., Bobot, F., Sighireanu, M., Yakobowski, B.: Exploiting pointer analysis in memory models for deductive verification. In: Enea, C., Piskac, R. (eds.) VMCAI 2019. LNCS, vol. 11388, pp. 160–182. Springer, Cham (2019). https://doi.org/10.1007/978-3-030-11245-5_8
5. Brat, G., Navas, J.A., Shi, N., Venet, A.: IKOS: a framework for static analysis based on abstract interpretation. In: Giannakopoulou, D., Salaün, G. (eds.) SEFM 2014. LNCS, vol. 8702, pp. 271–277. Springer, Cham (2014). https://doi.org/10.1007/978-3-319-10431-7_20
6. Calcagno, C., Distefano, D.: Infer: an automatic program verifier for memory safety of C programs. In: Bobaru, M., Havelund, K., Holzmann, G.J., Joshi, R. (eds.) NFM 2011. LNCS, vol. 6617, pp. 459–465. Springer, Heidelberg (2011). https://doi.org/10.1007/978-3-642-20398-5_33
7. Chow, F., Chan, S., Liu, S.-M., Lo, R., Streich, M.: Effective representation of aliases and indirect memory operations in SSA form. In: Gyimóthy, T. (ed.) CC 1996. LNCS, vol. 1060, pp. 253–267. Springer, Heidelberg (1996). https://doi.org/10.1007/3-540-61053-7_66

8. Conway, C.L., Dams, D., Namjoshi, K.S., Barrett, C.: Pointer analysis, conditional soundness, and proving the absence of errors. In: Alpuente, M., Vidal, G. (eds.) SAS 2008. LNCS, vol. 5079, pp. 62–77. Springer, Heidelberg (2008). https://doi.org/10.1007/978-3-540-69166-2_5

9. Cornish, J.R.M., Gange, G., Navas, J.A., Schachte, P., Søndergaard, H., Stuckey, P.J.: Analyzing array manipulating programs by program transformation. In: Proietti, M., Seki, H. (eds.) LOPSTR 2014. LNCS, vol. 8981, pp. 3–20. Springer, Cham (2015). https://doi.org/10.1007/978-3-319-17822-6_1

10. Cuoq, P., Kirchner, F., Kosmatov, N., Prevosto, V., Signoles, J., Yakobowski, B.: Frama-C: a software analysis perspective. In: Eleftherakis, G., Hinchey, M., Holcombe, M. (eds.) SEFM 2012. LNCS, vol. 7504, pp. 233–247. Springer, Heidelberg (2012). https://doi.org/10.1007/978-3-642-33826-7_16

11. Filliâtre, J.-C., Marché, C.: Multi-prover verification of C programs. In: Davies, J., Schulte, W., Barnett, M. (eds.) ICFEM 2004. LNCS, vol. 3308, pp. 15–29. Springer, Heidelberg (2004). https://doi.org/10.1007/978-3-540-30482-1_10

12. Gopan, D.: Numeric program analysis techniques with applications to array analysis and library summarization. Ph.D. thesis, University of Wisconsin (2007)

13. Gurfinkel, A., Kahsai, T., Komuravelli, A., Navas, J.A.: The SeaHorn verification framework. In: Kroening, D., Păsăreanu, C.S. (eds.) CAV 2015. LNCS, vol. 9206, pp. 343–361. Springer, Cham (2015). https://doi.org/10.1007/978-3-319-21690-4_20

14. Gurfinkel, A., Navas, J.A.: A context-sensitive memory model for verification of C/C++ programs. In: Ranzato, F. (ed.) SAS 2017. LNCS, vol. 10422, pp. 148–168. Springer, Cham (2017). https://doi.org/10.1007/978-3-319-66706-5_8

15. Illous, H., Lemerre, M., Rival, X.: A relational shape abstract domain. In: Barrett, C., Davies, M., Kahsai, T. (eds.) NFM 2017. LNCS, vol. 10227, pp. 212–229. Springer, Cham (2017). https://doi.org/10.1007/978-3-319-57288-8_15

16. Jourdan, J., Laporte, V., Blazy, S., Leroy, X., Pichardie, D.: A formally-verified C static analyzer. In: POPL, pp. 247–259 (2015)

17. Journault, M., Miné, A., Monat, R., Ouadjaout, A.: Combinations of reusable abstract domains for a multilingual static analyzer. In: Chakraborty, S., Navas, J.A. (eds.) VSTTE 2019. LNCS, vol. 12031, pp. 1–18. Springer, Cham (2020). https://doi.org/10.1007/978-3-030-41600-3_1

18. Journault, M., Miné, A., Ouadjaout, A.: Modular static analysis of string manipulations in C programs. In: Podelski, A. (ed.) SAS 2018. LNCS, vol. 11002, pp. 243–262. Springer, Cham (2018). https://doi.org/10.1007/978-3-319-99725-4_16

19. Kuderski, J., Navas, J.A., Gurfinkel, A.: Unification-based pointer analysis without oversharing. In: FMCAD, pp. 37–45 (2019)

20. Miné, A.: Field-sensitive value analysis of embedded C programs with union types and pointer arithmetics. In: LCTES, pp. 54–63 (2006)

21. Moy, Y.: Automatic modular static safety checking for C programs. Ph.D. thesis, Université Paris-Sud (2009)

22. Rakamarić, Z., Emmi, M.: SMACK: decoupling source language details from verifier implementations. In: Biere, A., Bloem, R. (eds.) CAV 2014. LNCS, vol. 8559, pp. 106–113. Springer, Cham (2014). https://doi.org/10.1007/978-3-319-08867-9_7

23. Rakamarić, Z., Hu, A.J.: A scalable memory model for low-level code. In: Jones, N.D., Müller-Olm, M. (eds.) VMCAI 2009. LNCS, vol. 5403, pp. 290–304. Springer, Heidelberg (2008). https://doi.org/10.1007/978-3-540-93900-9_24

24. Sui, Y., Xue, J.: SVF: interprocedural static value-flow analysis in LLVM. In: CC, pp. 265–266 (2016)

25. Venet, A.: A scalable nonuniform pointer analysis for embedded programs. In: Giacobazzi, R. (ed.) SAS 2004. LNCS, vol. 3148, pp. 149–164. Springer, Heidelberg (2004). https://doi.org/10.1007/978-3-540-27864-1_13

26. Wang, W., Barrett, C., Wies, T.: Cascade 2.0. In: McMillan, K.L., Rival, X. (eds.) VMCAI 2014. LNCS, vol. 8318, pp. 142–160. Springer, Heidelberg (2014). https://doi.org/10.1007/978-3-642-54013-4_9

27. Warren, R., Hermenegildo, M.V., Debray, S.K.: On the practicality of global flow analysis of logic programs. In: ICLP, pp. 684–699 (1988)

NSV 2021

Formal Verification of Neural Network Controllers for Collision-Free Flight

Daniel Genin[1]([envelope]), Ivan Papusha[1], Joshua Brulé[1], Tyler Young[1],
Galen Mullins[1], Yanni Kouskoulas[1], Rosa Wu[2], and Aurora Schmidt[1]

[1] The Johns Hopkins University Applied Physics Laboratory,
11100 Johns Hopkins Road, Laurel, MD, USA
Daniel.Genin@jhuapl.edu
[2] Defense Nuclear Facilities Safety Board, Washington DC, USA

Abstract. We investigate a method for formally verifying the absence
of adversarial examples in a neural network controller. Our approach
applies to networks with piecewise affine activation units, which may
be encoded symbolically as a piecewise affine mapping from inputs to
outputs. The approach rests on characterizing and bounding a critical
subset of the state space where controller action is required, partitioning this critical subset, and using satisfiability modulo theories (SMT)
to prove nonexistence of safety counterexamples on each of the resulting
partition elements. We demonstrate this approach on a simple collision
avoidance neural network controller, trained with reinforcement learning
to avoid collisions in a simplified simulated environment. After encoding the network weights in SMT, we formally verify safety of the neural
network controller on a subset of the critical partition elements, and
determine that the rest of the critical set partition elements are potentially unsafe. We further experimentally confirm the existence of actual
adversarial collision scenarios in 90% of the identified potentially unsafe
critical partition elements, indicating that our approach is reasonably
tight.

Keywords: Reinforcement learning · Satisfiability modulo theory ·
Formal verification

1 Introduction

Advances in machine learning and artificial intelligence (AI) have enabled a wide
variety of applications, such as self-driving vehicles, surveillance and delivery
drones, and autonomous ships. However, the successful adoption of such complex AI systems will require advances in our means for ensuring their safety and

A. Schmidt—This work was supported through JHU/APL internal R&D funds.
The views expressed herein are solely those of the authors, and no official support or
endorsement by the Defense Nuclear Facilities Safety Board or the U.S. Government
is intended or should be inferred.

© Springer Nature Switzerland AG 2022
R. Bloem et al. (Eds.): NSV 2021/VSTTE 2021, LNCS 13124, pp. 147–164, 2022.
https://doi.org/10.1007/978-3-030-95561-8_9

reliable operation. Many AI systems use reinforcement learning to train by optimizing a reward function. However, the unconstrained maximization of rewards leads to a variety of operational issues such as reward hacking, unsafe exploration, and catastrophic forgetting [1, 21]. In safety-critical systems, we must be able to guarantee that the system will behave according to the expectations of the users and all those who could be affected by the system.

While much attention is being paid to the existence of vulnerabilities of neural network (NN) controllers posed by adversarial examples [4], there are also ample examples of unexpected and tragic accidents, where misbehavior by autonomous systems has resulted in loss of life without any malicious input manipulation [3].

We present an approach for certifying safety of NN-based controllers for cyber-physical systems over a full continuous state space. This can be useful, for example, when addressing stringent safety requirements such as airworthiness certification. The approach combines recent successes in applying SMT and MIP solvers to NN verification, *e.g.*, [2, 5, 7, 13–15], with an efficient computation for identifying the boundary of the viable (safeable) set, which we the call *critical* subset (illustrated in Fig. 1).

The procedure for computing critical states is based on a type of reachability analysis, called *safeable* analysis [10, 18], which was originally developed for verification of the Airborne Collision Avoidance System X (ACAS X) [17]. Safeable analysis computes an approximation of the reachable set for sequences of future controller commands to determine which current commands can be made safe in the future. A notion of safeability was formally verified with the Coq theorem prover in [17], and those proofs extend to the analysis presented here. Although safeable analysis is particularly well adapted to controllers for kinematic systems, such as collision avoidance controllers, the approach presented in this paper may be applied to general systems where reachability guarantees are required.

The main innovation of our approach is the idea that safety verification needs to be performed only on the set of *critical states*. A controller that generates a safe command in every critical state is guaranteed to be safe regardless of its commands on the rest of the state space. This follows because critical states separate the safeable states from the unsafe states, and any system trajectory passing from safeable into unsafe or failing *must* pass through the critical set. Conversely, a controller that fails to resolve any of the critical states cannot be guaranteed safe, even when it performs well in simulations. This is particularly relevant for NN controllers because they are trained in idealized training environments, *e.g.*, with perfect sensing, where the controller may be able to easily steer the system away from the critical states and never learn safe behavior for those states.

We rely on an SMT solver to evaluate the safety of an NN control function with respect to an established safe command range, computed using safeable analysis. Because we use a piecewise constant overapproximation for the safe command range, which can be computed independently before being given as a constraint to SMT, our approach can support systems with general nonlinear dynamics and also allows for straightforward parallelization. Scalability of this procedure is driven primarily by the NN size and complexity. In our work, we use the open-source Z3 SMT solver [23].

We demonstrate feasibility of the proposed approach by applying it to a small network trained to maneuver a simulated aircraft vertically to avoid collisions with an adversarial intruder. We discretize the region of state space that contains all trajectories starting a fixed time before a potential collision into 23.2M hypercubes. We then compute a sound overapproximation of the critical subset, which contains just under 185k hypercubes, or about 0.8% of the accessible volume. We then use SMT to soundly classify critical hypercubes into two types: ones where the NN controller command is guaranteed safe over the entire cube, and ones where it cannot be guaranteed safe.

We use simulations to confirm that critical set forms an "impenetrable" barrier around the unsafe set: every collision scenario in the 185k scenario simulations passed through the critical set. Surprisingly, the NN controller failed to learn the correct response for most critical states, just under 90%. We also observe that in spite of the overapproximation used for computing critical states, to keep the verification time short, the false positive rate is below 11.5%, *i.e.*, about 88.4% of the visits to the failing hypercubes resulted in collisions. Our **contributions** are as follows: (1) verification of a classically trained reinforcement learning (RL) network, (2) demonstration of the use of envelopes and conservative approximations to create specifications to reduce the size of the input domain that must be verified, and (3) application to a commercial aircraft collision avoidance-inspired simulation.

1.1   Prior Work

The problem of verification of cyber-physical systems involving AI and neural network components has led to recent promising developments [26]. For example, Katz et al. [14,15] have demonstrated provably sound verification of local robustness properties, and Huang et al. [8] demonstrated that it is possible to provably rule out local existence of adversarial examples in image classification networks. While these works, and others, pioneered the use of SMT solvers for NN verification, applications are limited to NNs with piecewise linear units, such as ReLU and Hardtanh. Despite this limitation, a wide variety of safety critical NNs can be systematically analyzed. An alternative approach to robustness verification based on abstract interpretation was developed in [6]. VERISIG [9] extends verification to networks with sigmoid activation units by transforming the NN into a hybrid system and leveraging hybrid systems analysis tools. Recently, competitions and benchmarks such as VNN-COMP and ARCH-COMP20 [11] have spurred further innovations. An excellent survey of this rapidly expanding field is provided in [19].

The RELUPLEX NN verification tool developed in [14] was applied to verifying NN-based vertical aircraft collision avoidance controller [16]) in [13]. While work of Julian et al. [13] is focused on proving absence of safety violations on a subset of the state space, the current work demonstrates how to certify NN controller safety over the whole state space and, if safety cannot be guaranteed, identify the minimal set of states where the NN controller may be adjusted to yield a provably safe policy. More recent work appears in [12,20].

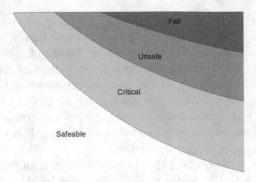

Fig. 1. Notional state space separated into safeable, critical, unsafe, and failing subsets.

2   Safe, Safeable and Critical States

One of the fundamental components of the present work is the notion of *safe-ability*, originally developed in [10]. Safeability is a property of the current state and the range of available controller commands that guarantees that the current command, which is potentially unsafe when applied for unbounded time, can be made safe by applying a different command at the next (discrete) controller iteration. Safeability can be expressed as a predicate over the state space, whose *true* level set corresponds to the maximal set of states from which collision avoidance can be guaranteed.

Safeability is important because it allows analysis of safety for sequences of commands that may be taken in the future. For example, in the case of aircraft collision avoidance, a practical controller implementation will not attempt to deconflict aircraft that are tens of miles apart even if they are on a potential collision course. The intruder or ownship may change course, the uncertainty in intruder position at the time of potential future closure may be far too high, *etc.*. However, the commands of the controller can be deemed safe as long as the current state is safeable for all possible controller commands, since a safe collision avoidance command can still be taken on the next controller iteration.

Safeability is a function of the current state and the range of available control commands. Therefore, it can be decided without the knowledge of the actual control law. Since the controller may safely exercise any command for the states in the safeable subset, it is natural to consider what happens at the boundary of this set. Adjacent to the safeable set lies a set of states we call *critical* [18]. These are states where safety cannot be definitively guaranteed in the future for all controller commands in the present; *i.e.*, only a subset of all controller commands can be definitively guaranteed to result in future safety.

A controller that selects a safe command in every critical state is guaranteed to be safe, because every trajectory terminating in failure must pass through a critical state.

Thus, the absence of counterexamples on the critical subset is equivalent to safety across the entire state space.

2.1 Setup

We consider a restricted subset of dynamics in [17] by constraining the horizontal motion to the straight-line, head-on geometry. The horizontal velocities of the aircraft are equal and fixed throughout the encounter. Vertical dynamics are constrained only by the maximal acceleration of the aircraft.

Following [17], we eliminate horizontal dynamics by summarizing the relevant horizontal information into a *horizontal conflict interval*. This is a time interval $[t_1, t_2]$ during which the aircraft may be proximate horizontally, and hence must be separated vertically to avoid collision. The duration $T = t_2 - t_1$ of the horizontal conflict interval depends on the horizontal distance at which aircraft can be considered to be safely separated and can be allowed to cross vertically. Because in our setup the horizontal velocities are fixed, the duration of the horizontal conflict interval is fixed at $T = D/(2v_x)$, where D is the horizontal keep away distance and v_x is the horizontal velocity.

Following standard aviation practice, we define the keep-away region to be a cylinder of radius R and half-height H, centered on the aircraft. This volume provides a buffer to account for sensor uncertainty, so that collisions may be avoided given typical position and altitude uncertainty. A breach of this cylindrical collision region is called a Near Mid-Air Collision (NMAC).

After eliminating the horizontal dynamics, the state space of the collision avoidance problem becomes three dimensional, comprising relative vertical position z and velocity v, and time until entry into horizontal conflict t_1. We define the relative vertical distance $z = z_i - z_o$, where the subscripts i and o stand for intruder and ownship, respectively. Similarly, the relative vertical velocity is $v = v_i - v_o$. Since we are considering purely vertical collision avoidance, the control input is vertical ownship acceleration $u = a_o$.

The following sections will be concerned with the safety of control inputs generated by the neural network controller in a specific relative configuration given by (z, v, t_1). Therefore, we need to compute the minimum/maximum vertical accelerations that allow the ownship to avoid NMAC by safely passing above/below the intruder aircraft. Note that this is somewhat different from the safety predicate in [17], which is a Boolean function that checks the safety of a maneuver specified by bounds on a_o in a given state. However, the underlying safety criteria that ensure separation between future envelopes of the two aircraft, are the same.

2.2 Reachability Computation

The key idea in [17] is to model the separation between reachable envelopes that encompass the space of possible future trajectories, subject to specified velocity and acceleration constraints. Using envelopes instead of individual trajectories allows for natural modeling and accounting of the uncertainties implicit and explicit in the collision avoidance system. The analysis of envelopes is tractable in the collision avoidance setting because the edges are piecewise linear and quadratic functions, arising out of second-order integrator dynamics. Despite the simplicity of the edges, the envelope non-determinism includes and allows reasoning about the safety of general non-polynomial trajectories that satisfy acceleration bounds.

We can guarantee the absence of NMAC if either of the two following conditions are true:

$$\forall t \in [t_1, t_2], \ z_i(t) - z_o(t) > H \qquad \text{[safe above]} \qquad (1)$$
$$\forall t \in [t_1, t_2], \ z_i(t) - z_o(t) < -H. \qquad \text{[safe below]} \qquad (2)$$

Following the established convention of relative coordinates $z = z_i - z_o$, $v = v_i - v_o$, and $a = a_i - a_o$, the safety equations determining minimum and maximum relative acceleration can be derived as follows: the ownship can keep the intruder above itself during the horizontal conflict interval $[t_1, t_2]$ by maintaining over the interval $[0, t_2]$ a constant relative acceleration a satisfying

$$\forall t \in [t_1, t_2], \ z + vt + \frac{at^2}{2} > H. \qquad \text{[safe above]} \qquad (1')$$

Similarly, it can keep the intruder below by choosing a constant relative acceleration satisfying

$$\forall t \in [t_1, t_2], \ z + vt + \frac{at^2}{2} < -H. \qquad \text{[safe below]} \qquad (2')$$

For a fixed z, v, t_1, and t_2, the safety condition $(1')$ imposes a lower bound

$$a \geq a_{\min}(z, v, t_1, t_2) \equiv$$
$$\inf \left\{ a \ \middle| \ \forall t \in [t_1, t_2], \ z + vt + \frac{at^2}{2} > H \right\} \qquad (3)$$

on the allowed relative acceleration a in the safe above case. (To see that it is indeed a lower bound, note that if some a satisfies $(1')$ in the time interval $[t_1, t_2]$, then so does $a + \epsilon$ for all $\epsilon \geq 0$.) Similarly, the safety condition $(2')$ imposes an upper bound

$$a \leq a_{\max}(z, v, t_1, t_2) \equiv$$
$$\sup \left\{ a \ \middle| \ \forall t \in [t_1, t_2], \ z + vt + \frac{at^2}{2} < -H \right\}. \qquad (4)$$

The lower and upper bounds $a_{\min}$ and $a_{\max}$ depend on the specific values of relative position, velocity, and entry into horizontal conflict; they reflect the minimum and maximum relative acceleration that the ownship must undertake in the configuration (z, v, t_1), in order for the intruder to pass safely above or below at the required vertical separation. These relative acceleration bounds (3) and (4), in turn, limit the vertical acceleration input u of the ownship in the two cases,

$$u < a_i - a_{\min}(z, v, t_1, t_2) \qquad \text{[safe above]} \qquad (5)$$
$$u > a_i - a_{\max}(z, v, t_1, t_2). \qquad \text{[safe below]} \qquad (6)$$

Note that the right-hand sides of (5) and (6) depend on the measured intruder quantities a_i, z_i, v_i, horizontal conflict entry t_1, and the ownship state. The horizontal conflict exit time $t_2 = t_1 + T$, where T is assumed fixed, can be thought of as purely a function of t_1. Therefore, we can drop dependence of $a_{\min}$ and $a_{\max}$ on t_2 when notationally convenient.

Explicit expressions for $a_{\min}$ and $a_{\max}$ are cumbersome to compute manually because of the large number of cases involving relative timing of the horizontal conflict interval and the orientation of the parabola in the left-hand sides of (1') and (2'). Broadly, we know that a computable expression exists because the sets involved in computing $a_{\min}$ and $a_{\max}$ are semialgebraic. To minimize the likelihood of human error, we used MATHEMATICA's [27] implementation of cylindrical algebraic decomposition and Reduce[] to eliminate the quantifier over t, and symbolically solved the polynomial equations for a (see the appendix).

2.3 Safe States

Following the previous discussion, the ownship is guaranteed to avoid collision starting from state (z, v, t_1) if it maintains a constant relative acceleration $a(t) = a$ over $t \in [0, t_2]$ satisfying either the safe above or safe below condition,

$$a_{\min}(z, v, t_1) < a \ \lor \ a < a_{\max}(z, v, t_1). \qquad \text{[safe } a] \qquad (7)$$

This is not always possible because for some states $a_{\min}$ and $a_{\max}$ will exceed the maximum *achievable* relative acceleration. Since intruder acceleration is uncontrolled, the worst case must be assumed to guarantee that collision can be definitively avoided. Both the ownship and intruder have acceleration (input) bounds such that ownship inputs, u, must obey $\underline{a}_o \leq u \leq \overline{a}_o$ and intruder acceleration, a_i, must follow $\underline{a}_i \leq a_i \leq \overline{a}_i$. Combining the worst case intruder with the ownship limitations, we obtain fixed constants for the minimum and maximum achievable relative accelerations, under the assumption that the intruder may accelerate up to its maximum in the opposite direction as the ownship. The achievable relative accelerations are therefore given by $\underline{a} = \overline{a}_i - \overline{a}_o$ and $\overline{a} = \underline{a}_i - \underline{a}_o$. This implies that the ownship can choose an input u satisfying (7), and therefore definitively avoid NMAC, when

$$a_{\min}(z, v, t_1) \leq \overline{a} \ \lor \ \underline{a} \leq a_{\max}(z, v, t_1). \qquad \text{[safe]} \qquad (8)$$

We will call states (z, v, t_1) satisfying (8) *safe*.

2.4   Safeable States

The definition of safe states is overly conservative because it requires that a current constant acceleration must be chosen to guarantee safety at a future horizontal conflict time that may be very far in the future. Applying such a definition to a real controller will result in a controller that seeks to resolve the possibility of future collisions even when the collision time is so far in the future that a later adjustment to acceleration would suffice.

A more flexible definition of safety is based on the notion of *safeability*, developed in [10]. A state is safeable if it can be made safe at the next time of control action selection (we assume a discrete-time control law) in the worst-case evolution during the current time-step. To simplify notation we introduce a one-step extrapolation operator

$$\phi(\tau; z, v, t_1, \alpha) \equiv \left(z + v\tau + \frac{\alpha\tau^2}{2}, v + \alpha\tau, t_1 - \tau \right), \tag{9}$$

where τ is the controller time-step and α is the anticipated relative acceleration. We can write the safeable condition in terms of ϕ as follows

$$\Sigma_\tau(z, v, t_1) \equiv \forall t \in [t_1, t_2], \ \underline{a} \le a_{\max}(\phi(\tau; z, v, t_1, \bar{a}))$$
$$\vee \ a_{\min}(\phi(\tau; z, v, t_1, \underline{a})) \le \bar{a} \tag{10}$$

Note that the state is propagated with the worst-case relative acceleration for the corresponding clause, $\underline{a}$ for the intruder passing safely above and $\bar{a}$ for the intruder passing safely below. If τ is set to 0, then (10) reduces to (8). Simplifying the notation, we thus refer to the predicate (8) as $\Sigma_0(z, v, t_1)$.

The key consequence of safeability of a state is that the state may be guaranteed to be safe at the next controller action selection time even if it is not safe with the current acceleration command. This property of safeability allows us to develop a definition of controller safety based on the notion of *critical states* that we introduce next.

2.5   Critical States

A *critical state* is one for which a safe acceleration command exists in the present moment (Σ_0) but for which there is no acceleration command that will definitively (for all possible intruder actions) guarantee safety at the next controller time step (Σ_τ)

$$\Sigma_0(z, v, t_1) \wedge \neg\Sigma_\tau(z, v, t_1). \tag{11}$$

In other words, a critical state is the last point along an unsafe trajectory at which an action could be taken that preserves safety. Detailed treatment of the state space partitioning into safeable and critical states was originally introduced in [18] and is closely related to the ModelPlex approach developed in [22].

2.6 Satisfiability Modulo Theory

To prove safety properties of a neural network in-the-loop, we first encode the controller ReLU network as constraints in the Z3 SMT solver [23]. It has been recently shown [14,24] that by introducing intermediate variables and encoding the internal neural layers as a logical combination of linear constraints involving the introduced variables, it is possible to automatically prove or disprove input/output properties of the neural network when treated as a function. For more details about the mechanics of encoding neural networks in SMT, see $e.g.$, [14] and [25, §2.1].

3 Safety Verification

The analysis in this section is based on the observation that transition to an undesirable state ($e.g.$, NMAC) is always preceded by a traversal of a *critical* state. It follows that *a controller that resolves, i.e., generates a safe action in, every critical state is guaranteed to be safe, regardless of its actions on the rest of the state space*. Conversely, a controller that fails to resolve any of the critical states cannot be guaranteed safe, even when it performs well in simulations.

Next, we describe how to validate controller performance on the critical set. In theory, the task is simple: the predicate (11) describes the set of critical states and the predicate (7) determines whether a given state is safe for a specified relative acceleration command a. In principle, all that remains is to evaluate (7) with acceleration commanded by the controller over the set where (11) holds. In practice, this is non-trivial because (10) depends on nonlinear functions a_{min} and a_{max} and commanded acceleration is determined by the NN controller, which is a complex (although in our case, piecewise linear) function. Moreover, it would be useful to have more than just a yes/no answer. If the controller fails to resolve all of the critical cubes (cubes that contain critical states), it would be useful to know (1) what proportion of the critical cubes are unresolved by the controller and (2) where in the state space they are located.

The nonlinearity of expressions for a_{min} and a_{max} and the complexity of the NN controller put computing exact answers to these questions beyond the capabilities of existing tools. However, with judicious use of conservative, piecewise-constant overapproximations for a_{min} and a_{max}, and SMT solvers, we can compute very good approximations to both questions posed above for the example NN controller described in Sect. 5.

We begin by subdividing the state space into a collection of cubes $\mathcal{G}$, over which the safety analysis will be carried out. We used a grid partition with uniform step sizes for this study because it is straightforward to implement, but, overall, the same approach would work for grid partitions with adaptive step size. As expected, the accuracy of the computations increases with decreasing cube size, increasing the number of cubes that need to be analyzed. We found that, for our example model, even relatively large cubes produced decent results. Furthermore, the per cube analysis lends itself to parallelization, so we do not expect the trade-off between accuracy and cube size to be a significant bottleneck for moderate dimensional state spaces.

On each cube, the bound $a_{\min}$ is approximated from above, and $a_{\max}$ from below. Let

$$\lceil a_{\min} \rceil (C) \equiv \max_{(z,v,t) \in C} a_{\min}(z, v, t) \tag{12}$$

$$\lfloor a_{\max} \rfloor (C) \equiv \min_{(z,v,t) \in C} a_{\max}(z, v, t), \tag{13}$$

where C is a compact subset of the state space, e.g., grid partition cube. This ensures that the cube-wise equivalent of (7) given by

$$\forall\, (z, v, t1) \in C,\ \lceil a_{\min} \rceil (C) < a \vee a < \lfloor a_{\max} \rfloor (C)$$

has a solution only if every point within the cube is guaranteed to have a solution for (7). Computing the bounds $\lceil a_{\min} \rceil$ and $\lfloor a_{\max} \rfloor$ is straightforward due to the monotonicity of $a_{\min}$ and $a_{\max}$, which guarantees that the maximum and minimum over a partition cube both occur at the corners.

Similarly, we can define a cube-wise safeable predicate by replacing $a_{\min}$ and $a_{\max}$ in (10) with the corresponding overapproximations

$$\Sigma_\tau(C) \equiv \forall t \in [t_1, t_2],\ \underline{a} \le \lceil a_{\min} \rceil (\phi(\tau; C, \underline{a})) \vee \lfloor a_{\max} \rfloor (\phi(\tau; C, \bar{a})) \le \bar{a}, \tag{14}$$

where

$$\phi(\tau; C, \alpha) \equiv \bigcup \{ c \in \mathcal{G} \mid \exists (z, v, t) \in C,\ \phi(\tau; z, v, t, \alpha) \cap c \ne \emptyset \} \tag{15}$$

is the grid-adapted propagation operator. It is now straightforward to extend the critical state predicate (10) to cubes by substituting the cube-wise safeable predicate (14) by

$$\Sigma_0(C) \wedge \neg \Sigma_\tau(C). \tag{16}$$

Using the cube-wise safety predicate above, it is now possible to identify the critical cubes (as illustrated in Fig. 2), which are defined by the property that at least one point within the cube is critical. The union of all critical cubes overapproximates (contains) the set of critical states defined by (11), and that overapproximation becomes increasingly accurate with decreasing grid partition size.

We now proceed to evaluate NN controller safety on the set of critical cubes. For each cube C, we compare the acceleration commanded by the NN controller at every point of the cube with the conservative bounds $\lceil a_{\min} \rceil (C)$ and $\lfloor a_{\max} \rfloor (C)$. This is a task at which modern SMT solvers excel. For this purpose, we developed the Python package LANTERN ("safer than a torch")[1] for encoding general PYTORCH neural networks as SMT expressions in Z3 [23]. It should be mentioned that as our experiments focus on the state space decomposition and formal verification strategy, the choice to use Z3 was made purely

---

[1] https://github.com/JHUAPL/lantern-smt.

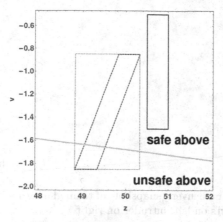

Fig. 2. An example critical cube (black) shown in relative coordinates, with its worst case one-step projection (blue) and its grid overapproximation (green). Lower part of the cube, whose projection falls below the orange line, cannot be guaranteed safe. (Color figure online)

for convenience—other more specialized SMT solvers and similar translation packages could be used to similar effect.

Finally, we iterate over all critical cubes, querying the SMT solver to evaluate the cube-wise safety predicate (3). Every critical cube is identified as either resolved or unresolved. Note that unresolved critical points within critical cubes are not guaranteed to always result in NMAC. This is because in developing the safeable predicate (10), we made conservative worst-case assumptions about relative acceleration of the ownship and intruder.

4   Collision Avoidance Controller

4.1   Training a Network with an RL Game

We developed a 2D flight simulator to train and test the NN controller for vertical collision avoidance. In the simulation, an ownship is set on a head-on collision course with an opposing intruder; the ownship seeks to evade while the intruder attempts to collide. Repeated iterations of this scenario are run, each with a randomly-selected initial vertical offset between the ownship and intruder.

The two aircraft are positioned horizontally 800 pixels (px) apart from one another, with the ownship on the left and intruder on the right (see Fig. 3). The ownship has a constant v_x (rightward velocity) of 7.5 px/s, while the intruder is moving left at -7.5 px/s. Both aircraft begin with zero vertical velocity. As a controlling action, the ownship can apply up to a ± 0.2 px/s^2 and intruder up to ± 0.15 px/s^2 acceleration in the z (vertical) dimension. The opponent's acceleration is limited to 75% of the RL agent's acceleration, so that the RL agent can have a reasonable chance of avoiding collision.

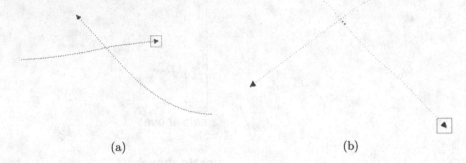

(a)   (b)

Fig. 3. Minimal dodge maneuvers: snapshots of trained network behavior. The ownship (with NMAC box) starts on left, intruder on right.

The intruder is randomly assigned a starting altitude of ±500 px relative to the ownship. The system state is defined completely by the x and z positions and corresponding velocities of both aircraft. Network inputs are provided in relative coordinates,

$$(x, z, \dot{x}, \dot{z}) = (x_i - x_o, z_i - z_o, \dot{x}_i - \dot{x}_o, \dot{z}_i - \dot{z}_o). \qquad (17)$$

Finally, the NMAC area is a rectangle with a width and height of 50 px centered on the ownship.

4.2 Shaping Policy Behavior

Several key factors affect the strategies that are adopted by the RL agent for this game: opponent behavior, opponent performance capabilities, and reward functions. The opponent agent was designed to actively seek collision with the RL agent in order to pose a worst-case collision threat. To that end, the intruder is designed to know the ownship acceleration and pursue a parabolic trajectory that directly collides at the time step of vertical alignment. With horizontal speeds of both aircraft fixed, collision is only possible in the center of the screen.

Reward and penalty functions were used to influence the RL agent's trained behavior away from undesired strategies:

- *NMAC Penalty*: The agent is punished (negatively rewarded) by 5 points for each time-step at which the center point of the opponent is within the 50×50 px safety box.
- *Fuel Penalty*: The agent is punished by the amount $0.2 \cdot |u|$, where u is the commanded ownship acceleration.
- *Distance from Horizontal Middle Plane Penalty*: The agent is punished an amount equal to

$$0.0001 \cdot \left| \frac{\mathtt{map\_height}}{2} - \mathtt{agent\_height} \right|,$$

providing a cumulative punishment for distance from the center line. This helps minimize distance from the original mission trajectory, and also avoids a trivial solution where the RL agent flies off-screen as soon as possible to avoid interaction with the opponent.

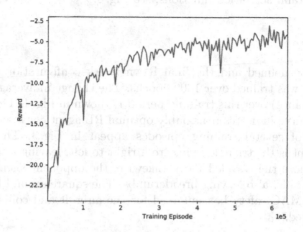

Fig. 4. Reward function over the RL training period, trained with a sequence of 600,000 episodes of play.

Fig. 5. Selected controller network architecture

4.3 Network Selection: Algorithm and Hyperparameters

With the learning environment defined, an RL-trained network and configuration was selected and configured to adapt to that environment. In selecting the network, we considered the performance of the RL agent at the problem, the minimization of the number of units in each hidden layer, and the use of only ReLU activation functions.

To achieve these goals, we benchmarked learning agent performance over a multidimensional spread of algorithm and hyperparameter configurations. All combinations of the following were evaluated:

– *RL Algorithm*: Vanilla Policy Gradient, Trust Region Policy Optimization, Proximal Policy Optimization, Deep Deterministic Policy Gradient, Twin Delayed DDPG, or Soft Actor-Critic.

- *Hidden Layers*: [8, 8] (two hidden layers of eight nodes), [16, 16], or [32, 32].
- *Activation Function*: ReLU, LeakyReLU, or Hardtanh.

We experimentally chose the network architecture resulting in the best objective value: Proximal Policy Optimization with a [16, 16] hidden layer configuration and Hardtanh activation functions; see Fig. 5.

5   Results

With the game defined and the final RL network configuration selected, the learning agent was trained over 1600 epochs. The change in average reward per cycle (performance) over this training period is shown in Fig. 4. The asymptotic performance curve indicates reasonably optimal RL agent convergence.

Examples of several training episodes appear in Fig. 3. The boxed RL-controlled agent is the triangle flying from right to left, leaving a trail of breadcrumbs to denote the traveled path. Likewise, the opponent agent approaches from the right side, also leaving breadcrumbs. The square around the RL agent denotes the NMAC safety box enforced for the aircraft and collision locations are shown in red.

Table 1. Verification results for all hypercubes

Total Hypercubes	23,200,000
Hypercubes identified as critical	184,936 (100%)
Failing critical cubes	163,518 (88.4%)
Verified safeable critical cubes	21,418 (11.5%)

Table 2. Testing of the Network and Safety Guarantees

Total test scenarios	181,147
Number with collisions	12,678
Collision scenarios predicted by unsafe cube traversal	12,678
Collision scenarios not traversing unsafe cube	0
Total number visited critical cubes	1,722
Total visited safe cubes	635
Total visited failing cubes	1,087

Table 1 shows the total number of hypercube partitions that were identified as critical (see Sect. 3) out of the 23.2 million total cubes. Only 11.5% of these critical cubes were verified as satisfying the safeability requirements. We tested inputs sampled at random from the states inside failing critical cubes (these start the game in locations other than the usual starting positions), and over 90% of those states led to collisions, showing that these unverified cubes are largely not due to overapproximation of safety bounds. Table 2 shows the results over 181,147 tests. Fewer than 7%, or 12,678, scenarios resulted in collision. All collisions were preceded by visiting a nonsafeable critical cube. However, we see that fewer than 1% of the 184,936 critical cubes were visited during these tests. To test how frequently the network avoids ever visiting a critical state we tested 57,750 scenarios. Only 5700 scenarios (or 9.9%) ever visited a critical hypercube. From these results, we see that the RL network achieved its 93% success rate by steering the game away from critical states and would not be robust to unexpected events that put the system into a critical, yet resolvable state (Fig. 6).

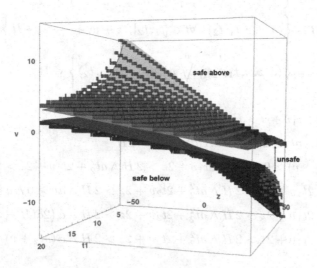

Fig. 6. Safety boundaries defined by level sets $a_{\min}(z, v, t_1) = \bar{a}$ (blue) and $a_{\max}(z, v, t_1) = \underline{a}$ (orange) in (z, v, t_1) space. Resolved critical cubes shown in green and unresolved in red. (Color figure online)

6 Conclusion

We have demonstrated a novel approach to verifying a neural network controller by partitioning the input space and using SMT solvers to prove safety only on the portions critical to safe operation. We showed this technique can guarantee a network is free from counterexamples to safety over continuous regions of the input space. Further, this technique identifies the critical areas where a network could be tuned to verify safety. Future work will focus on the use of efficient solvers to adjust the networks to be provably safe as well as scaling to larger networks.

Appendix

The minimum (maximum) relative acceleration $a_{\min}$ ($a_{\max}$) allowed so that the intruder passes safely above (below) the ownship is given by the following functions

$$a_{\min}(z, v, t_1, t_2) \equiv \inf\{a \mid (a, z, v, t_1, t_2) \in A\} \tag{18}$$

$$a_{\max}(z, v, t_1, t_2) \equiv \sup\{a \mid (a, z, v, t_1, t_2) \in B\}, \tag{19}$$

where

$$A \equiv \left\{ (a, z, v, t_1, t_2) \mid \forall t \in [t_1, t_2], \ z + vt + \frac{at^2}{2} > H \right\}$$

$$= \left\{ (a, z, v, t_1, t_2) \mid \bigvee_{i=1}^{6} \psi_A^{(1)}(a, z, v, t_1, t_2) \right\} \subseteq \mathbf{R}^5 \tag{20}$$

$$B \equiv \left\{ (a, z, v, t_1, t_2) \mid \forall t \in [t_1, t_2], \ z + vt + \frac{at^2}{2} < -H \right\}$$

$$= \left\{ (a, z, v, t_1, t_2) \mid \bigvee_{i=1}^{6} \psi_B^{(i)}(a, z, v, t_1, t_2) \right\} \subseteq \mathbf{R}^5, \tag{21}$$

$$\psi_A^{(1)} \equiv a = 0 \wedge t_1 v + z > H \wedge H < t_2 v + z$$

$$\psi_A^{(2)} \equiv v = 0 \wedge at_1^2 + 2z > 2H \wedge at_2^2 + 2z > 2H$$

$$\psi_A^{(3)} \equiv a (at_1 + v) > 0 \wedge at_1^2 + 2t_1 v + 2z > 2H \wedge at_2^2 + 2t_2 v + 2z > 2H$$

$$\psi_A^{(4)} \equiv at_1^2 + 2t_1 v + 2z > 2H \wedge at_2^2 + 2t_2 v + 2z > 2H \wedge av \geq 0 \wedge a \neq 0$$

$$\psi_A^{(5)} \equiv at_1^2 + 2t_1 v + 2z > 2H \wedge at_2^2 + 2t_2 v + 2z > 2H \wedge a \left(2a(H - z) + v^2\right) < 0$$

$$\psi_A^{(6)} \equiv at_1^2 + 2t_1 v + 2z > 2H \wedge at_2^2 + 2t_2 v + 2z > 2H \wedge a (at_2 + v) < 0,$$

$$\psi_B^{(1)} \equiv a = 0 \wedge H + t_1 v + z < 0 \wedge H + t_2 v + z < 0$$

$$\psi_B^{(2)} \equiv v = 0 \wedge at_1^2 + 2(H + z) < 0 \wedge at_2^2 + 2(H + z) < 0$$

$$\psi_B^{(3)} \equiv a (at_1 + v) > 0 \wedge at_1^2 + 2(H + z) + 2t_1 v < 0 \wedge at_2^2 + 2(H + z) + 2t_2 v < 0$$

$$\psi_B^{(4)} \equiv at_1^2 + 2(H + z) + 2t_1 v < 0 \wedge at_2^2 + 2(H + z) + 2t_2 v < 0 \wedge av \geq 0 \wedge a \neq 0$$

$$\psi_B^{(5)} \equiv a \left(2a(H + z) - v^2\right) < 0 \wedge at_1^2 + 2(H + z) + 2t_1 v < 0$$
$$\wedge \ at_2^2 + 2(H + z) + 2t_2 v < 0$$

$$\psi_B^{(6)} \equiv at_1^2 + 2(H + z) + 2t_1 v < 0 \wedge a (at_2 + v) < 0 \wedge at_2^2 + 2(H + z) + 2t_2 v < 0$$

Note that the sets A and B are semialgebraic. For the decomposed dynamics, we have $t_2 = t_1 + T$, where T is the fixed horizontal conflict duration. The infimum in $a_{\min}$ be determined by computing the infimum over each semialgebraic component $\psi_A^{(i)}$ and keeping track of the valid sets. Similarly, the supremum in $a_{\max}$ can be found by maximizing a over each $\psi_B^{(i)}$.

References

1. Amodei, D., Olah, C., Steinhardt, J., Christiano, P., Schulman, J., Mané, D.: Concrete problems in AI safety, July 2016. arXiv:1606.06565 [cs.AI]
2. Bak, S., Tran, H.-D., Hobbs, K., Johnson, T.T.: Improved geometric path enumeration for verifying ReLU neural networks. In: Lahiri, S.K., Wang, C. (eds.) CAV 2020. LNCS, vol. 12224, pp. 66–96. Springer, Cham (2020). https://doi.org/10.1007/978-3-030-53288-8_4
3. National Transportation Safety Board: Preliminary report released for crash involving pedestrian, Uber Technologies Inc, test vehicle (2018). https://www.ntsb.gov/news/press-releases/Pages/NR20180524.aspx. Accessed 23 Sept 2020
4. Chen, T., Liu, J., Xiang, Y., Niu, W., Tong, E., Han, Z.: Adversarial attack and defense in reinforcement learning-from AI security view. Cybersecurity 2(1), 1–22 (2019). https://doi.org/10.1186/s42400-019-0027-x
5. Dutta, S., Chen, X., Jha, S., Sankaranarayanan, S., Tiwari, A.: Sherlock - a tool for verification of neural network feedback systems. In: ACM International Conference on Hybrid Systems: Computation and Control (HSCC), pp. 262–263. Association for Computing Machinery, New York (2019)
6. Gehr, T., Mirman, M., Drachsler-Cohen, D., Tsankov, P., Chaudhuri, S., Vechev, M.: AI^2: safety and robustness certification of neural networks with abstract interpretation. In: IEEE Symposium on Security and Privacy (SP), pp. 3–18 (2018)
7. Huang, C., Fan, J., Li, W., Chen, X., Zhu, Q.: ReachNN: reachability analysis of neural-network controlled systems. ACM Trans. Embed. Comput. Syst. 18(5s) (2019)
8. Huang, X., Kwiatkowska, M., Wang, S., Wu, M.: Safety verification of deep neural networks. In: Majumdar, R., Kunčak, V. (eds.) CAV 2017. LNCS, vol. 10426, pp. 3–29. Springer, Cham (2017). https://doi.org/10.1007/978-3-319-63387-9_1
9. Ivanov, R., Weimer, J., Alur, R., Pappas, G.J., Lee, I.: Verisig: verifying safety properties of hybrid systems with neural network controllers. In: ACM International Conference on Hybrid Systems: Computation and Control (HSCC), pp. 169–178 (2019)
10. Jeannin, J., et al.: Formal verification of ACAS X, an industrial airborne collision avoidance system. In: Girault, A., Guan, N. (eds.) International Conference on Embedded Software, EMSOFT 2015, Amsterdam, The Netherlands, 4–9 October 2015. ACM (2015)
11. Johnson, T.T., et al.: ARCH-COMP20 category report: artificial intelligence and neural network control systems (AINNCS) for continuous and hybrid systems plants. In: Frehse, G., Althoff, M. (eds.) International Workshop on Applied Verification of Continuous and Hybrid Systems (ARCH20). EPiC Series in Computing, vol. 74, pp. 107–139 (2020)
12. Julian, K.D., Kochenderfer, M.J.: Reachability analysis for neural network aircraft collision avoidance systems. J. Guid. Control. Dyn. 44(6), 1132–1142 (2021)
13. Julian, K.D., Sharma, S., Jeannin, J.B., Kochenderfer, M.J.: Verifying aircraft collision avoidance neural networks through linear approximations of safe regions. In: AIAA Spring Symposium (2019). arXiv:1903.00762 [cs.SY]
14. Katz, G., Barrett, C., Dill, D.L., Julian, K., Kochenderfer, M.J.: Reluplex: an efficient SMT solver for verifying deep neural networks. In: Majumdar, R., Kunčak, V. (eds.) CAV 2017. LNCS, vol. 10426, pp. 97–117. Springer, Cham (2017). https://doi.org/10.1007/978-3-319-63387-9_5

15. Katz, G., et al.: The marabou framework for verification and analysis of deep neural networks. In: Dillig, I., Tasiran, S. (eds.) CAV 2019. LNCS, vol. 11561, pp. 443–452. Springer, Cham (2019). https://doi.org/10.1007/978-3-030-25540-4_26

16. Kochenderfer, M.J., Holland, J.E., Chryssanthacopoulos, J.P.: Next generation airborne collision avoidance system. Lincoln Lab. J. **19**(1), 17–33 (2012)

17. Kouskoulas, Y., Genin, D., Schmidt, A., Jeannin, J.-B.: Formally verified safe vertical maneuvers for non-deterministic, accelerating aircraft dynamics. In: Ayala-Rincón, M., Muñoz, C.A. (eds.) ITP 2017. LNCS, vol. 10499, pp. 336–353. Springer, Cham (2017). https://doi.org/10.1007/978-3-319-66107-0_22

18. Kouskoulas, Y., Schmidt, A., Jeannin, J.B., Genin, D., Lopez, J.: Provably safe controller synthesis using safety proofs as building blocks. In: 7th International Conference in Software Engineering Research and Innovation (CONISOFT), pp. 26–35 (2019)

19. Liu, C., Arnon, T., Lazarus, C., Barrett, C., Kochenderfer, M.J.: Algorithms for verifying deep neural networks (2019)

20. Lopez, D.M., Johnson, T., Tran, H.D., Bak, S., Chen, X., Hobbs, K.L.: Formal methods for intelligent aerospace systems. In: Verification of Neural Network Compression of ACAS Xu Lookup Tables with Star Set Reachability. AIAA SciTech Forum (2021)

21. McCloskey, M., Cohen, N.J.: Catastrophic interference in connectionist networks: the sequential learning problem. In: Psychology of Learning and Motivation, vol. 24, pp. 109–165. Elsevier (1989)

22. Mitsch, S., Platzer, A.: ModelPlex: verified runtime validation of verified cyber-physical system models. Formal Methods Syst. Des. **49**(1), 33–74 (2016). Special issue of selected papers from RV 2014

23. de Moura, L., Bjørner, N.: Z3: an efficient SMT solver. In: Ramakrishnan, C.R., Rehof, J. (eds.) TACAS 2008. LNCS, vol. 4963, pp. 337–340. Springer, Heidelberg (2008). https://doi.org/10.1007/978-3-540-78800-3_24

24. Papusha, I., Topcu, U., Carr, S., Lauffer, N.: Affine multiplexing networks: system analysis, learning, and computation, April 2018. arXiv:1805.00164 [math.OC]

25. Papusha, I., Wu, R., Brulé, J., Kouskoulas, Y., Genin, D., Schmidt, A.: Incorrect by construction: fine tuning neural networks for guaranteed performance on finite sets of examples. In: 3rd Workshop on Formal Methods for ML-Enabled Autonomous Systems (FoMLAS), July 2020. arXiv:2008.01204 [cs.LG]

26. Platzer, A.: The logical path to autonomous cyber-physical systems. In: Parker, D., Wolf, V. (eds.) QEST 2019. LNCS, vol. 11785, pp. 25–33. Springer, Cham (2019). https://doi.org/10.1007/978-3-030-30281-8_2

27. Wolfram Research Inc: Mathematica, Version 12.1, Champaign, IL (2020). https://www.wolfram.com/mathematica

An Efficient Summation Algorithm for the Accuracy, Convergence and Reproducibility of Parallel Numerical Methods

Farah Benmouhoub[1(✉)], Pierre-Loic Garoche[2], and Matthieu Martel[1,3]

[1] LAMPS Laboratory, University of Perpignan, Perpignan, France
{farah.benmouhoub,matthieu.martel}@univ-perp.fr
[2] ENAC, Toulouse, France
pierre-loic.garoche@enac.fr
[3] Numalis, Montpellier, France

Abstract. Nowadays, parallel computing is ubiquitous in several application fields, both in engineering and science. The computations rely on the floating-point arithmetic specified by the IEEE754 Standard. In this context, an elementary brick of computation, used everywhere, is the sum of a sequence of numbers. This sum is subject to many numerical errors in floating-point arithmetic. To alleviate this issue, we have introduced a new parallel algorithm for summing a sequence of floating-point numbers. This algorithm which scales up easily with the number of processors, adds numbers of the same exponents first. In this article, our main contribution is an extensive analysis of its efficiency with respect to several properties: accuracy, convergence and reproducibility. In order to show the usefulness of our algorithm, we have chosen a set of representative numerical methods which are Simpson, Jacobi, LU factorization and the Iterated power method.

Keywords: Floating-point arithmetic · Accurate summation ·
Numerical accuracy · Numerical methods · Convergence ·
Reproducibility

1 Introduction

Scientific computing relies heavily on floating-point arithmetic as defined by the IEEE754 Standard [1,8,17]. It is therefore sensitive to round-off errors, and this problem tends to increase with parallelism. In floating-point computations, in addition to rounding errors, the order of the computations affects the accuracy of the results. For example, let us calculate in IEEE754 single precision (Binary32) the sum of three values x, y and z, where $x = 10^9$, $y = -10^9$ and $z = 10^{-9}$. We obtain

$$((x + y) + z) = ((10^9 - 10^9) + 10^{-9}) = 10^{-9}, \tag{1}$$

$$(x + (y + z)) = (10^9 + (-10^9 + 10^{-9})) = 0. \tag{2}$$

© Springer Nature Switzerland AG 2022
R. Bloem et al. (Eds.): NSV 2021/VSTTE 2021, LNCS 13124, pp. 165–181, 2022.
https://doi.org/10.1007/978-3-030-95561-8_10

Equations (1) and (2) show that for the same mathematical expression, a sum of three operands, different orderings of the computations yield different results. In the floating-point arithmetic, we note that, for the same values of x, y and z, and for the same arithmetic operation, we obtain two different results because of parsing the three values differently. In fact, many summation algorithms exist in the literature. Some of them are based on compensated summation methods [13, 16, 18, 21–23] with or without the use of the error-free transformations to compute the error introduced by each accumulation. Others are based on manipulating the exponent and/or the mantissa of the floating-point numbers in order to split data before starting computations [5, 6].

In a similar approach, we proposed in [2] a new algorithm for accurately summing n floating-point numbers. This algorithm performs computations only within working precision, requiring only an access to the exponents of the values. The idea is to compute the summands according to their exponents without increasing the complexity. More precisely, the complexity of the algorithm is linear in the number of elements, just like the naive summation algorithms. The main contribution of the present article is to show that this algorithm improves simultaneously the parallel execution time, the reproducibility and convergence of computations through the increase of their numerical accuracy as follows:

1. *numerical accuracy improvement* is illustrated on computations of MPI implementations of Simpson's rule and the LU factorization method.
2. *convergence acceleration* is showcased on both Jacobi's method and the iterated power method compared to versions of these methods which use a simple summation algorithm. Past results [4] show that improving the accuracy of computation also leads to accelerate the convergence of iterative sequential algorithms. Our motivation is therefore to parallelize these two methods focusing first on accuracy and obtaining, as a side effect, a better convergence.
3. Last, *reproducibility of numerical computation in the context of parallel summation* is supported by the reduction on numerical errors. Indeed, the combination of the non-associativity of floating-point operations like addition and computations done in parallel may affect reproducibility. The intuitive solution used to ensure reproducibility is to determine a deterministic order of computation. Another method is based on reduction or elimination of round-off errors, i.e. by improving the numerical accuracy of computations that we will further see in this article. This is illustrated on Simpson's rule and a simple matrix multiplication.

A last contribution is an experimental comparison of the execution time of our algorithm with respect to the similar approach proposed by Demmel and Hida [5]. Indeed, Demmel and Hida algorithm [5] has a time complexity of $O(n \log n)$ because of an additional sorting step, compared to our summation algorithm which involve no explicit sorting and has a complexity in $O(n)$. Our solution has a greater space complexity but this can be addressed with sparse datastructures. Execution time of the two approaches are compared in Sects. 3.1 and 3.2.

The rest of the paper is organized as follows. Section 2 recalls elements of floating-point arithmetic and the related work on some existing summation methods proposed to improve the numerical accuracy of computations. We also present our parallel summation algorithm. Section 3 focuses on the improvement of numerical accuracy, based on two experiments, Simpson's rule and a LU factorization. Section 4 focuses on the impact of accuracy on the convergence speed. It is based on experiments on Jacobi's method and the Iterated Power Method. Last, we focus on reproducibility in Sect. 5, based on two experiments: the Simpson's rule and a matrix multiplication. We conclude in Sect. 6.

2   Background

This section introduces some useful notions used in the remainder of this article. Section 2.1 provides some background of the floating-point arithmetic as defined by the IEEE754 standard [1,8,17]. Section 2.2 discusses related work. Our algorithm introduced in [2], is presented in Sect. 2.3.

2.1   Floating-Point Arithmetic

Following the IEEE754 Standard, a floating-point number x in base β is defined by

$$x = s \cdot m \cdot \beta^{exp-f+1} \tag{3}$$

where

- $s \in \{-1, 1\}$ is the sign,
- $m = d_0 d_1 .... d_{f-1}$ is the mantissa with digits $0 \leq d_i < \beta$, $0 \leq i \leq f - 1$,
- f is the precision,
- exp is the exponent with $exp_{min} \leq exp \leq exp_{max}$.

The IEEE754 Standard defines binary formats with some particular values for f, exp_{min} and exp_{max} which are summarized in Table 1. Moreover, the IEEE754 Standard defines four rounding modes for elementary operations over floating-point numbers. These modes are towards $+\infty$, towards $-\infty$, towards zero and towards nearest, denoted by $\circ_{+\infty}$, $\circ_{-\infty}$, $\circ_0$ and $\circ_\sim$, respectively.

   The behavior of the elementary operations $\diamond \in \{+, -, \times, \div\}$ between floating-point numbers is given by

$$v_1 \diamond_\circ v_2 = \circ(v_1 \diamond v_2) \tag{4}$$

where $\circ$ denotes the rounding mode such as $\circ \in \{\circ_{+\infty}, \circ_{-\infty}, \circ_0, \circ_\sim\}$. By Eq. (4), we illustrate that, in floating-point computations, performing an elementary operation $\diamond_\circ$ with rounding mode $\circ$ returns the same result as the one obtained by an exact operation $\diamond$, then rounding the result using $\circ$. The IEEE754 Standard also specifies how the square root function must be rounded in a similar way to Eq. (4) but does not specify the round-off of other functions like sin, log, etc. In this article, without loss of generality, we consider that $\beta = 2$. We assume the rounding mode to the nearest. In floating-point computations, absorption and cancellation may affect the numerical accuracy of computations. An absorption occurs when adding two floating-point numbers with different orders of magnitude. The small value is absorbed by the large one. A cancellation occurs when two nearly equal numbers are subtracted and the most significant digits cancel each other.

Table 1. Binary formats of the IEEE754 Standard.

Format	#total bits	f bits	exp bits	exp_{min}	exp_{max}
Half precision	16 bits	11	5	-14	$+15$
Single precision	32 bits	24	8	-126	$+127$
Double precision	64 bits	53	11	-1122	$+1223$
Quadruple precision	128 bits	113	15	-16382	$+16383$

2.2 Related Work

Summation of floating-point numbers is one of the most basic tasks in numerical analysis. Research work has focused on improving the numerical accuracy [5,6,13,16,18,21] or reproducibility [7] of the computations involving summations. There are many sequential and parallel algorithms for this task. Surveys of them being presented in [11,12]. Floating-point summation is often improved by compensated summation methods [13,16,18,21–23] with or without the use of error-free transformations to compute the error introduced by each accumulation. We detail some of the compensated summation algorithms further in this section. The accuracy of summation algorithms can also be improved by manipulating the exponent and the mantissa of the floating-point numbers in order to split data before starting computations [5,6]. This approach is the one employed by our algorithm and it is explained in details in Sect. 2.3.

Compensated Summation Methods: The idea is to compute the exact rounding error after each addition during computations [13]. Compensated summation algorithms accumulate these errors and add the result to the result of the summation. The compensation process can be applied recursively yielding cascaded compensated algorithm. Malcolm [16] describes cascading methods based on the limited exponent range of floating-point numbers. He defines an extended precision array e_i where each component corresponds to an exponent. To extract and scale the exponent, Malcolm uses an integer division, without requiring the division to be a power of 2. If the extended precision has $53+k$ bits in the mantissa, then, obviously, no error occurs for up to 2^k summands and $\sum_{i=1}^{n} p_i = \sum_{i=1}^{n} e_i$. The summands p_i are added with the respect to decreasing order into the array element corresponding to their exponent. Note that such an algorithm requires twice as much running time compared to our algorithm.

Rump et al. [18,21,22] proposed several algorithms for summation and dot product of floating point numbers. These algorithms are based on iterative application of compensations. An extension of the compensation of two floating-point numbers to vectors of arbitrary length is also given and used to compute a result as if computed with twice the working precision. Various applications of compensated summation method have been proposed [9,10]. Thévenoux et al. [24] implement an automatic code transformation to derive a compensated programs.

Also, we mention the accurate floating-point summation algorithms introduced by Demmel and Hida [5,6]. Given two precision f and F with $F > f$, Demmel and Hida's algorithms use a fixed array accumulators $A_0, ...A_N$ of precision F for summing n floating-point numbers of precision f such that $S = \sum_{i=1}^{n} s_i$. These algorithms require accessing the exponent field of each s_i to decide to which accumulator A_j to add it. More precisely, each A_j accumulating the sum of the s_i where e leading bits are j. Then, these A_j are sorted in decreasing order to be summed. Consequently, complexity of these algorithms is equal to $O(n \log n)$, because of the sorting step.

Parallel Approaches: In addition to the existing sequential algorithms, many other parallel algorithms have been proposed. Leuprecht and Oberaigner [15] describe parallel algorithms for summing floating-point numbers. The authors propose a pipeline version of sequential algorithms [3,20] dedicated to the computation of exact rounding summation of floating-point numbers. In order to ensure the reproducibility, Demmel and Nguyen [7] introduce a parallel floating-point summation method based on a technique called pre-rounding to obtain deterministic rounding errors. The main idea is to pre-round the floating-point input values to a common base, according to some boundary, so that their sum can later be computed without any rounding error. The error depends only on both input values and the boundary, contrary to the intermediate results which depend on the order of computations.

2.3   Accurate Summation Algorithm

In this section, we describe our summation algorithm introduced in [2] for accurately summing n floating-point numbers. Our algorithm enjoys the following set of properties. First, it improves the numerical accuracy of computations without increasing the cost of complexity compared to the naive algorithm. Second, it performs all the computations in the original working precision without using accumulators of higher precision. Last, using this new algorithm, we increase the numerical accuracy and, as a side effect and shown in the next sections, we also improve the execution time and reproducibility of summation.

For the algorithm detailed hereafter, we assume that we have P processors and n summands (with $n \gg P$). We assign n/P summands to each processor. For computing the sum $S = \sum_{i=1}^{n} s_i$, $\forall 0 \leq i < P$ processor i computes $\sum_{j=i \times n/P}^{(i+1) \times n/P - 1} s_j$. Then a reduction – a last sum – is done to compute the final result. First of all, Algorithm 1 allocates an array called *sum_by_exp* which is created and initialized at 0 for all its elements before starting the summations. The array *sum_by_exp* has $exp\_max - exp\_min + 1$ elements. Let us assume that the exponents of summands range from exp_min to exp_max. The main idea is to sum all the summands whose exponent is 2^i in the cell *sum_by_exp*$[i + bias]$ such as $bias = -exp\_min$, this avoids most absorptions while avoiding to sort explicitly the array. Let $exp\_(s_i)$ denote the exponent of s_i in base 2. For computing the sum $S = \sum_{i=1}^{n} s_i$, each value s_i is added to the appropriate cell *sum_by_exp*$[exp\_s_i + bias]$ according to its exponent. For parallelism, each processor has an *sum_by_exp* array to sum locally. In order to obtain its local final

Algorithm 1 Accurate summation with local sum at each processor

1: Initialization of the array sum_by_exp
2: total_sum=0.0
3: **for** i=0 : p_row **do**   ▷ p_row: rows number of each processor
4:     exp_s_i=getExp(s[i])+bias   ▷ *getExp*: function used to compute exponent
5:   in base 2
6:     sum_by_exp[exp_s_i]=sum_by_exp[exp_s_i]+s[i]
7: local_sum=0.0   ▷ Summing locally in order of increasing exponents
8: **for** i=0 to exp_max-exp_min+1 **do**
9:     local_sum=local_sum+sum_by_exp[i]
                                                    ▷ Total sum by processor 0
10: MPI_Reduce(&local_sum, &total_sum, 1, Mpi_float, Mpi_sum, 0,Mpi_comm_world)

result, we add these values in increasing order. Once the final local sums are computed, a reduction is done and the processor receiving the result of the reduction gets the total sum. To emphasize the property regarding the cost of complexity mentioned above, we note that the cost of Algorithm 1 is $O(n)$, no sorting being performed and the access to the data to be summed being done only once.

Let us mention that another refined implementation of Algorithm 1 has been proposed in [2]. This second implementation shares a common idea with Algorithm 1 which is related to the way that the summands are added and differs from Algorithm 1 in that the final sum is not carried out in the same way. The advantage of this other implementation is that the summation results are more accurate than those of Algorithm 1. Concerning its drawback, the cost of complexity will be higher in the constant of the $O(n)$ while being linear. In the following sections, we evaluate the simpler and most cost-effective version of Algorithm 1 regarding accuracy, convergence speed for iterative schema and reproducibility. We note that our implementations are done in the C programming language with MPI, compiled with MPICC 3.2, and made them run on an Intel i5 with 7.7 GB memory. Let us also note that for our experiments, we report numerical values relying on thousands separators, typesetting 1234567.89 as $1, 234, 567.89$.

3   Numerical Accuracy

In this section, we first evaluate the numerical accuracy of our algorithm introduced in Sect. 2.3. Secondly, we address the issue of the compromise between numerical accuracy and running time of the studied algorithms. We take into consideration two examples, namely Simpson's rule and the LU factorization method. For each example, we have implemented two parallel versions, using MPI [19]. The first one, called original program uses simple sums: to sum n values $x_1, ..., x_n$ it computes $(((x_1 + x_2) + x_3) + ... + x_n)$. The second program uses Algorithm 1 and is called, the accurate program. The experiments are carried out for several numbers of processors.

3.1   Simpson's Rule

Our first example computes the integral $C \times \int_0^b f(x)dx$ of mathematical functions f using Simpson's rule. The Simpson's rule is a numerical method that approximates the value of a definite integral of a function f using quadratic polynomials. We measure the efficiency of our algorithm on this example by computing the absolute errors between both the results of the original and accurate programs with respect to the analytical solution of the integral, as shown in Fig. 1. We integrated the following functions $C \times \cos(x)$, $C \times (1/x^2 + 1)$ and $C \times \tanh(x)$ with $C = 10^6$, and b ranging in $[2; 5]$. The number of processors P ranges in $[2; 8]$. Each processor computes a part of the integral.

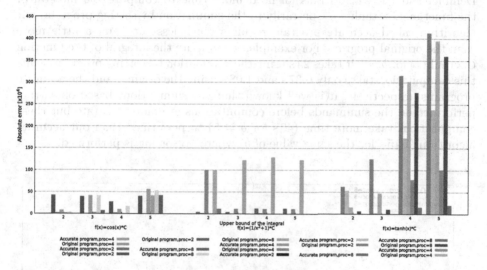

Fig. 1. The absolute errors between the original program and the accurate one for the integral computation of three different functions $(C \times \cos(x), C \times (1/x^2 + 1)$ and $C \times \tanh(x))$ with the corresponding analytical result by varying the upper bound of the integral $b = 2, 3, 4, 5$.

For the first experimentation, let us take the function $C \times \cos(x)$ as an example. As it is observed in Fig. 1, the absolute errors of the original program are larger than those of the accurate program of several order of magnitude. To better illustrate, let us consider the value 3 of the x-axis corresponding to the upper bound of the integral. We notice that the absolute errors of the original program are $392, 700.198$, $411, 541.22875$ and $414, 048.5725$ for $P = 2$, $P = 4$ and $P = 8$, respectively. In contrast to the accurate program where the absolute errors computed for the same example are $3, 238.3225$, $32, 419.6975$ and $77, 805.5725$, respectively. In the same way, we note that the results of the second function $C \times (1/x^2 + 1)$ and the third function $C \times \tanh(x)$ are similar to those of the first function $C \times \cos(x)$. Moreover, the results of the $C \times \tanh(x)$ function show that the results computed by the original Simpson's rule performed on a large upper bound of the integral are those which have larger absolute errors. Indeed, for $P = 2$ the absolute errors computed for the upper bound equal to 2,3,4 and 5 are $621, 315.3125$, $1, 253, 797.375$, $3, 166, 450.745625$ and $4, 130, 976.360625$ respectively.

The second experiment measures the execution time (in seconds) of the original program, accurate program and another program based on sorting. The choice of this last program is motivated by the main idea of Demmel and Hida algoritms [5]. Let us consider the third function $C \times \tanh(x)$ for $P = 8$, Fig. 2 displays the running time in seconds taken by each program (original program, accurate program and summation by sorting) to compute the integral of this function. The results show that the summation program based on sorting like Demmel and Hida algorithms [5] need more time to compute the integral of the function $C \times \tanh(x)$. Contrarily to the summation by sorting program, our algorithm called accurate program requires much less time and a little more than the original program. For example, to compute the integral of the function $C \times \tanh(x)$ for $b = 2$ it takes 24 s using the summation by sorting program, while this computation takes only 0.37 s and 1.08 s using the original and the accurate programs, respectively. It is well known that the summations based on sorting performed on the summands before computations are more accurate but these computations take more time (49 s for $b = 5$) to performed than our accurate algorithm (1.15 s for the same value of b) where no sorting is performed.

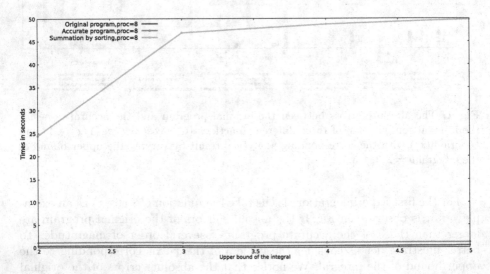

Fig. 2. Execution time of the original program, accurate program and summation algorithm by sorting for the integral computation of the function $C \times \tanh(x)$.

3.2 LU Factorization

Our second example is the parallel LU factorization method. This method consists in rewriting a matrix A as the product of a lower triangular matrix L and an upper triangular matrix U such that $A = LU$. The LU factorization method is a very common algorithm which can be used e.g. to solve linear systems or to compute the determinant of a matrix. In the parallel case, the matrix A is divided into blocks of rows and each processor performs its computations on a given block. For our experiments we generated square matrices of various dimensions $n \in [200, 800]$ with increment of 100. These matrices contain values chosen to introduce ill-conditioned sums [14]. In our case, we consider 30% of large values among small and medium. By small, medium and large values we mean respectively, of the order of 10^{-7}, 10^0 and 10^7. This is motivated by the IEEE754 single precision arithmetic. Also, we take vectors x with the same proportions of large values among small and medium as for the matrices.

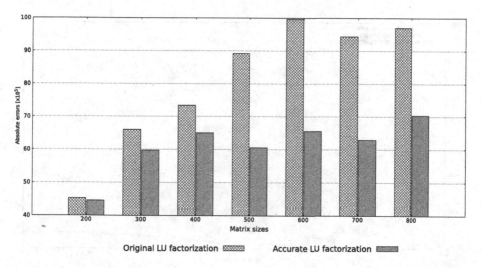

Fig. 3. The absolute errors of the LU factorization by the original and accurate algorithm for matrix of different sizes.

The first experimentation consists of comparing the numerical accuracy of the LU factorization carried out using the original and accurate programs. Let us consider a matrix A and vector x. We start by computing the solution vector given by $Ax = b$. This vector is considered as the exact solution. Next, we apply the original LU factorization program to the matrix A with $P = 16$ processors in order to obtain L_{orig} and U_{orig}. In the same way, we factorize the matrix A using the accurate LU factorization into L_{acc} and U_{acc}. We compare the new vector solutions $b_{orig} = L_{orig} \times U_{orig} \times x$ and $b_{acc} = L_{acc} \times U_{acc} \times x$ with the exact solution b. Figure 3 represents the absolute errors between the computed solutions after factorization and the exact solution. These experiments show significant improvements: while the difference between the absolute errors of the original and the accurate program are already up to an order of 10^5 for our smallest matrices ($n = 200$), it reaches up to an order of 10^7 for large ones ($n = 600$). More precisely, for $n = 200$ the absolute errors are $452, 1984$ and $445, 6448$ for the original and the accurate LU factorization, respectively. We obtain $996, 1472$ and $655, 3600$ for $n = 600$. Thus, we conclude from this experimentation that the accurate program shows its efficiency in terms of numerical accuracy when we handle large matrices, i.e. when various types of absorptions and cancellation have been introduced.

By the second experimentation, we want to show the running time taken by each LU factorization program for a set of matrices of size varying from 200 to 800 with $P = 16$. Figure 4 summarizes the execution time taken by each algorithm (original program, accurate program and summation by sorting) to compute the LU factorization.

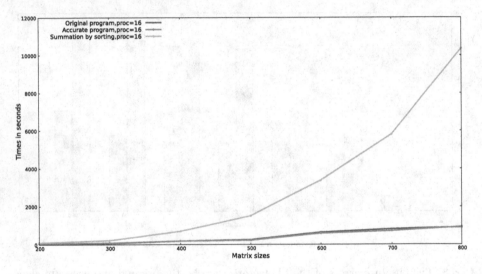

Fig. 4. Execution time of the original program, accurate program and summation algorithm by sorting of the LU factorization.

We notice in Fig. 4 that the summation algorithm based on sorting requires much more time to compute the LU factorization. Besides, accurate program needs much less time than summation algorithm by sorting and a little more than the original algorithm. To better illustrate, let us take a matrix of size $n = 300$. We remark that the execution takes only 66 s and 90 s with original program and accurate program, respectively, while the summation by sorting program requires 224 s for the same computation. Let us also remark that the running time obtained for the summation by sorting program for the large matrices are much larger than those obtained for the smallest one. In fact, the execution time increase from 101 s to approximately 2 h for matrices sizes 200 and 800, respectively, using the summation algorithm by sorting.

4   Convergence of Iterative Methods

In this section, we focus on the impact of accuracy on the number of iterations required by numerical iterative methods to converge. For our experiments, we consider two iterative methods: Jacobi's method and Iterated Power method. As in the previous section, we implemented two versions of the same algorithm, the original one and our accurate version. We observed the impact on the convergence, comparing their respective number of iterations.

4.1   Jacobi's Method

The Jacobi's method is a well known numerical method used to solve linear systems of the form $Ax = b$. In this method, an initial guess, an approximate solution x^0, is selected and is iteratively updated until finding the solution x^k of the linear system. More precisely, this method iterates until $|x_i^{(k+1)} - x_i^k| < \varepsilon$. In our case, the parallelization of the Jacobi's method is done according to the row-wise distribution. Jacobi's method is stable whenever the matrix A is strictly diagonally dominant, i.e. its satisfies the property of Eq. (5).

$$\forall i \in 1, \ldots, n, \qquad |a_{ii}| > \sum_{j \neq i} |a_{ij}|. \tag{5}$$

We examine the impact of accuracy on the convergence speed for the systems of sizes 10 and 100. While the chosen systems were stable with respect to the sufficient condition of the stability given by Eq. (5), they are close to instability with $\forall i \in 1, \ldots, n, |a_{ii}| \approx \sum_{j \neq i} |a_{ij}|$. Figures 5 represents the difference between the number of iterations of the original and the accurate programs. Let us take the first system of size $n = 10$. We notice that for various values of ε varying from 10^{-2} to 10^{-5}, the convergence speed in terms of number of iterations increases from 59 to 2,029. For the second system when $n = 100$, we remark that the number of iterations reduced are larger than those computed for the system $n = 10$ for the same values of ε. For instance the number of iterations reduced for $\varepsilon = 10^{-2}$ and $\varepsilon = 10^{-5}$ are 861 and 10,946, respectively. From these two examples, we conclude that the smallest values of ε are those which have a large difference between the original and the accurate programs in terms of the number of iterations. Also, for a given value of ε, the accurate program shows its efficiency on the convergence speed on large matrices compared to small ones.

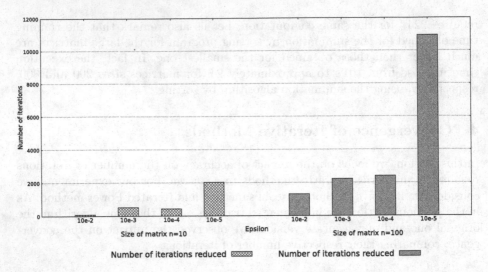

Fig. 5. Difference between number of iterations necessary for the original and the accurate programs to achieve the convergence of the Jacobi method.

4.2 Iterated Power Method

The Iterative Power method is particularly useful for estimating numerically the largest eigenvalue and its corresponding eigenvector. The idea is to fix an arbitrary initial vector $\mathbf{x}^{(0)}$ which contains a single non-zero elements. Then, we build an intermediary vector $\mathbf{y}^{(1)}$ such that $\mathbf{A}\mathbf{x}^{(0)} = \mathbf{y}^{(1)}$. In order to obtain the vector $\mathbf{x}^{(1)}$, we renormalize $\mathbf{y}^{(1)}$ so that the selected component is again equal to 1. For the next iteration, we use $\mathbf{x}^{(1)}$ as a selected vector. The iterative process is repeated until convergence. We assume that, the parallelization of the Iterated Power method is done according to the row-wise distribution. Let us take a square matrix $\mathbf{A}$ of the form:

$$A = \begin{pmatrix} d & a_{12} & \cdots & a_{1j} \\ a_{21} & d & \cdots & a_{2j} \\ \vdots & & & \vdots \\ a_{i1} & a_{i2} & \cdots & d \end{pmatrix}$$

We assume that $a_{ij} = 0.01$ and $d \in [300.0, 500.0]$ following the methodology introduced in [4]. Figure 6 summarizes the difference between the number of iterations of the original and the accurate Iterated Power method. As it is observed in Fig. 6, the accurate program accelerates the convergence speed of the Iterative Power method by reducing the number of iterations needed to converge. Indeed, for the matrix size $n = 100$ with various values of the diagonal and using $P = 4$ we show that the number of iterations reduced increases from 205 to 340.

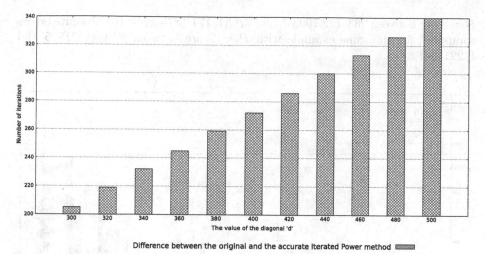

Fig. 6. Difference between number of iterations of original and accurate Iterated Power method ($n = 100$, $d \in [300, 500]$ with increment of 20).

5   Reproducibility

In this section, we aim at evaluating the efficiency of Algorithm 1 on the improvement of reproducibility. Figures 7 and 8 give results of reproducibility for Simpson's rule and Matrix Multiplication, respectively. During our experiments, we consider the original and the accurate programs of each method. We compare the results of each of them on several processors and their respective results with only one processor.

5.1   Simpson's Rule

Let's take again the example of Simpson's rule already introduced in Sect. 3. In practice, improving the numerical accuracy often improves reproducibility. We measure the efficiency of our algorithm on this example by computing the absolute errors between both the results of the original and the accurate programs by varying the number of processors from 2 to 8 and their respective program with only one processor, as shown in Fig. 7. Let us consider several mathematical functions $C \times \cos(x)$, $C \times (1/x^2 + 1)$ and $C \times \tanh(x)$ with $C = 10^6$, and b ranging in $[2; 5]$. For example, for $f(x) = C \times \cos(x)$ with $P = 2$, the results show that the absolute errors of the original program are larger (between $105, 553.117187$ and $703, 687.4375$) than those of the accurate program (between $47, 938.1875$ and $195, 067.296875$) as it is observed in Fig. 7. Also, we can observe in Fig. 7 that the results of integrals computed by the original program performed on a large number of processors $P = 8$ are those which have a larger absolute errors. As an example, the absolute errors computed for the function $C \times \tanh(x)$ with

$P = 8$ are between $233, 122.109375$ and $3, 637, 171.1875$ while the absolute errors computed for the same example with $P = 2$ are between $87, 960.921875$ and $1, 221, 541.8750$.

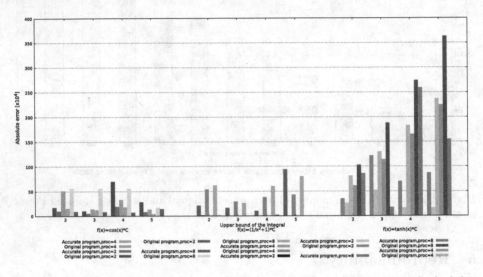

Fig. 7. The reproducibility of the integral computations using Simpson method of the original program and the accurate one depending on the number of processors.

5.2   Matrix Multiplication

The computation of the matrix-matrix multiplication based on floating-point addition and multiplication which are non-associative operations is prone to accuracy problems. Moreover, the out of order execution of arithmetic operations on different or even similar parallel architectures are different, reproducibility of the results is not guaranteed. In this context, we address the problem of reproducibility in the case of matrix multiplication. To parallelize this method, we assume that each matrix is divided into sub-matrices of the size n/P. For our experiments, we consider square matrices of various dimensions $n \in [200, 800]$ with increment of 200. These matrices contain a variety of floating-point values chosen with difference in magnitude. More precisely, they are made of 50% of large values (of the order of 10^7) among small (of the order of 10^0) and medium (of the order of 10^{-7}). Figure 8 represents the percentage of accuracy computed between the original and the accurate programs carried out using $P = 8$ and their respective result using only one processor. The results show that for different matrix sizes, the percentage of accuracy of the original program ranges from 3% to 13%. Contrarily to the original program, the percentage linked to the accurate program described in this article is equal to 100% for each matrix which confirms the usefulness of Algorithm 1.

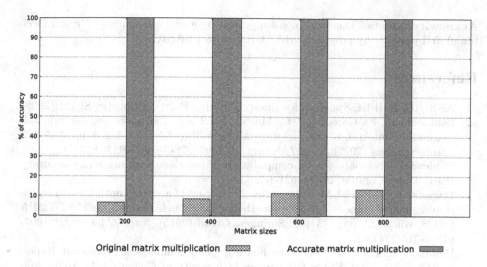

Fig. 8. The reproducibility of the matrix-matrix multiplication for different size of matrices.

6   Conclusion and Future Work

In this article, we have focused on the impact of accuracy on both the reproducibility and convergence speed of numerical algorithms. The originality of this article is to study the impact that a new accurate summation algorithm has on the accuracy of numerical methods involving sums. In this work, we have experimented our algorithm on several representative numerical methods by comparing the original and the accurate programs of each of them. The experiments show the usefulness of our algorithm on the improvement of reproducibility. Also, the results obtained show the efficiency of our algorithm to reduce the number of iterations required by numerical iterative methods to converge. More precisely, the accurate program converge more quickly than the original one without loss of accuracy. In a future work, we would like to refine our algorithm by adding a test phase after line 4 of Algorithm 1, i.e. before adding the value s_i to the appropriate cell of the array sum_by_exp. Indeed, if we have a large set of values to be summed with the same exponent, the result produced can have a larger exponent than the initial one. Therefore, a loss of accuracy can be caused during the computations of the local sums. An interesting perspective consists in feeding our algorithms [2] with a static analysis. Our idea is to rely on static analysis to detect the exponents range of a given set of values that will be summed. Once this range is accurately computed, one can use our summation algorithm and obtain more accurate floating-point results. Further, it will be interesting to explore the impact of our algorithms in the context of neural networks. Our goal is to improve the numerical accuracy of computations by using the accurate summation algorithms [2] as a replacement for their summation algorithms.

Acknowledgments. This work was supported by a regional funding (Region Occitanie) and partially by project ANR-17-CE25-0018 FEANICSES.

References

1. ANSI/IEEE. IEEE Standard for Binary Floating-Point Arithmetic. SIAM (2008)
2. Benmouhoub, F., Garoche, P.-L., Martel, M.: Parallel accurate and reproducible summation. In: Arai, K. (ed.) Intelligent Computing. LNNS, vol. 283, pp. 363–382. Springer, Cham (2022). https://doi.org/10.1007/978-3-030-80119-9_21
3. Bohlender, G.: Floating-point computation of functions with maximum accuracy. IEEE Trans. Comput. **26**(7), 621–632 (1977)
4. Damouche, N., Martel, M., Chapoutot, A.: Impact of accuracy optimization on the convergence of numerical iterative methods. In: Falaschi, M. (ed.) LOPSTR 2015. LNCS, vol. 9527, pp. 143–160. Springer, Cham (2015). https://doi.org/10.1007/978-3-319-27436-2_9
5. Demmel, J., Hida, Y.: Accurate floating point summation. Technical Report UCB/CSD-02-1180, EECS Department, University of California, Berkeley, May 2002
6. Demmel, J., Hida, Y.: Accurate and efficient floating point summation. SIAM J. Sci. Comput. **25**(4), 1214–1248 (2003)
7. Demmel, J., Nguyen, H.D.: Parallel reproducible summation. IEEE Trans. Comput. **64**(7), 2060–2070 (2015)
8. Goldberg, D.: What every computer scientist should know about floating-point arithmetic. ACM Comput. Surv. **23**(1), 5–48 (1991)
9. Graillat, S., Langlois, P., Louvet, N.: Algorithms for accurate, validated and fast polynomial evaluation. Jpn. J. Ind. Appl. Math. **26**(2–3), 191–214 (2009)
10. Graillat, S., Ménissier-Morain, V.: Compensated Horner scheme in complex floating point arithmetic. In: Proceedings 8th Conference on Real Numbers and Computers, Santiago de Compostela, Spain, pp. 133–146 (2008)
11. Higham, N.: The accuracy of floating point summation. SIAM J. Sci. Comput. **14**(4), 783–799 (1993)
12. Higham, N.: Accuracy and Stability of Numerical Algorithms. Society for Industrial and Applied Mathematics (1996)
13. Kahan, W.: A survey of error analysis. In: IFIP Congress (1971)
14. Langlois, P., Martel, M., Thévenoux, L.: Accuracy versus time: a case study with summation algorithms. In: Proceedings of the 4th International Workshop on Parallel and Symbolic Computation, PASCO '10, New York, NY, USA, pp. 121–130. Association for Computing Machinery (2010)
15. Leuprecht, H., Oberaigner, W.: Parallel algorithms for the rounding exact summation of floating point numbers. Computing **28**(2), 89–104 (1982). https://doi.org/10.1007/BF02241816
16. Malcolm, M.: On accurate floating-point summation. Commun. ACM **14**(11), 731–736 (1971)
17. Muller, J.M., et al.: Handbook of Floating-Point Arithmetic, Birkhäuser (2010)
18. Ogita, T., Rump, S., Oishi, S.: Accurate sum and dot product. SIAM J. Sci. Comput. **26**(6), 1955–1988 (2005)
19. Pacheco, P.: An Introduction to Parallel Programming, 1st edn. Morgan Kaufmann Publishers Inc., San Francisco (2011)
20. Pichat, M.: Correction d'une somme en arithmetique a virgule flottante. Numer. Math. **19**(5), 400–406 (1972). https://doi.org/10.1007/BF01404922

21. Rump, S.: Ultimately fast accurate summation. SIAM J. Sci. Comput. **31**(5), 3466–3502 (2009)
22. Rump, S., Ogita, T.: Fast high precision summation. Nonlinear Theory Appl. IEICE **1**, 2–24 (2010)
23. Rump, S., Ogita, T., Oishi, S.: Accurate floating-point summation part I: faithful rounding. SIAM J. Sci. Comput, **31**(1), 189–224 (2008)
24. Thévenoux, L., Langlois, P., Martel, M.: Automatic source-to-source error compensation of floating-point programs: code synthesis to optimize accuracy and time. Concurr. Comput.: Pract. Exp. **29**(7), e3953 (2017)

Modeling Round-Off Errors
in Hydrodynamic Simulations

William Weens[1,2], Thibaud Vazquez-Gonzalez[1],
and Louise Ben Salem-Knapp[1,3(✉)]

[1] CEA DAM DIF, 91297 Arpajon Cedex, France
{william.weens,thibaud.vazquez-gonzalez,louise.bensalem-knapp}@cea.fr
[2] Université Paris-Saclay, CEA, Laboratoire en Informatique Haute Performance
pour le Calcul et la simulation, 91680 Bruyères-le-Châtel, France
[3] Université Paris-Saclay, CNRS, ENS Paris-Saclay, Inria,
Laboratoire Méthodes Formelles, 91190 Gif-sur-Yvette, France

Abstract. The growth of the computing capacities makes it possible
to obtain more and more precise simulation results. These results are
often calculated in *binary64* with the idea that round-off errors are not
significant. However, exascale is pushing back the known limits and the
problems of accumulating round-off errors could come back and require
increasing further the precision. But working with extended precision,
regardless of the method used, has a significant cost in memory, computation time and energy and would not allow to use the full performance
of HPC computers. It is therefore important to measure the robustness of
the *binary64* by anticipating the future computing resources in order to
ensure its durability in numerical simulations. For this purpose, numerical experiments have been performed and are presented in this article.
Those were performed with *weak floats* which were specifically designed
to conduct an empirical study of round-off errors in hydrodynamic simulations and to build an error model that extracts the part due to round-off
error in the results. This model confirms that errors remain dominated
by the scheme errors in our numerical experiments.

Keywords: Floating-point · Round-off error · Hydrodynamics ·
HPC · Exascale

1 Industrial and Scientific Context

The HPC industry applies to an ever-increasing number of scientific domains—
biology, molecular dynamics, meteorology, astrophysics, aerodynamics, etc. It
must therefore evolve regularly to adapt to theoretical and material changes,
as well as to new regulatory or commercial demands. The list of usual requirements for HPC simulation codes is then increased by new needs. To name a
few requirements: improving speed, robustness, accuracy and maintainability,
energy efficiency, portability on heterogeneous resources (GPU or FPGA type
accelerators), or the measurement of uncertainties in the results [12].

© Springer Nature Switzerland AG 2022
R. Bloem et al. (Eds.): NSV 2021/VSTTE 2021, LNCS 13124, pp. 182–196, 2022.
https://doi.org/10.1007/978-3-030-95561-8_11

In this context, simulations must both improve and guarantee the results while relying on constantly renewed computing resources (HPC) (GP-GPU) and on parallel computing (MPI, Multithreading, Vectorization) of which performance increases year after year. The strategy commonly used to take advantage of the possibilities promised by the *exascale* consists in relying on the exploitation of proven models and schemes and in increasing the size of the problem studied—such as the size of the mesh, the number of particles, elements, etc. This strategy of improved accuracy leads to a contradiction since finite precision calculations also introduce errors. Indeed, by increasing the size of the simulated problems, the number of operations also increases, thus degrading the results contrary to the expected effect. Therefore, in order to guarantee the quality of the results, it is important to measure the optimal point between their improvement by adding information versus their degradation by round-off errors due to floating-point arithmetic. In other words, in the current context, the question addressed here could be summarized as follows: *Is binary64 sufficient for exascale computing?*

The use of the common theoretical tools such as interval arithmetic, Taylor series or probability do not provide satisfactory answers to this question [6,8,11, 23]. Because of the large number of operations in a simulation and the complexity of the programs, the bounds obtained to frame the error are too large to be useful. This is why new approaches have emerged and recent advances in formal proofs have allowed the determination of thin theoretical bounds for framing the error for a finite differences scheme on the wave equation [4] and the Runge-Kutta method [5]. The bounds obtained are compatible with the tolerances of the industry but for simulations of more complex problems, the empirical approach remains unavoidable today in order to detect the real weight of round-off errors in the numerical results.

In this paper, we focus on the measurement of numerical error in hydrodynamic simulations [7], which are the skeleton model of many more complete physical models. A new analysis tool, the *weak floats*, has been developed to improve the traditional empirical approach—extended precision—which is too slow to be conducted on large meshes. After introducing our approach, Sect. 2 describes the implementation of the *weak floats* within a numerical error model. In Sect. 3, the framework of the hydrodynamic applications is detailed: the equations, the discretisation method, the details of the HPC implementation and the test cases used. In Sect. 4, the numerical results are presented. The tests are performed in dimension 1, using Godunov type numerical schemes of order 1. Also using several test cases of reference [24] with the floating types of the IEEE-754 standard [14] and the *weak floats*. Finally, the versatility of the developed tools, their ease of use, and their speed allowed us to obtain sufficient data to conclude this study, while realizing a proof of principle of their application for empirical analysis. By extrapolating the data obtained to exascale, an attempt is made to answer the problematic of required arithmetic precision for the exascale in the conclusion.

2   Model of the Numerical Error

2.1   Measurement of the Error Due to Floating-Point Arithmetic

We are interested in the numerical error, denoted ε^{num}, which we define as the deviation between the theoretical result from the mathematical model, y^{model}, and the result obtained by the simulation, $y^{simulation}$. In this work, we focus on the case where y^{model} and $y^{simulation}$ are space-time fields. Using the L_2 norm:

$$\varepsilon^{num} := ||y^{model} - y^{simulation}||_{L_2} . \qquad (1)$$

This numerical error ε^{num} has two sources: the error due to the discretization of the equations ε^{scheme} and the error created by finite precision computations ε^{float}.

Every numerical scheme introduces errors. But if the scheme is consistent, the discretization error ε^{scheme} can be seen as the error caused by the lack of information. Therefore, it is sufficient to add information (cells, particles, etc.) to decrease this error—the decrease of the error compared to the injected information defines the order of the scheme. Processing this additional information involves more calculations and therefore more operations. The error from finite precision computations ε^{float} can be seen as the accumulation of errors due to rounding committed for each operation [17,20]. We understand then that these two sources of errors will counteract each other. To be more precise, to reduce ε^{scheme}, we must do more operations but each operation can introduce an additional round-off error increasing then ε^{float}. Therefore there is a minimum for the numerical error ε^{num} which corresponds to a certain problem size that should not be exceeded.

Figure 1 illustrates (on a floating-point number) what this divergence point means. When the simulation is not accurate enough, the last bits of the mantissa do not contain relevant information (gray pattern error), so the round-off error is hidden. As the calculations proceed, the round-off error accumulates in the last bits and moves up to the significant part of the information. If it exceeds the area of irrelevant information, then the round-off error appears and spoils the relevant information.

In a simulation, this backtracking process is complex. The round-off errors can be compensated, amplified, and occur more or less quickly in certain cells and on certain quantities. The error can contaminate the cell or spread. This behavior depends on the code but also on the input data.

The possibility of detecting round-off errors ε^{float} in a numerical simulation implies constraints on the choice of the numerical experiment. A study can be conducted only if: i) the problem is mathematically well defined, at least in some configurations, ii) there exists convergent numerical schemes to solve the problem, iii) there exists implementations of these schemes that do not introduce systematic errors (via non-ordered sums on sets for example), iv) the software/component stack (libraries, compilers, chips) is reliable, v) reproducibility[1]

---

[1] If several realizations of the same experiment under identical conditions give exactly identical results, then the experiment is said to be reproducible.

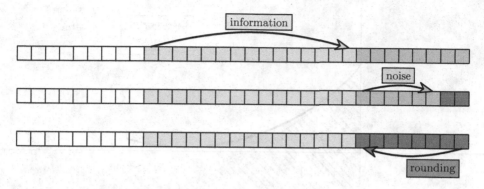

Fig. 1. Idealized illustration of the encounter between the round-off error (red) and the relevant information (blue) in a floating-point number. The irrelevant information (gray) is the scheme error. (Color figure online)

is ensured, vi) the computational speed is high enough to explore large problem sizes.

2.2   Error Model on an Explicit Numerical Scheme

Similarly to an ordinary differential equation [2], the expected behavior of the numerical error for a one-dimensional problem discretized by a numerical scheme of order 1 is:

$$\varepsilon^{num} \leq C_1 h + C_2 h^{-1}, \tag{2}$$

where C_1, C_2 are constants specific to the case studied and to the scheme, and h a parameter characterizing the finiteness of discretization of the equations (for example equal to the space step for a 1D spatial discretization). C_1, C_2 are abstract constants defined to bound the error in mathematical proofs and their numerical values are usually not to be found.

The convergence order of the scheme can be seen in the first member $C_1 h$. Without round-off errors, the numerical error would tend toward 0 with h, giving results more and more accurate. The second member $C_2 h^{-1}$ is identified as the accumulation of the round-off error, which depends on the number of operations and thus on the space step. Indeed, in the case of explicit schemes, the number of iterations in time of the simulation N_{it}—on which depends N_{op} the number of operations—depends on the time step Δt, itself constrained by Courant-Friedrichs-Lewy (CFL) number [19,27] which relates it to the space step h.

When the number of cells becomes infinite, the asymptotic behavior of the two components of the numerical error is:

$$\lim_{h \to 0} \varepsilon^{scheme} = 0, \quad \lim_{h \to 0} \varepsilon^{float} = +\infty. \tag{3}$$

The decomposition of the numerical error into two sources is illustrated qualitatively in Fig. 2 by showing the part of ε^{num} due to discretization in blue hatch-

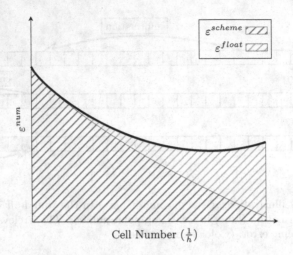

Fig. 2. Qualitative representation of the behavior of the numerical error and of its components with a convergent scheme.

ing and the part due to round-off errors in green hatching. This illustration allows to interpret the results presented in the following sections.

It is important to note that when ε^{float} becomes significant compare to ε^{scheme}, then the results deviate quickly from the analytical solution and the curve diverges. The simulation loses all its meaning and the total error (the measured one) suddenly increases. The quantity of interest that seemed relevant to us is the number of cells at which the divergence occurs. This divergence point depends on the floating-point precision and is written N_{div}^{double} for *binary64* numbers.

2.3 Weak Floats

To certify that the code is used within a valid domain, it is necessary to obtain an estimate of the divergence point of the *binary64* N_d^{double}. It is precisely for this purpose that the *weak floats* have been developed.

The idea of *weak floats* is to use precisions smaller than the *binary64*, to find the divergence points for these sub-precisions, and to extrapolate the values in order to estimate the divergence point of the *binary64*. A similar approach exploiting a sub-precision has been used in [15].

To speed-up the computation, operations between *weak floats* are carried out on a CPU stem type (*binary32*, *binary64*, etc.), which mantissa size is higher than the *weak floats* mantissa, then the result is truncated and rounded. The *weak floats* have therefore the same number of exponent bits as the chosen stem type (*binary64* in our simulations). Due to the truncation and rounding operations, it is impossible for the compilers to use many optimizations. The execution is thus largely slowed down by the *weak floats* while the precision is reduced.

In the following, *weak N* designates a *binary64* floating-point number of which only the N first *bits* of the mantissa are used, the others being truncated (thus a precision of $N + 1$ *bits* with the implicit *bit*).

N.B. All *weak floats* are thus numbers obtained by two rounding operations. The first operation is the rounding operation of the IEEE-754 standard on the *binary64* (hardware) and the second is the one of the weak floats (software). With the nearest rounding mode (*nearest*), the double rounding is not equal to the last rounding $\circ_m(\circ_n(x)) \neq \circ_m(x))$ with $m < n$ (see [21]). This double rounding is thus a rounding mode in itself, different from those of the standard; it has no significant impact on the production of round-off errors and does not produce a visible bias on the results.

3   Description of the Numerical Experience

3.1   Mathematical Model

The hydrodynamic equations—also called Euler's equations—are a good candidate to evaluate the impact of round-off errors. This system of coupled differential equations is at the heart of many numerical simulations performed in industry and academia. It still contains a large number of open problems both numerically and theoretically, but it can be solved numerically with schemes of which the convergence is proven and exact solutions exist for certain initial conditions.

The system of Euler's equations for a fluid is written:

$$\partial_t \begin{pmatrix} \rho \\ \rho u \\ \rho E \end{pmatrix} + \boldsymbol{\nabla} \cdot \begin{pmatrix} \rho u \\ \rho u \otimes u + p\mathbb{I}_3 \\ (\rho E + p)u \end{pmatrix} = \mathbf{0}, \tag{4}$$

with ρ, E, p and u respectively the density, the total specific energy, the pressure and the velocity vector of the considered fluid.

The system of Eq. (4) is closed using an equation of state relating pressure, energy and density. Only the ideal gas law is used in the following. This equation of state is written:

$$p = (\gamma - 1)\rho e, \tag{5}$$

with γ the polytropic coefficient and e the specific internal energy of the fluid and $E = e + \frac{u^2}{2}$.

3.2   Numerical Schemes

The study of the impact of round-off errors is based on comparisons of results from simulations performed with a finite volume numerical scheme based on Godunov's method [9], widely documented in the literature [19, 27]. Briefly, a cell grid discretization is performed on the spatial domain and the scheme provides a method to compute fluxes among each cell for each time step. The working quantities of the method are the averaged values in the volume of each cell, hence the name finite volume method.

In his founding paper of 1959, Godunov introduced a new discretization for hyperbolic systems of conservation laws such as the Euler's equations using the solution of the Riemann problem. In the original version of the method, Godunov uses an exact solver. Later, Lax-Friedrichs [18] and Rusanov [22] independently developed an approximate solver, much less expensive in computation time and accurate to the order of the scheme. Many other Riemann solvers exist and the quality of each of them depends on the domain of use. This study explores the impact of round-off errors on the Rusanov solver.

The convergence of the scheme is only possible if the time step Δt respects the CFL condition [19, 27]:

$$\Delta t \leq C \frac{h}{\max\limits_{\{i \in N\}} (|u_i + c_i|, |u_i - c_i|)}, \tag{6}$$

with the dimensionless CFL constant C, N the number of cells, h the space step, and u_i, c_i the fluid velocity and the sound velocity in the cell i.

3.3   Software and Hardware Environment HPC

As mentioned above, the convergence of the numerical scheme and the reproducibility of the results obtained by the computational code are essential for the study of round-off errors. The possibility for the scheme to perform numerical simulations on a very large number of cells is an additional constraint which requires the development of a code capable of exploiting HPC resources.

In order to respect all the imperatives stated above, the VARIANT code developed for this study is entirely parallelized by sub-domain of calculation. Communication between all sub-domains is provided using the MPI library. Load balancing on the sub-domains is ensured by an equal division of all sub-domains, taking into account the domain edge cells, without any conditional branching on the computations to be performed in each cell (no test on the cell values to select the operations). Each sub-domain with its edge cells is itself processed in parallel using *multithreading*.

One executable is compiled for each type of the floating-point number. These types are: *binary32*, *binary64* or *weak floats*. All the rounding modes of the standard IEEE 754 [14] are implemented for the *weak floats* (with a nuance for the nearest mode, see Sect. 2.3).

3.4   Test Cases

The behavior of the numerical scheme implemented is studied using several test cases from the literature. These specific test cases were selected for this study because they have an analytical solution allowing precise measurements of the numerical error. They also involve several characteristics found in large-scale numerical simulations performed in industry or academia (shock, contact discontinuity, relaxation, large displacement, etc.).

The Sod's Shock Tube. [24] is a two-state Riemann problem. The computational domain $[0, 1]$ is separated at the position $x = 0.5$, the state on the left has a density $\rho = 1$ and a high pressure $p = 1$ and the state on the right has a density $\rho = 0.125$ and a low pressure $p = 0.1$. Both fluids are described by the ideal gas law (5) with a coefficient $\gamma = 1.4$. This 1D test is performed with Neumann boundary conditions (wall type). At the initial time, both fluids are at rest, i.e. without initial velocity. As soon as $t > 0$, the pressure difference will create a shock which will propagate towards the right. The gas on the left will expand and the gas on the right will compress. The exact solution is given by the solution of a Riemann problem.

The Double Rarefaction or Centered Rarefaction. Is a 1D test which consists in separating a fluid in the middle of the domain $[0, 1]$ to create a vacuum. We initially define a constant pressure $p = 0.4$ and a constant density $\rho = 1$. The internal energy is calculated with the Eq. (5) and the velocities are constant and opposite. The left half of the domain goes to the left and the right half of the domain goes to the right, which results in a low density in the center and two expansion profiles that meet. The exact solution is also given by solving a Riemann problem.

Advection of a Gaussian and a Crenel. This one-dimensional test transports a density profile at constant velocity. This test involves a constant velocity $u = 1$ and a constant pressure $p = 1$. The first advection case transports a density profile which has a centered Gaussian shape and the second one transports a crenel. The advection of the density profile being performed at constant speed on a numerical domain $[0, 1]$ with periodic boundary conditions, the analytical solution of the density profile at the final time $t_f = 4$ (corresponding to 4 full turns of the numerical domain) is given by $\rho(x, t_f) = \rho(x, 0)$.

4   Results and Discussions

The results on the different 1D cases are presented in this section, using several precisions and a Godunov scheme type of order 1, with the Rusanov solver.

To understand what is hidden in a numerical error, the first result presented is the test case of the advection of the Gaussian with different precisions (variations on the size of the mantissa). The following results are compared on graphs in logarithmic scale. On the x-axis is the cell number and on the y-axis is the difference in L^2 norm between the average density per cell $\bar{\rho}$ obtained by the simulation and the analytical solution (in practice the formula is a finite sum over each cell volume).

$$\varepsilon^{num} := \|\bar{\rho}_{sim.} - \bar{\rho}_{exact}\|_{L^2} \tag{7}$$

Next, to isolate the effect of round-off errors alone, the CFL number and the final time are varied. Finally, the divergence point is measured and its relation with the size of the mantissa is quantified.

4.1   Variation on the Size of the Mantissa

Where the round-off error causes the results to diverge

Figure 3 is a summary of a set of simulations concerning the advection of a Gaussian simulated with different *weak floats*. Each point of each curve is the numerical error ε^{num} of a complete simulation. On this figure, it is first interesting to notice that the evolution of the error is consistent with the prediction of the qualitative model—Eq. (2) and Fig. 2. We can also observe that the *binary64* follows the order of the scheme while the other precisions diverge from its curve. The divergence point of each type of floating-point number increases with the size of the mantissa.

The *binary64* does not seem to be affected by round-off errors. The convergence is still valid even at 1 million cells. The computation time required to reach the divergence point of the *binary64* is too large and this point cannot be directly determined numerically.

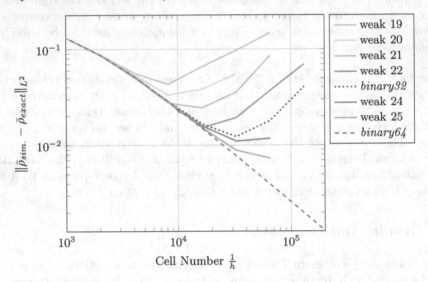

Fig. 3. Error curve of the advection of a Gaussian simulated with different precisions using a Rusanov solver at order 1.

4.2   Variation on the CFL Number

Where we isolate the round-off error

Figure 4 presents a simulation of the Gaussian advection case at order 1 with the Rusanov solver using different CFL numbers C. The CFL numbers used are 0.5 (default), 0.25 and 0.125. The mantissa sizes shown are 21 and 23 (*binary32*).

These curves highlight the contribution of the round-off error in the total numerical error. For the same simulation, the decrease of the CFL number will

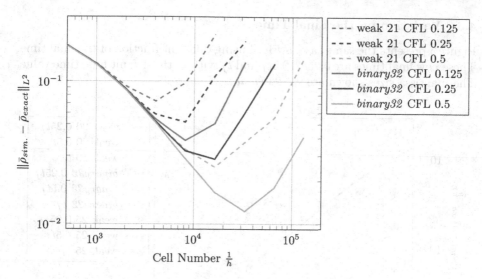

Fig. 4. Error curve of the advection of a Gaussian simulated with different CFL numbers using a Rusanov solver at order 1. *binary32* in solid line and *weak floats 21* in dashed line. The same color is used for a given CFL number. (Color figure online)

increase the number of iterations without significantly decreasing the error due to the scheme, as long as the state is converged. The only cause of the increase of the error is then the increase of the number of operations (since all the other parameters are identical). With each division of the CFL number, the divergence point decreases for each precision used (see Table 1). Finally, the smaller the mantissa is, the smaller the divergence point will be ($N_{div}^m \sim m$). It confirms that the error is due to a defect in the ability of the mantissa to absorb the round-off error of the calculations. This effect does not show up in the formula (2), which invalidate its simplicity and requires a more complete model to be developed.

Table 1. Mantissa size, CFL, number of iterations and divergent mesh size.

Mantissa size	CFL	N_{it}	N_{div}
21	0.5	161 338	3 968
21	0.25	182 143	2 240
21	0.125	227 634	1 408
23	0.5	343 495	8 448
23	0.25	395 539	4 864
23	0.125	519 364	3 200
25	0.5	666 172	16 384
25	0.25	832 242	10 240
25	0.125	1 124 164	6 912

4.3   Variation on the Final Time

Figure 5 presents the same case as Fig. 4 using different fraction of the final time. These new final times are $0.25t_f$, $0.5t_f$ and t_f with t_f the default final time value. The mantissa sizes shown are 20, 23 ($binary32$) and 25.

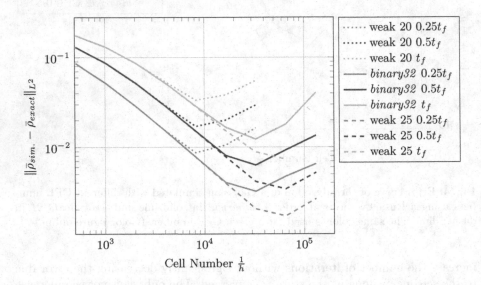

Fig. 5. Error curve of the advection of a Gaussian simulated with different final times using a Rusanov solver at order 1. *binary32* in solid line, *weak floats 20* in dotted line and *weak floats 25* in dashed line. The same color is used for a given final time.

The variation of the final time in Fig. 5, like the variation of the CFL number, isolates the effect of the number of operations. By increasing the final time, the simulated cases are different. Since it is a transport of a Gaussian on a periodic domain, only the number of turns of the domain changes. The numerical error then becomes larger when the case simulates more turns but the curves remain parallel to each other. However, with more operations, the accumulation of round-off errors is larger and the point of divergence decreases as shown in Table 2.

Table 2. Mantissa size, final time and divergent mesh size.

Mantissa size	$0.25t_f$	$0.5t_f$	t_f
20	4864	4608	3968
23	10240	9728	8448
25	20480	19456	16384

4.4   Prediction of the Divergence Point

Where we build up an error model

By varying the CFL number, the final time and the mantissa size, we observe a quasi-linearity of the divergence point between mantissa size and number of operations.

A systematic search for the divergence point for a given test case confirms this linearity as shows in Fig. 6. This figure plots the divergence point obtained with respect to the mantissa. By linear regression, we can see that the linearity (in logarithmic scale) is very close from each experimental observation and each case can be fit with great accuracy with two parameters α, β by a basic model: $2^{\alpha m + \beta}$ where m is the size of the mantissa.

The test cases seem to produce round-off errors regularly during the calculation. The error production rate increases linearly with respect to the mantissa. Concretely, this implies that an additional *bit* in the mantissa allows to increase exponentially the number of cells needed (and thus of operations) to reach the divergence point. The divergence point is not doubled for each additional bit because with more cells, the results become more accurate and require more bits in the mantissa.

Although the cases used are different, it is quite remarkable that a single linear model is sufficient to represent accurately the round-off error produced in the simulations. We think that this result can be related to an analogous numerical experiment conducted in [26].

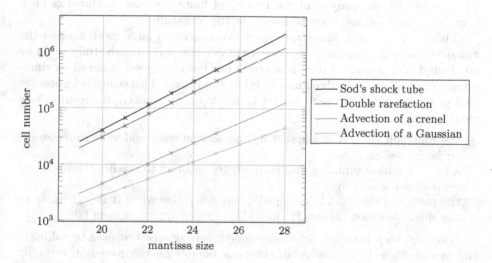

Fig. 6. Number of cells of the divergence point as a function of the mantissa size for four cases. The curves are plotted in logarithmic scale on the y-axis. The lines are obtained by linear regression.

We used the linear model $2^{\alpha m + \beta}$, to extrapolate divergence point of the different test cases for *binary64*. Once the parameters α and β are calibrated by linear regression for each case, the extrapolated point is then simply given by the formula applied with $m = 52$. We conclude that in dimension one, the number of operations needed to make the *binary64* diverge is 220 million cells with 9 billion iterations for the Gaussian advection and 286 billion cells with 251 billion iterations for the Sod's shock tube (see Table 3). These values are orders of magnitude greater than the capacities of exascale supercomputers.

Table 3. Extrapolation of the number of cells needed to observe the divergence of the *binary64* as a function $2^{\alpha m + \beta}$ with the parameters obtained by linear regression.

Test case	Number of cells	Number of iterations	α
Double rarefaction	6.98×10^{10}	5.75×10^{10}	0.659
Advection of a crenel	2.75×10^{9}	9.82×10^{10}	0.600
Advection of a Gaussian	2.21×10^{8}	8.99×10^{9}	0.509
Sod's shock tube	2.86×10^{11}	2.51×10^{11}	0.710

5   Conclusion

The question of round-off errors is of prominent concern for all HPC simulation codes ([10,15,25], etc.). Although the problem is addressed in many textbooks ([1,2,13,16,17]), an analysis of the impact of finite precision arithmetics on a complete computational code is missing in the literature.

Thanks to the *weak floats* and the performances on large mesh sizes of the massively parallel computational code VARIANT [29], an in-depth study could be conducted. The impact of round-off errors has been analyzed in detail on simulations of ideal gas hydrodynamics in HPC conditions. This study is important as it gives confidence on the future HPC developments. Indeed, the results show that:

- the round-off error is dominated by the scheme error and validate *binary64* on large meshes;
- a linear model is sufficient and surprisingly accurate to predict the round-off error in our simulations.
- the tools and the model developed could determine when it is legitimate to use single precision (*binary32*) in addition to an approach as in [28].

The next step is to get rid of the dependence on the test-case to calibrate the model. Since it is possible to compute bounds on the round-off error on each routine of the code and since these routines are common to the majority of numerical schemes, it is possible to assemble the theoretical bounds to give an estimate of a global bound on the round-off error [3]. Theoretical bounds are wider than empirical bounds but they allow to validate any initial condition including chaotic and turbulent cases.

References

1. Ascher, U.M., Greif, C.: A First Course in Numerical Methods. Society for Industrial and Applied Mathematics, USA (2011)
2. Atkinson, K.E., Han, W., Stewart, D.: Euler's method, chap. 2, pp. 15–36. Wiley, Hoboken (2011)
3. Boldo, S., Ben Salem-Knapp, L., Weens, W.: Bounding the round-off error of the upwind scheme for advection, submitted
4. Boldo, S., Clément, F., Filliâtre, J.C., Mayero, M., Melquiond, G., Weis, P.: Wave equation numerical resolution: a comprehensive mechanized proof of a C program. J. Autom. Reason. **50**(4), 423–456 (2013). https://doi.org/10.1007/s10817-012-9255-4
5. Boldo, S., Faissole, F., Chapoutot, A.: Round-off error and exceptional behavior analysis of explicit Runge-Kutta methods. IEEE Trans. Comput. (2019)
6. Chapoutot, A., Alexandre dit Sandretto, J., Mullier, O.: Validated explicit and implicit Runge-Kutta methods. In: Small Workshop on Interval Methods. Prague, Czech Republic (2015)
7. Euler, L.: Principes généraux du mouvement des fluides. Mémoires de l'Académie Royale des Sciences et des Belles Lettres de Berlin **11**, 274–315 (1755)
8. Gautschi, W.: Numerical Analysis: An Introduction. Birkhauser Boston Inc., Cambridge (1997)
9. Godunov, S.K.: Eine Differenzenmethode für die Näherungsberechnung unstetiger Lösungen der hydrodynamischen Gleichungen. Mat. Sb., Nov. Ser. **47**, 271–306 (1959)
10. Harvey, R., Verseghy, D.L.: The reliability of single precision computations in the simulation of deep soil heat diffusion in a land surface model. Clim. Dyn. **46**(11), 3865–3882 (2016). https://doi.org/10.1007/s00382-015-2809-5
11. Henrici, P.: Error propagation for difference methods. In: The SIAM Series in Applied Mathematics. Wiley, New York (1963)
12. Heroux, M.A., et al.: ECP software technology capability assessment report (2020). www.exascaleproject.org
13. Higham, N.J.: 2. Floating point arithmetic, pp. 35–60. SIAM (2002)
14. IEEE: IEEE Standard for Floating-Point Arithmetic. Institute of Electrical and Electronics Engineers IEEE Std 754-2008, pp. 1–70 (2008)
15. Izquierdo, L.R., Polhill, J.G.: Is your model susceptible to floating-point errors? J. Artif. Soc. Soc. Simul. **9**(4), 1–4 (2006)
16. Kahan, W.: Pracniques: further remarks on reducing truncation errors. Commun. ACM **8**(1), 40 (1965)
17. Knuth, D.E.: The art of computer programming. In: Seminumerical Algorithms, 3rd edn, vol. 2. Addison-Wesley, Boston (1997)
18. Lax, P.D.: Weak solutions of nonlinear hyperbolic equations and their numerical computation. Commun. Pure Appl. Math. **7**(1), 159–193 (1954)
19. LeVeque, R.J.: Finite volume methods for hyperbolic problems. In: Cambridge Texts in Applied Mathematics, Cambridge University Press (2002)
20. Muller, J.M., et al.: Handbook of Floating-Point Arithmetic, 2nd edn. Birkhäuser Boston (2018). ACM G.1.0; G.1.2; G.4; B.2.0; B.2.4; F.2.1. ISBN 978-3-319-76525-9
21. Muller, J.M., et al.: Handbook of Floating-point Arithmetic, 2nd edn. Birkhäuser, Basel (2018)
22. Rusanov, V.V.: The calculation of the interaction of non-stationary shock waves with barriers. Zh. Vychisl. Mat. Mat. Fiz, pp. 267–279 (1961)

23. Alexandre dit Sandretto, J., Chapoutot, A.: Validated simulation of differential algebraic equations. In: Small Workshop on Interval Methods, Prague, Czech Republic (2015)
24. Sod, G.A.: A survey of several finite difference methods for systems of nonlinear hyperbolic conservation laws. J. Comput. Phys. **27**(1), 1–31 (1978)
25. Spiegel, S.C., Huynh, H., DeBonis, J.R.: A survey of the isentropic euler vortex problem using high-order methods, chap. 1, p. 1 (2015). https://arc.aiaa.org/
26. Thornes, T., Düben, P., Palmer, T.: A power law for reduced precision at small spatial scales: experiments with an SQG model. Q. J. R. Meteorol. Soc. **144**(713), 1179–1188 (2018)
27. Toro, E.F.: Riemann Solvers and Numerical Methods for Fluid Dynamics. Springer, Heidelberg (2009). https://doi.org/10.1007/b79761
28. Váňa, F., et al.: Single precision in weather forecasting models: an evaluation with the IFS. Mon. Weather Rev. **145**(2), 495–502 (2017)
29. Weens, W.: Toward a predictive model to monitor the balance between discretization and rounding errors in hydrodynamic simulations. In: SIAM Conference on Parallel Processing for Scientific Computing (2020)

Author Index

Printed in the United States
by Baker & Taylor Publisher Services

Printed in the United States
by Baker & Taylor Publisher Services